HAZOR

THE REDISCOVERY OF A GREAT CITADEL
OF THE BIBLE

YIGAEL YADIN

Weidenfeld and Nicolson

Weidenfeld and Nicolson
11 St John's Hill
London SW 11

Weidenfeld and Nicolson Jerusalem
19 Herzog Street
Jerusalem

9.0GL

Designed by Alex Berlyne for Weidenfeld and Nicolson
Jerusalem

Maps by Carta, Jerusalem; plans drawn by Talma Levin;
index compiled by Orly Ophrat

ISBN 297 76845 X

Composed and bound by Keterpress Enterprises, Jerusalem;
printed by Japhet Press, Tel Aviv, Israel, 1974

HAZOR

endpaper The stelae temple in area C
frontispiece Aerial view of area B

Contents

Foreword

Those readers who are acquainted with the two predecessors in this series, *Masada* and *Bar-Kokhba*, will find basic similarities and differences between them and the present work. Like the other books, *Hazor*, too, is a personal account written for the lay reader; like them it aims to tell not only *what* we found in our excavations but *how* we found it, thus letting the reader share our moments of anxiety and excitement alike; and as in the other two books, the text and photographs are intimately interwoven, like a lecture accompanied by slides. Most of the photographs were taken during the dig – the black and white by the expedition photographers, Messrs Schweig, Volk, and Radovan, the colour by the author – and if, as a result of the field conditions, they may occasionally lack technical perfection, this is compensated for by their being authentic, thus telling much more than words could describe.

The basic difference between *Hazor* and the other books emanates from the difference inherent in the material itself. Here we are dealing with a classic archaeological dig: the excavation of an ancient mound (*tell*) of over twenty strata, representing the remains of many cities built one on top of the other and covering a span of 3,000 years. The fascination of archaeology is further heightened at Hazor, for the site is not just any ancient city, but one which is biblical in all its aspects. For many of us, the names of Joshua, Sisera, Deborah, Solomon, Ahab and Jezebel – to mention but a few – are associated with chapter and verse; here they are connected with strata, buildings and artefacts: X is a chapter in the Book of Kings; in Hazor, X is the stratum of the city built by Solomon. To many crucial problems in biblical research – like the date of the Exodus and the conquest of Canaan, the battles of Deborah and the building activities of Solomon and Ahab – the spade has literally dug up solutions. For this reason, *Hazor* may appeal not only to those who wish to learn more about archaeology and its methods, but also to those who are interested in the Bible, the history of the Holy Land and the people of Israel.

This book could never have been written, of course, were it not for the excavations. I am deeply indebted to all those who helped in this respect, as mentioned in the following pages, and I wish here to reiterate my profound gratitude to the late James A. de Rothschild, to whose interest and generosity the expedition owes so much. I was privileged to have a wonderful staff to share the work (see list on page 276). As in many enterprises of this kind, where the joint efforts of many – each contributing in his or her own way – bring about the end product, at Hazor, too, we experienced a feeling of team work in the true sense of the word.

I am grateful to John Curtis of Weidenfeld and Nicolson, who showed much interest and encouraged me throughout the writing of this book. My particular thanks are due to the staff of Weidenfeld and Nicolson Jerusalem, especially to Alex Berlyne, the book's designer, for his intelligent approach and patient efforts to balance my ever-increasing demand for more illustrations and my insistence that the photographs appear by their corresponding text with the limitations of the book; and to Ina Friedman, who edited the manuscript for press and while reading it critically offered valuable advice and raised pertinent questions that compelled me to further elucidate certain points. As with my previous books, my wife, Carmella, helped me in more ways than one. The book is dedicated to the blessed memory of W.F. Albright, the greatest of biblical archaeologists, a great humanist, an inspiring teacher and a true friend. Much of his teaching is embedded in these pages.

I began writing *Hazor* in August of 1973 and completed it – no easy task – during the trying days following the Yom Kippur war. Let us hope that when it is read, the clouds will have passed from this part of the world and the reader will be able to look back into history without worry about the present and the future.

Jerusalem   Y.Y.

Passover 1974

To Professor William Foxwell Albright,
scholar, teacher and friend,
in memoriam

1 Why Hazor?

Strange as it may seem, practically nothing was known about the Canaanite and Israelite cultures of the northern part of the Holy Land, and in particular of the Galilee, until we began our excavations on the site of ancient Hazor. The prospect of opening up a new field of knowledge was, in itself, strong enough a motive for selecting the site for excavation. But our attention was drawn to Hazor for other compelling reasons as well: the important role played by the city in the history of the country in biblical times; its enormous size and peculiar features, unparalleled by any other site in the country; and the abundance of references to it in extra-biblical sources covering a period from the second millennium BC through the first century AD (with only a few gaps) and a geographical range that spans almost the entire Fertile Crescent – making Hazor almost unique among Palestinian cities. We were therefore in a position to reconstruct the history of Hazor from historical documents and then confront our theories with the results of the excavations – an exciting situation in archaeological practice. Furthermore, some of the most controversial and acute problems in biblical history concern Hazor, and only the spade could help solve them. The best way to start this account, therefore, is by presenting all we knew about Hazor, from both biblical and external sources, prior to the excavations. Let us begin with the biblical sources, which have, after all, attracted scholars for years.

Perhaps the most important biblical reference to Hazor is the one concerning Joshua's wars in the north against Jabin, king of Hazor. According to the Bible, Jabin was the head of the Canaanite league, or coalition, that fought against Joshua, and his role was momentous in the whole sequence of the Israelite conquest of Canaan. Here is what the Bible tells us after it describes Joshua's victories against the kings of southern Canaan (Joshua 11:1–5):

> When Jabin king of Hazor heard of this, he sent to Jobab king of Madon, and to the king of Shimron, and to the king of Achshaph, and to the kings who were in the northern hill country, and in the Arabah south of Chinneroth, and in the lowland, and in Naphoth-dor on the west, to the Canaanites in the east and the west, the Amorites, the Hittites, the Perizzites, and the Jebusites in the hill country, and the Hivites under Hermon in the land of Mizpah. And they came out, with all their troops, a great host, in number like the sand that is upon the seashore, with very many horses and chariots. And all these kings joined their forces and came and encamped together at the waters of Merom, to fight with Israel.

The *tell* of Hazor viewed from the south-west. In the foreground, the road leading from Tiberias to the north; in the background, snowcapped Mount Hermon

Hazor and the Bible

Joshua *versus* Jabin

The Bible then proceeds to describe how Joshua smashed the Canaanite
league that assembled near the water of Merom, somewhere in northern
Galilee (Joshua 11:10–13):

> And Joshua turned back at that time, and took Hazor, and smote its
> king with the sword; for Hazor formerly was the head of all those kingdoms.
> And they put to the sword all who were in it, utterly destroying them;
> there was none left that breathed, and he burned Hazor with fire. And all
> the cities of those kings, and all their kings, Joshua took, and smote them
> with the edge of the sword, utterly destroying them, as Moses the servant of
> the Lord had commanded. But none of the cities that stood on mounds
> [*tells*] did Israel burn, except Hazor only; that Joshua burned.

The main interest in these descriptions is the compiler's, or editor's,
gloss, which tries to explain why Hazor alone was the target of Joshua's
wrath. Obviously, when this account was written, or edited, centuries
later, Hazor was no longer a city of prime importance, which is why
the editor added that 'Hazor *formerly* was the head of all those kingdoms'
(referring to the city's status on the eve of Joshua's conquest).

This quotation from the Book of Joshua clearly indicates the importance of Hazor at the time of the conquest, and viewed in isolation it is
not at all controversial. Yet this same reference generated a heated
debate among biblical scholars because Jabin, king of Hazor, is mentioned again in the Book of Judges (which follows Joshua in both the
canon and chronology), this time in connection with the famous
Deborah *versus* Sisera   battle of Deborah against Sisera. The battle is dealt with in both chapters
4 and 5. Chapter 5 contains the famous Song of Deborah, but makes no
mention of either Hazor or Jabin (19–21):

> The kings came, they fought;
>   then fought the kings of Canaan,
> at Ta'anach, by the waters of
>   Megiddo;
>   they got no spoils of silver.
> From heaven fought the stars,
>   from their courses they fought
>   against Sisera.
> The torrent Kishon swept them
>   away,
>   the onrushing torrent, the torrent
>   Kishon.

So far, so good. But a prose version of the same battle preserved in
chapter 4 provides us with the following historical background to the
clash:

> And the people of Israel again did what was evil in the sight of the Lord,
> after Ehud died. And the Lord sold them into the hand of Jabin king of
> Canaan, who reigned in Hazor; the commander of his army was Sisera,
> who dwelt in Harosheth-ha-goiim (1–2).

Then, at the end of that chapter, when the victory over Sisera was complete, we are told:

> So on that day God subdued Jabin the king of Canaan before the people of Israel. And the hand of the people of Israel bore harder and harder on Jabin the king of Canaan, until they destroyed Jabin king of Canaan (23–4).

If Hazor was destroyed and Jabin killed in the times of Joshua, decades before the period of the Judges, how is it possible that the city and its king again figured so prominently in these later battles? It was precisely the answer to this question that we wanted to elicit with the help of the spade – and indeed we did, as will be recounted later.

Discrepancy?

Hazor is again mentioned in the Bible in I Kings 9:15: 'And this is the account of the forced labour which King Solomon levied to build the house of the Lord and his own house and the Millo and the wall of Jerusalem and Hazor and Megiddo and Gezer.' The verse implies that following the fall of Canaanite Hazor, there was no proper city on the site until Solomon rebuilt it, along with the other two strategic cities. In the whole saga of biblical archaeology, there are few cases in which so many owe so much to so few words, and one of the most exciting subjects dealt with in the following chapters is how this verse from Kings helped us in our excavations at Hazor, as well as at Megiddo and Gezer.

Hazor and Solomon

The last biblical reference to Israelite Hazor is in II Kings 15:29 and relates that the city fell to the hosts of Tiglath-pileser III, the mighty Assyrian emperor who conquered northern Israel, including Hazor, in 732 BC: 'In the days of Pekah king of Israel Tiglath-pileser king of Assyria came and captured . . . Hazor, Gilead, and Galilee, all the land of Naphtali; and he carried the people captive to Assyria.' Tragic as this event may have been for the population of northern Israel, for

The end of Israelite Hazor

The soldiers of Tiglath-pileser III storming a fortified city – perhaps Hazor – shown in a relief from the monarch's palace at Nimrud

us archaeologists it is a priceless piece of information. After all, we thrive on destructions of ancient cities. In this case, we hoped that should we find the city destroyed by Tiglath-pileser, the biblical verse would give us a good peg on which to hang our absolute chronology.

The Maccabees and Josephus

One further reference in Jewish historical writings to an actual event concerning Hazor is preserved in the First Book of Maccabees 11:67, where we are told that Jonathan the Maccabee fought against Demetrius in 147 BC on the 'Plain of Hazor'. It is impossible, of course, to know whether this remark indicates the existence of an actual settlement at that time, or whether – as the location of Hazor was still known – the plain adjacent to it was simply called by that name. Here again, it was the role of the spade to provide an answer. Finally, the last mention of Hazor is in the writings of the famous Jewish historian Josephus Flavius (*Antiquities* V.199). It has no historical value concerning the ancient periods, but it is of great help in identifying the location of Hazor. Indeed, Josephus says that Hazor lay 'over the Lake Semechonitis', today called Lake Huleh in Upper Galilee.

Evil upon Hazor

Without detracting from the importance of the biblical references to Hazor, one should remember that the Bible is a source of information about that city only from Joshua onwards. What about its earlier history? Here we are indeed fortunate to have abundant references in Egyptian and Mesopotamian inscriptions. The first mention of Hazor in any historical document is contained in the so-called Egyptian Execration Texts. In the first half of the second millennium BC, the Egyptians practised a strange magical rite in which they cursed their actual or potential enemies. Two sets of testimonies of this practice are preserved. In the first, the names of Egypt's enemies in the west, south and east (including those in Canaan) were written on pottery vessels that were then broken, in the belief that this act, performed in ceremony, might bring evil upon the enemy. This set of Execration Texts is most probably from the period of the 12th Dynasty, about the nineteenth or beginning of the eighteenth century BC. From these vessels we learn that there were as yet no fortified cities proper in Canaan. References are mainly to rulers of political centres, as well as to heads of various tribal confederacies ruling over larger units or provinces. In most cases, two, three or four people are mentioned as heads of the more important families in these centres. However, in the second group of texts, written on clay figurines depicting captive enemies, only one ruler is mentioned in conjunction with each place – an obvious indication that by that time some of the tribal units scattered over large geographical areas had begun to settle down in places as semi-nomads or perhaps already as city dwellers.

Unfortunately, Egyptologists do not agree about the precise date of this second group of Execration Texts; some place them in the nineteenth century and others in the eighteenth century. But their importance cannot be underestimated; and, in fact, one of our aims in

An Egyptian Execration Text that specifically mentions Hazor as an enemy of Egypt

the excavations was to determine their date. For it is in the second group of these Execration Texts that Hazor is mentioned for the first time, among the other potential enemies of Egypt in Canaan. Moreover, they provide us with a very precious piece of information: the name of the ruler of Hazor, a certain Gt'i. Nothing else is known about him. His name seems, in all probability, to be non-Semitic, which is particularly interesting because some of the other rulers in the same texts bear names that are clearly derived from the West Semitic onomasticon.

While mention of Hazor in the Execration Texts must be given its due, the really valuable data concerning the status of the city before the Israelite conquest comes from the other end of the Fertile Crescent through archives discovered in the famous city of Mari, on the right bank of the Euphrates. Excavations conducted by the distinguished French archaeologist André Parrot uncovered the palaces of the kings of Mari, and in them were over 25,000 inscribed clay tablets arranged in orderly royal archives. For a while, in the eighteenth century BC, the city was ruled by Shamshi-Adad I, the great Assyrian king; but most of the archives are related to the last king of Mari, one Zimri-Lim, a contemporary of the great Hammurabi of Babylon. The documents, not all of which have yet been published, mention Hazor several times and in contexts that indicate it was one of the most important cities in the entire Fertile Crescent. In fact, it is the only city of the Holy Land mentioned, except for an occasional reference to the neighbouring city of Dan.

Among the Mari documents were various types of diplomatic

left A vertical aerial photograph of the excavated palace at Mari, where over 25,000 tablets were found arranged in royal archives

right A typical clay tablet with cuneiform inscription from Mari. In several of these documents, from the times of Hammurabi, Hazor is mentioned (section in black) as one of the most important centres of the Fertile Crescent

Hazor and Hammurabi

correspondence. In one of these letters, Baḫdi-Lim, chamberlain of Mari's palace during the reign of Zimri-Lim, informs his master of the following:

> To my Lord
> speak
> Thus speaks Baḫdi-Lim
> Thy servant:
> A group of messengers from Hazor
> and Qatna has arrived here.

Further on in the same letter, he announces:

> Two messengers from Babylon
> who have long since resided at Hazor,
> With one man from Hazor
> as their escort, are crossing
> to Babylon.

What a precious piece of information! We learn that the king of Babylon, Hammurabi, had special ambassadors residing at Hazor for a considerable length of time. In yet another letter, Baḫdi-Lim reports the movement of emissaries in the opposite direction: 'Further, a group of travellers in transit from Babylon . . . on their way to Yamḫad, Qatna, Hazor . . . have arrived here. Shall I let them go or stop them?' And a most important document from Mari published only recently tells us of the following:

> 30 minas tin, for Ibni-Adad king of Hazor
> . . . .
> 20 minas tin for Ibni-Adad
> for the second time; . . .
> 20 minas tin for Ibni-Adad for the third time.

Thus we learn of the important trade in tin alloy, which was imperative for the production of bronze. We see that the king of Hazor received three successive tin shipments from Mari, totalling 70 minas, that is, about 35 kilograms. The most valuable piece of information, however, is the name of the ruler of Hazor, Ibni-Adad, designated as 'king of Hazor.' His name is given in the Accadian form of the West Semitic name Yabni-Hadad, 'the god Hadad has created'. Scholars have suggested that the form of the name of the king of Hazor mentioned in the Bible – Yabin (Jabin being the Anglicized version) – is indeed short for the full theophoric formula. If this is true, then Yabin may have been a royal dynastic name of the kings of Hazor for quite a time.

Egypt again For the next references to Hazor we must go back to Egypt. Nearly every Pharaoh of the New Kingdom (sixteenth–thirteenth centuries BC) mentions Hazor among towns he conquered in Canaan. Some-

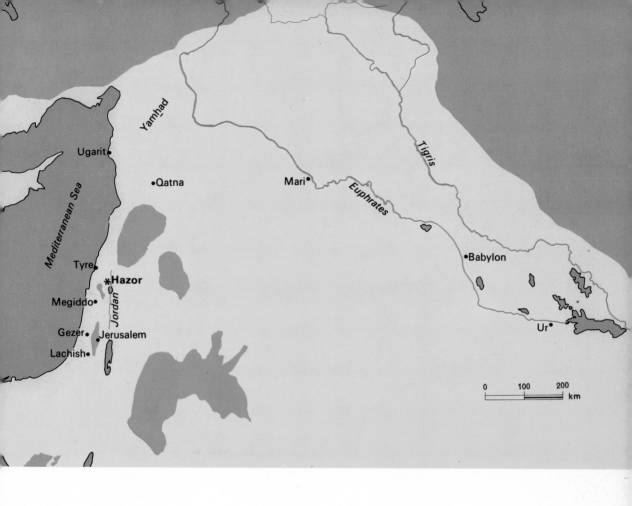

times it is very difficult to tell whether Hazor had actually been conquered; or whether it was just under the control of the Pharaoh; or,
indeed, whether any suggestion of either conquest or control was
merely an idle boast of the king. Still, the very fact that Hazor is
mentioned in these lists is of prime historical importance and, for us,
valuable for dating purposes. The earliest of these references goes
back to Thutmose III (the famous Pharaoh of the early fifteenth century BC who captured Megiddo and recorded this battle in great
detail). Hazor is next mentioned in the reign of Amenophis III (around
1400 BC) and again in the days of Seti I (around 1300 BC). An interesting
allusion to Hazor is found in one of the Egyptian papyri from the
thirteenth century in which Hori, a royal official, challenges a military
scribe to answer a number of military and topographic questions. **A military quiz**
The context of the reference seems to be something like an ancient
military quiz. One of the questions Hori asks is: 'Where does the
Mahir [a swift military courier] make the journey to Hazor? What
is its stream like?' The questions embody the valuable topographic
hint that Hazor lay not far away from a river – probably the Jordan.

By far the most important reference to Hazor in the first half of the

A clay tablet from el-Amarna which was sent by Abdi-Tirshi, king of Hazor

fourteenth century BC is no doubt to be found in the so-called el-Amarna letters. El-Amarna, in Middle Egypt, is the present-day name for the site in which the famous 'heretical' king Amenophis IV (Akhenaten) established a city in around 1360 BC. It was practically abandoned twenty years later. But in this briefly populated site were found the archives of the 'foreign office' of Akhenaten and his father, Amenophis III, which contained hundreds of clay tablets inscribed in cuneiform in Accadian, the *lingua franca* of the day. Among them were many letters from the kings of the cities of Canaan, most of them Egyptian vassals. It is most entertaining, in a way, to read today about the petty intrigues of petty kings who ruled thousands of years ago. They complained about each other incessantly to the mighty Pharaoh, and we have both the complaints and the replies. Not one king admits to being guilty of disloyalty to the Pharaoh; on the contrary, it is always his rival who is charged with that sin. The el-Amarna archive is the most important source of information about the Holy Land in the period preceding Joshua. It demonstrates that the country was ruled by numerous petty kings, a situation also reflected in the Book of Joshua itself. But it is precisely here that we realize the importance of Hazor's ruler: he alone was singled out by the title of 'king' and was referred to as such by himself and the other rulers. In one of these letters, the king of Hazor proclaims that he is safe-guarding the cities of the Pharaoh until the latter's arrival, which indicates, no doubt, that the king of Hazor's rule extended beyond the city itself.

The unfortunate Abdi-Tirshi

A further letter from the king of Hazor includes two more valuable bits of information. First, we learn that the name of the king was Abdi-Tirshi ('servant of Tirshi', *i.e.*, the deity). Second, there is an allusion to some intrigue against him: 'Let my lord the King remember all that was done against the city of Hazor – your city – as well as against your servant.' We actually do not know what all this means and can only surmise that it has something to do with a court intrigue within the city of Hazor. Or it may be a reference to the incursions by the *Habiru* (pronounced Khabiru), marauding bands that harassed some of the cities of Canaan at that time (some scholars identified them as the Hebrews). Another letter, this time from Abi-Milki, king of Tyre, informs the Pharaoh that: 'The king of Hazor left his city and joined the *Habiru*.' Complete chaos seems to have reigned in Canaan as the result of the *Habiru* incursions, because the letter concludes with the words: 'Let the King know that they [the *Habiru*] are hostile to the Supervisor. The King's land is falling into the hands of the *Habiru*. Let the King ask the High Commissioner, who is familiar with Canaan.'

An ambitious king

Whatever calamities befell Abdi-Tirshi from time to time, we do know that he was a very ambitious king, and his rule expanded far beyond the city of Hazor itself. In another letter, written by Ayab, ruler of Ashtaroth in Cis-Jordan, we read that the ruler of Hazor 'took from me three cities.' These pieces of information show clearly that a remote ancestor of Jabin who ruled about 100 years before him was a mighty and ambitious ruler whose kingdom embraced a considerable part of northern Canaan. It is to this period, the fourteenth–thirteenth centuries BC, on the eve of Joshua's conquest, that the biblical description 'head of all those kingdoms' refers.

Summing up the information about Hazor from the written sources, we had cause to hope, even before our excavations began, that we might find remnants of cities ranging from the beginning of the second millennium to the first or second centuries BC, a span of over 2,000 years. We discovered them indeed, and even more than expected.

Where was the site of Hazor? Several suggestions have been offered over the years; but the first modern scholar, as far as we know, who correctly suggested that Hazor was located on the site called by the Arabs Tel el-Qedaḥ (or Tell Waggās, as it is also known, after the name of a village nearby) was J.L. Porter. In 1875 he published a book entitled *Handbook for Travellers in Syria and Palestine* in which he wrote: 'We soon afterwards crossed a deep glen [*i.e.*, Wadi el-Waggās] on whose northern bank is a scarped mound and beside it a broad terrace which was apparently the site of the town. Upon it now stands the little village of Waggās. The ancient and long-lost Hazor might possibly have stood on this spot.' In a later book (*The Giant Cities of Bashan and Syria*, 1881), he not only repeats his conviction, but adds some interesting details about the site as he saw it.

Where was Hazor?

Beside where I sat was the mouth of the ravine of Hendaj. [This time he approached the site from the north.] Mounting my horse, I followed a broad path, like an old highway, up its southern bank, and soon came upon the ruins of an ancient city. Not a building – not even a foundation, was perfect. Large cisterns, heaps of stones, mounds of rubbish, prostrate columns, the remains of a temple and an altar with a Greek inscription – such were the ruins strewn over this site. I thought at the time that these might be the ruins of Hazor, and I have since become more and more confirmed in the belief.

This ingenious suggestion was not only not taken up by scholars at the time, it was even forgotten; and the credit for identifying the site of Tell el-Qedaḥ with Hazor and bringing it to the attention of modern scholars should go to John Garstang, who not only re-identified the site with Hazor in 1926, but was also the first to conduct excavations there. Garstang, who was Director of Antiquities of the British Mandatory administration of Palestine, was absorbed with the problems of Israel's ancient history, particularly in the period of Joshua and the Judges. For this reason he later on conducted excavations in Jericho as well.

Tell el-Qedaḥ occupies an ideal strategic location in northern Galilee that fits perfectly all the known data concerning the site of

A strategic location

A vertical aerial photograph of Hazor. Note the 'bottle-shaped' *tell* and the earthen ramparts of the enclosure

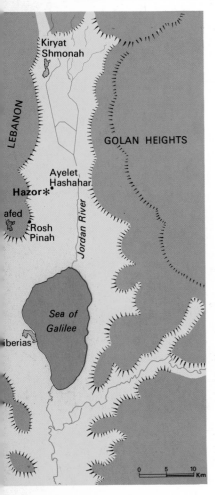

Hazor. It lies 15.5 kilometres, as the crow flies, north of the Sea of Galilee and about 8 kilometres below the southern tip of Lake Huleh. I might just as well state now, before describing our excavations, that the identification of Tell el-Qedaḥ with Hazor is now absolutely certain. A fragment of a clay tablet with a cuneiform inscription found on the site, as a result of our excavations, records a case of litigation, conducted in the presence of the king, concerning real estate in Hazor. Thus Hazor becomes one of the very few biblical cities whose identification has been confirmed by a written document found on the site!

The site   What attracted the attention of earlier scholars was not only the

strategic position of the site, but particularly its unique topographic features; and it is vital for the understanding of our excavations to describe these in detail. The site is, in fact, composed of two distinct parts: a *tell* proper and a vast rectangular plateau, or enclosure, to its north and east. The *tell* itself is 'bottle' shaped, with its 'neck' in the west and its 'base' in the east. It rises to about 40 metres above the bed of Wadi el-Waggās and is 540 metres long and some 260 metres wide at the bottom. Thus the total area at the foot of the mound is about 100 dunams, or 25 acres; while at the top, which is of course narrower, it covers only 15 acres, roughly the area of Megiddo. Impressive as it is,

An aerial view of the western tip of the *tell*, looking south-east. Note the steep slope of the mound and the springs near the highway. The photograph was taken after the excavations and shows the citadel discovered in this area

the *tell* is hardly different from scores of *tells* in the Holy Land. The present-day road to the north, towards Syria and Lebanon, skirts the mound on the south and east. Near the road, the bed of Wadi el-Waggās is covered with a thicket of shrubs, due to the many springs along its course in close vicinity to the mound. These springs, together with the strategic position and the large and fertile fields in the immediate area, must have attracted the first settlers to the site.

The unique feature of the site, though, is not the *tell* proper but the huge rectangular enclosure lying to its north and partially to its east. The northern part of the enclosure is about 1 kilometre from north to south and about 700 metres, on the average, from east to west, thus extending over an area of 170 acres in all. The eastern spur measures 400 metres from east to west and 250 metres from north to south, making its area 25 acres. The total area of the enclosure, therefore, is 200 acres. Several sides of the enclosure, in particular the western one, are protected by huge earthen ramparts. Until the beginning of our excavations, the enclosure was considered by all scholars to represent a huge fortified camp. It was difficult to imagine it as a well-built city, some ten or twenty times larger than Megiddo or even Jerusalem in the time of King David. But the stupendous ramparts and the incredible efforts that had been invested in its defence cast some doubts on the encampment theory, and one of our main objectives was to probe into the nature of this so-called enclosure or fortified camp.

The site was first excavated by Garstang in 1928, but, unfortunately, no report was ever published and most of the records were burned in Liverpool during World War Two. Some indications of the results of Garstang's excavations were embodied in short descriptions, accompanied by a rough sketch, in his book *Joshua, Judges* (1931). Except for two spots on the *tell* proper, and despite his note that 'extensive soundings were made upon the site', it was impossible to ascertain where he had dug in the enclosure. When we began our excavations in 1955, we lacked access to the files of the Department of Antiquities of Palestine, which were stored in the Rockefeller Museum in East Jerusalem (then under Jordanian rule). Only in 1969, following the Six Day War and after the completion of our excavations, did his report become available to me. While it is not extensive, it is accompanied by a more detailed sketch indicating the many soundings he carried out in the enclosure. As it turned out, our ignorance of the information in Garstang's report back in 1955 was a kind of blessing in disguise, for had we known the exact spots of his soundings, some of the most significant discoveries of our expedition would probably have been passed by. It so happened that both Garstang and our team were attracted to the same areas; but unluckily for him, he just missed the mark and therefore reported that no important results were reached in them. Had we been armed with this report, in all likelihood we would have avoided the areas that Garstang had already probed, and as a result

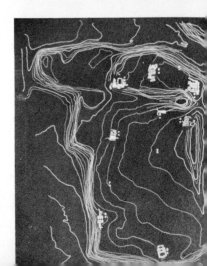

about half this book simply would not have been written at all!

Ever since I was a student, when I researched warfare in biblical lands in the light of archaeology for my Ph.D. thesis, I had been drawn to the site of Hazor and hoped to excavate it some day. Its unique fortifications, its association with the great battles of Joshua and the references to it in the period of Solomon and later Israelite kings were most alluring. But the dream had to be shelved at that time. While serving in the army during Israel's War of Independence and the following four years, I used to visit the site occasionally during military manoeuvres and was impressed afresh by its gigantic ramparts and unique features. When I resigned from the army at the end of 1952 to resume work on my Ph.D. thesis as a research fellow of the Hebrew

above A close aerial view, looking south, showing the 'bottle-shaped' *tell* (the 'neck' is on the right). In the foreground is the southern part of the enclosure, with part of its ramparts on the right
opposite A contour map of the site of Hazor, showing the *tell* in the south (top) and the enclosure (bottom)

Our excavations University, I spent two years in London and resolved to start a large-scale excavation on the site upon my return to Israel. The vastness of the area and the importance of the site required large-scale excavations and the best possible archaeological team. It was also imperative that the expedition be equipped with all the modern technical facilities available, photographic laboratories and surveying and drawing tools. I was extremely fortunate to have found in the late James A. de Rothschild a man not only generous, but with a deep love and understanding of the problems of the history of the Holy Land and the Jewish people, and he soon became enthusiastic about this project. Were it not for his help, and on upon his death for the help of his wife, Dorothy, I doubt that these excavations would ever have materialized, despite the invaluable aid we received from the Government of Israel, the Anglo-Israel Exploration Society and the Hebrew University.

The main excavations were carried out in four seasons of three months each during the summers of 1955–8. We employed up to 220 labourers at a time provided by the Government Labour Exchange from among the newly arrived North African immigrants who were settled in the neighbouring new settlement, also named Hazor. Their work was supervised by a team of about forty-five archaeologists, architects, pottery-restorers, photographers, draftsmen and senior students (see list of staff members at the end of the book). I knew that I would also need a first-class administrator to take all the administrative and technical problems off my hands and leave me free to concentrate on the archaeological aspects of the work. I was at that time still in London and, having heard of the availability of a former army officer whom I knew quite well from my service days, I wrote and asked if he would undertake the task, giving him details of the site, its size, what was required and so on. I was delighted to receive his acceptance a few days later and much amused by his letter, which included his estimate of the cost of the excavations. One large item in it was a bulldozer, with whose help he expected to level the *tell* completely and finish the excavations in a few weeks! Nevertheless, he was an excellent administrator and learned the tricks of the trade in no time.

In 1968, ten years after termination of the excavations, I returned to the site for another big season. Taken as a whole, the excavations of Hazor were among the most extensive ever carried out in the Holy Land, and I believe that they served as a true laboratory from which subsequent archaeologists of Israel emerged. Those who know who the leading archaeologists of Israel are today will easily recognize their names on our Hazor staff, though some of them were at that time students only. Nonetheless, the excavations were not an attraction for archaeologists or academics alone. The interest they provoked also brought a stream of tourists and many distinguished visitors.

Once the members of the staff were selected, we decided to build our own camp, consisting of three pre-fabricated barracks and a huge shed

for sorting and washing the pottery, near Kibbutz Ayelet Hashaḥar, just east of the site. Our staff was lodged in the kibbutz guest-house, today one of the most flourishing in the country, even featuring a duty-free shop for the thousands of tourists who visit it all year round. But when we began our dig, the entire guest-house consisted of two or three huts. While we take a bit of the credit for helping the kibbutz develop this branch of its economy, we were no less grateful to it for accommodating us in those days.

Our first task was to prepare the area grid. We managed to obtain a vertical aerial photograph of the site, as well as a photogrametric map based on it. The grid of the excavation was not parallel to the geographical one but was oriented by the bearings of the rectangular enclosure, for we believed that this would give us a better adjustment between the grid squares and the building plans. The whole area was then divided into large squares of 100 × 100 metres, each given a running number from west to east by row. In the excavated areas, each large square was further divided into sub-squares of 5 × 5 metres, which meant that one large square consisted of 400 small ones. The latter were marked by the letters A–U from west to east, and numbers 1–20 from south to north. Thus a full reference to any particular

left Technicians in the expedition camp restoring a huge jar of the 13th century BC
right David Ben Gurion, then Prime Minister and Minister of Defence, accompanied by the author, inspects a huge jar (similar to the one on the left)

Preparing the area

square may have read: 80/L-12. In the excavated areas, each of the small squares was marked with its letter and number and a concrete cube was sunk into the ground at its corner. The vastness of the site and its two distinctive components – the *tell* and the enclosure – dictated the need to start excavations in various areas simultaneously if we were to achieve any results at all. Every area chosen for excavation was supervised by a senior archaeologist and was marked by a separate letter: A, B, etc. Furthermore, because of the considerable distance between the excavated areas, and in order to ensure strict objectivity of the stratification in each area, we decided to mark the strata in each area independently. While the excavations were in progress, we employed two sets of numbers to designate the strata: Arabic numerals for the enclosure and Roman numerals for the upper mound. In the following chapters, I shall occasionally equate these two sets of numbers. Only later on, when it became possible to correlate the strata of the two areas, did we replace the Arabic numerals used in the enclosure with Roman ones, as is the accepted usage in archaeology.

Retrieving the data

The main problem in excavations is the precise and meticulous recording of the spots where objects are found in relation to the floors and walls of the respective buildings. In the photographs, one may notice from time to time numbers that mark what we call 'loci' (a *locus* is the Latin word used archaeologically to define a place, such as a room, a floor, an oven and so on). In order not to confuse findspots, and since numbers were the cheapest commodity at our disposal, we gave each area its own numbers: area A from 1,000 to 3,000; area B from 3,001 to 6,000 and so forth. Each area maintained its own numbered baskets, in which the sherds were accumulated daily for

left A photogrametric map of Hazor with the archaeological grid
right A surveyor preparing an area for excavations. Note the cubes for indicating the corners of the 5-metre square

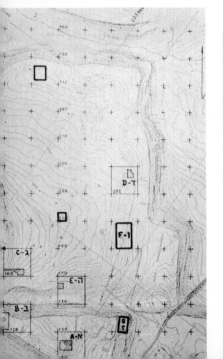

washing and classification. The finds themselves were then marked by our students with ink. Thus the inscription on sherd H57–B127/3 meant: Hazor, season of 1957, area B, basket 127, object number 3 in the basket. The supervisor of each area kept an independent list of baskets, marked in his field diary according to the *loci*, the absolute altitude, context and so on, so the number of the basket was the key to its exact provenance.

Another difficult problem in archaeological excavations is the disposal of the dug-up earth. What should one do with it? Some archaeologists just dump the earth nearby, only to regret it later when results show that it is precisely under that dump that a most important element of a building is located. Others just let the earth roll down the slope of the *tell*, which is a cheap method of disposal but may cause difficulties for future archaeologists. Because of Hazor's large-scale excavations, it was essential to find a basic solution to this problem right from the start. After deliberations, we decided to set up a network of small-gauge rails to carry little wagons drawn by a small engine. The network connected the excavated areas and lead to the western slope of the mound, where we built a special shoot to carry the earth away from the *tell*. The railway was quite efficient, but it was so slow that we named it 'The Hazor Express'. Because of the great distances separating the excavated areas, we installed field telephones between them, so I could be informed at any moment, wherever I happened to be, if anything special had turned up elsewhere. With the help of my station wagon, I could respond to the call in no time. On 1 August 1955 everything was set and ready for the beginning of the dig, and all of us were indescribably anxious to begin.

'The Hazor Express'

The construction of the 'shoot' on the western slope. 'The Hazor Express' brought the dug-up earth from the excavated areas, and at the bottom of the shoot (right), another network of wagons carried the earth further away from the site.

2 The First Confrontation

One of the biggest enigmas we hoped to solve during our excavations was the nature of the huge enclosure north of the *tell*. As already stated, this enclosure had also attracted the attention of Garstang, for it was a unique feature of Hazor – an area of 200 acres enclosed by a huge earthen rampart and further defended by a very deep and wide moat. What was it? Was it really just an enclosure, a camp area, a chariot parking-place, as suggested by Garstang and, in fact, accepted by most scholars up until our excavations? And if so, why was it defended by such formidable earth works, which necessitated the exertion of thousands of people for a long period? If not, could it be a city? And if it was a city, then it was obviously the largest in Israel and among the largest in the entire Fertile Crescent. In fact, if one reckons a population of about fifty inhabitants per 1,000 square metres, then the area of the enclosure could hold between 30,000 and 40,000 people, making it an enormous city!

Garstang's assertion that the enclosure was just a camp had, in his time, justifiable reasons, for similar enclosures were known in Egypt, Israel, and particularly Syria. Scholars had connected all of these with the huge chariot forces of the Hyksos hosts and therefore believed them to be camps. Likewise, in Garstang's time scholars thought it impossible that a city of such enormous dimensions (particularly in comparison with the other famous cities of the period, Megiddo and Beth-shan) could have existed at Hazor. If it had existed, then it was ten to fifteen times larger than contemporary cities in Canaan! Even conceding the logic of these arguments, and the apparent support provided by Garstang's trial trenches, it was hard to believe that such an enormous effort would have been invested in fortification just to defend a camp. One way or another, it was imperative that a problem of such prime importance be solved definitively, and we made up our minds to deal with it from the very beginning. But the nature of the enclosure was not the only question that faced us. There were two other problems of primary historical importance, particularly from a biblical viewpoint. The first: whether it was a camp or not, when was the enclosure destroyed – or rather, when did Joshua destroy it? The second: when was this camp, or city, or whatever established? This information was a vital prerequisite for the study of the material culture of ancient Palestine and its relations with the neighbouring countries.

After considerable deliberations with my colleague Jean Perrot, who

Why area C?

An oblique aerial view (looking north) of the entire site of Hazor. In the foreground are the springs, the highway and the *tell*. The earthen ramparts and moat are clearly visible (left) in the huge enclosure lying to the north of the *tell*

A close aerial view of area C (looking south), showing the extended trench on the slope of the rampart

was entrusted with supervising the excavations in the first area chosen in the enclosure, we selected an area in its south-west corner near the huge earthen rampart and close to the *tell* proper. This area had two advantages for a first trial dig. First, it was close to the earthen rampart, into which we intended to probe anyway in order to ascertain its method of construction (was it just a heap of earth, or was there some technique that made this earth hold together?). Second – an administrative consideration – it was near the *tell*, where our main dig was to be, and thus enabled us to move freely and without much effort between all the excavation areas, easing the logistic problems. The chosen area was called area C (areas A and B having been designated on the *tell* proper), and excavations there began on the first day of the first season, simultaneously with those on the *tell* above. It was here, as luck would have it, that we made the first and most important discovery of the entire expedition, one that already provided answers to the problems we had set out to solve.

The first major discovery

Before the excavations began, nothing could be seen on the surface except traces left by ploughshares and stalks of harvested wheat, as the whole area was cultivated by the farmers of neighbouring Rosh Pinah. We cut a long and narrow trench in the west, at the top of the earthen rampart, working in an easterly direction towards the heart of the enclosure. The trench was 70 metres long and 5 metres wide and was sub-divided into small squares, 5 × 5 metres each, separated from one another by a catwalk, for stratigraphic checking. Later on in the first season, we enlarged the area southwards, as shown in the photograph. The first days of the excavation were rather disappointing. As we progressed it became apparent that whatever lay beneath the surface had been badly mutilated by the ploughshares, while closer to the earthen rampart, where the slope began, we seemed to be digging in sterile soil – so much so that some members of our staff began to doubt the expediency of exploring any further. But there is a firm rule in excavations: do not give up before you are quite certain that you are really in virgin soil. And indeed, soon afterwards we were rewarded with the major discovery of the season and, I may now add, of all the five seasons of excavations. Just about 1 metre below the surface, we struck remains of buildings with cobble-stone floors, well preserved walls and great quantities of pottery. Here, indeed, we had the first indication that the area had not been an enclosure or camp but a fully built-up city.

A city!

Soon enough we were able to distinguish two phases in the structures – or rather, two strata – which we designated from top to bottom as IA and IB. As a rule, when excavators are certain that strata are truly separate, they are designated different numbers. In this case, the differentiation of strata was not so clear at the beginning, and we had

The foundations of buildings with cobble-stone floors, the first discovery indicating that the enclosure was indeed a city

The two phases (IA–IB) of the last Canaanite city are clearly seen in this photograph. The numbers indicate various *loci*

6215

the impression that many houses and structures of the lower phase had been re-used, with raised floors and alterations, in the upper and last city to exist on the site. So we were careful to mark both strata with the same number, using letters to indicate the two phases. In due course, as excavations progressed, we also understood what had puzzled us at the beginning – indeed, what nearly discouraged us from continuing the dig – why we seemed to be digging into sterile soil in some parts of the trench. It became clear that the area near the foot of the earthen rampart was covered with disintegrated mud bricks and clay material washed down from the top of the ramparts in past millennia. No wonder the soil was sterile; it sealed the last level of occupation! Once this discovery was made and the enigma solved, we extended the area to the south, where a series of buildings of these last two phases emerged – houses with huge courtyards surrounded by rooms. In many cases the top city had been abandoned in haste, to judge from the many vessels left intact on the floors of the houses.

Having ascertained that we were indeed digging in the remains of a huge, formidable city, the second – and, historically, perhaps much more important – question to be answered arose: when were these two top cities, and particularly the topmost one, destroyed? Since the destruction of the top level, this area had never been occupied again. Could it be that this huge city came to its end through the acts of Joshua's

opposite, top A general view of area C taken from the rampart, looking east towards Kibbutz Ayelet Hashahar. Note the density of the built-up area
opposite, bottom A schematic plan (right) of a complex of buildings with courtyards shown in the photograph (left). Courtyard 6215 is seen in the centre
bottom

left Huge quantities of broken vessels, many of which are great *pithoi*
right A basalt mortar and grinder found intact on the mud floor, indicating that the inhabitants left in haste

A girl from North Africa felt 'at home' operating the two grinding stones, which are over 3,000 years old

troops, as narrated in the Book of Joshua? If so, the possibility of dating this last destruction could help immensely in solving the much-debated problem of dating one of the most important events in the history of the Holy Land: the occupation of the country by the Israelites. A clue would be found, as usual and common in many other cases, in the pottery found on the floor.

Garstang believed that the last Canaanite settlement was destroyed by Joshua around 1400 BC, or, in archaeological terminology, at the end of the Late Bronze I period. This opinion, which accorded with his views on the date of the Exodus and the conquest of Canaan by the Israelites, baffled the many scholars who believed that these two events took place at least 100 years later. What was Garstang's main evidence for thus dating the destruction of Canaanite Hazor? Let us quote his own words:

The clue of Mycenaean pottery

... In L.B.A. [Late Bronze Age] there appears to have been only a surface occupation, in tents or huts, which was brought to a close by a general conflagration. Some two thousand five hundred fragments of pottery from the surface deposits were examined, and while L.B.A. was well represented, both by Cypro-Phoenician and local fabrics, no Mykenaen specimens were found ... as a whole and in round terms the complete absence of Mykenaen specimens, as at Jericho, suggests a date of destruction about 1400 B.C. ...

Since this was a vital point, and since Mycenaean pottery will be mentioned frequently in the course of describing the Hazor excavations, a few words about its importance to absolute dating in the archaeology of the Holy Land are in order.

The designation Mycenaean pottery is applied by archaeologists to a specially and easily recognized type of pottery that originated in mainland Greece, mainly within the Mycenaean culture, and was found all over the Aegean, as well as in Egypt and the eastern Mediterranean coasts. It is sub-divided into Mycenaean I, II and III. Since Mycenaean I and II are characteristic of the sixteenth and fifteenth centuries BC, our interest lies mainly in the so-called Mycenaean III type. Due to an interesting coincidence, its appearance in any dig serves as evidence – nearly the only firm testimony available to us – for absolute dating of strata to the fourteenth and thirteenth centuries. The reason for this extremely fortunate phenomenon is that a great quantity of this type of pottery was discovered in the short-lived city of el-Amarna, which was discussed in the previous chapter. Obviously, artefacts discovered there are of tremendous importance because they can be absolutely dated to the reign of Amenophis IV (1364–47 BC); and the fact that a certain type of Mycenaean III pottery was discovered at el-Amarna makes it a sure peg for absolute chronology throughout the Near East. The distinguished Swedish archaeologist Arne Furumark dedicated most of his life to the classification and dating of Mycenaean pottery, and according to his classification the type found in el-Amarna is, on the whole, Mycenaean IIIA. Thus this type, with some variants, is typical of the fourteenth

A typical Mycenaean IIIB stirrup jar found in Hazor

century BC. Another type, Mycenaean IIIB, is associated in Egyptian archaeology and other places with the thirteenth century BC, or roughly with Ramses II, believed by many scholars to be the Pharaoh of the Exodus. While Mycenaean II of the fifteenth century is found in the Holy Land, though in meagre quantities, the Mycenaean IIIA and IIIB types are found on nearly every site in Palestine and the neighbouring countries that was occupied during the fourteenth and thirteenth centuries BC.

We can now understand the reasoning behind Garstang's dating. Having found no Mycenaean pottery, he legitimately came to the conclusion that the occupation of the enclosure came to an end *prior* to the appearance of the Mycenaean pottery in the area, that is, roughly before 1400 BC. One can readily imagine our excitement, therefore, when we uncovered an abundance of Mycenaean pottery on the floor of the two topmost strata! As we carefully removed the earth, there emerged quantities of the IIIB type (typical of the thirteenth century) on the floors of the top level (1A) and of the IIIA type in the lower stratum (1B). These finds not only indicated that the settlement of 1B was the city of the notorious Abdi-Tirshi mentioned in the el-Amarna letters, but, even more important, they made it quite clear that the large city of Hazor in the enclosure (which we may, from now on, call the lower city, to distinguish it from the settlement discovered on the *tell* proper) was

A fine group of Mycenaean
IIIA vessels found in a tomb at
Hazor. Note the stirrup jars,
the pyriform-shaped vessel and
the cup

opposite, left Top of a
Mycenaean III figurine of a
woman. Note the 'choker' and
low '*décolleté*'

destroyed during the thirteenth century BC, while Mycenaean pottery
was still in use. According to Furumark, Mycenaean pottery went out
of fashion roughly around 1230 BC, so the evidence in hand, contrary
to Garstang's conclusions, shows that the city was destroyed around
1230 at the latest. As will be explained in due course, we have substantial
evidence to indicate that the destruction took place some time in the
third quarter of the thirteenth century, say between 1250 and 1230 BC.
This evidence was substantiated in all the other areas of the lower city
and is, indeed, among the most important and decisive archaeological
testimonies ever uncovered in excavations concerning the date of the
conquest by Joshua and, indirectly, of the Exodus itself.

Once we had determined more or less when the lower city was destroyed, we still had to resolve when this city of such phenomenal
dimensions had been established. For that purpose we deepened our
excavation during the first and second (1956) seasons, when the area
was supervised by Trude Dothan. Naturally, we had to remove the

upper strata; and as we extended our trenches mainly southwards, we left strata 1A and 1B only in the northern part of area C, owing to the special nature of the discoveries made there. As expected, under stratum 1B we came upon a new stratum, which was marked 2. It contained many residential buildings and pottery that proved them to belong to the Late Bronze I period (sixteenth–fifteenth centuries BC). Later on we made important discoveries pertaining to this stratum in other areas, all testifying to a period of flourishing culture. Considering that the city was founded on a thick layer of ash (evidence that a fire had destroyed its predecessor at the end of the Middle Bronze period), and in view of the fact that the remains pre-dated the fourteenth century, there is no doubt that stratum 2 represented the Hazor of Pharaoh Thutmose III, which – as we have learned from Egyptian documents – was a very important city.

Once photographed and drawn, the remains of the Late Bronze I city were likewise removed in various areas, and below them two strata, 3 and 4, were discovered, both from the Middle Bronze period. The lower of these, stratum 4, was built on virgin soil, so it was obviously the very first level of the lower city and therefore the first city to be founded here in the enclosure. We have said that both strata belonged to the Middle Bronze period, but they can be dated even more accurately to the last two phases thereof – which, by accepted dating, fall between the middle of the eighteenth century BC and the middle or the end of the sixteenth century BC – say about 1550 BC. Discoveries in these strata were numerous, but we were impressed most of all by the town-planning, particularly by the sewage systems in the houses. One of our finds was a beautiful sewage canal with an outlet made of basalt.

A corner of a Middle Bronze house (left) with a well-built sewage canal and outlet (right)

Gracious living

The houses themselves are also of considerable interest. One of the houses found in stratum 3 demonstrates how well planned and spacious the residential buildings of the quarter were. In its centre is a large court flanked by four rooms, two on the east and two on the west. It was in the south-east room that we discovered the sewage drain and its beautiful basalt outlet.

Infants buried in jars

Upon removing the floors of the lowest city to ascertain whether it was indeed the first city and was built on virgin soil, we encountered a surprising phenomenon. Under most of the floors (and one must remember that floors in this instance mean beaten-earth floors, which are often difficult to discern) we found many jars, seemingly intact, lying sideways in the virgin soil. Was this evidence of an even earlier

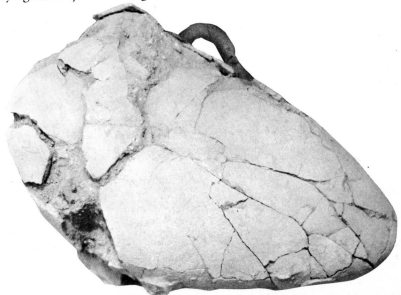

An infant burial jar as found under the floor
below, *left* An opened jar showing the crouching and squeezed skeleton
below right A similar jar showing a juglet for liquids near the head

city? Only when we opened the first jar did we see that they were infant burials. Scores of such burials – some of twins – were discovered. Sometimes the whole area under a floor was littered with them. Most of the jars contained juglets placed next to the skeletons, probably offerings of food and milk for the dead. Early in this century, when infant burials in jars were first discovered, archaeologists believed them to be evidence of child sacrifices; but now we know that it was a common practice, particularly in the Middle Bronze period, to bury infants under the floors of homes so that they might continue to live near their families. Had our case really been one of child sacrifices, we would have been forced to conclude that almost all the infants of those homes were sacrificed as offerings, which is obviously absurd. On the other hand, the large number of burials under some of the houses indicates a high rate of infant mortality, perhaps the result of an epidemic. As will be told, we found similar burials in other areas.

I recall an amusing episode in connection with these discoveries. When I first reported our finds, I mentioned the existence of the food and milk juglets in the jars. Sometime later I received a letter from a pediatrician in South Africa requesting a photograph of the milk bottle we had found, because it was important to his research on the sucking habits of babies!

In some of the jars we also found scarabs, but not as many as were found in graves of the same period uncovered in other areas. The popularity of scarabs in Canaan at that time was due to the proliferation and influence of Egyptian culture, for these objects, which are actually either seals or seal amulets, are Egyptian in origin, or were made under the influence of Egyptian prototypes, and they are very typical of the Middle Bronze period – particularly its second part, the so-called Hyksos period. They are carved like the common dung-beetle, *scarabeus sacer*, and the beetle-shaped seal amulets were also popular for rings because of their shape: convex back and flat bottom. The Egyptians considered beetles to have light-giving properties and associated them with the morning sun. In their paintings one sometimes sees the scarab rolling the globe of the sun with its hind legs, a design the Egyptians adapted from Nature: the beetle pushing the ball of dung, in which its eggs were laid and hatched. When they bear royal names, scarabs become very important for purposes of dating, or rather post-dating, for the objects found together with scarabs must be dated *later* than the Pharaoh whose name is inscribed on them. Unfortunately, none of the scarabs we found bore royal names, but their style and pseudo-hieroglyphs are most typical mainly of the Hyksos period.

Perhaps the single most important discovery of the Middle Bronze period in area C was a group of three large jugs found in a row of niche-like structures at the very foot of the earthen rampart. To our great amazement, the shoulder of one of the jugs bore an inscription

Three typical Hyksos scarabs found at Hazor, shown from three sides

The jar (above, left) with the oldest cuneiform inscription found in the Holy Land (above right and below)

The earliest cuneiform inscription found in Israel

in Accadian (the language of the Babylonians and Assyrians) in cuneiform script. This is a rare inscription, not only because it is the earliest one found in Israel but also because the cuneiforms were scratched on the fired pot, rather than indented with a wedge (which gave its name to this script) before firing, while above the inscription is a large symbol of a trident that was incised in the wet clay before firing. The inscription itself has been deciphered as a person's name, read differently by two scholars, though both agree that its first element is *Ish-me*, which means 'he heard'. The second element is definitely theophoric, as indicated by the determinative (star) preceding it, but scholars are divided about its reading: either 'Adad' (the deity), in which case the name would mean 'Adad heard'; or 'Ilam' (the word for god in the accusative), in which case it would mean 'he heard the god'. In all probability the name is that of the owner of the jar or, if the object was associated with a cult place, it might be the name of its donor. In any case, it is the earliest cuneiform inscription ever found in this part of the world and is also important for its indication of Babylonian influence on Hazor in this period. During the course of our excavations, further evidence of that influence was found in other areas. But in order to appreciate it completely, I shall defer discussion of this point until I have described the other finds.

The discoveries in area C, which indicated that the enclosure was indeed a city (established in the Middle Bronze period and destroyed during the final phase of the Late Bronze period), created a great sensation in the archaeological world – and a particular stir among one or two members of our own staff. One must remember that before we started excavations at Hazor, quite a number of scholars had already made up their minds one way or another about the nature of the enclosure. And those scholars whose views seemed to have been shattered by the new discovery could not immediately swallow these results. The opposition to our conclusions by at least one member of our own team served as a blessing in disguise. His argument against my basic conclusion was: 'Yes, it is true that in area C we found remains of buildings. But one should remember that this area of the enclosure is in the south-west corner, very close to the *tell*, and it is therefore possible that here, and only here, a small residential quarter existed.' Such an important challenge could not be ignored. So as early as 1955, during the first season, but particularly in the second season a year later, I decided to open up further areas of excavation in the enclosure areas D, E, F and so forth (which will be described in detail in later chapters). In all of them we encountered the same scene: foundation strata of the Middle Bronze II period and termination of the upper stratum in the Late Bronze period, as evidenced by the Mycenaean III pottery. But it so happened that all the areas selected for further excavation were on the fringe of the enclosure or were associated with a temple or some other prominent building, so the results did not entirely convince those who opposed the conclusion that the enclosure was indeed a city. They now argued that the finds in these areas only meant that structures of temples existed at random; but this did not indicate the existence of an entire city. So in 1957, during our third season, I decided to find a way of convincing even the die-hards and suggested the following 'deal' to my colleagues: 'Let us pick a random area, not associated with any visible building or stones, right in the centre of the enclosure and excavate a small 5 × 5 metre square. And let us agree that the results of our probe there would settle the matter once and for all. Should this little square yield buildings, as had the other areas, then we would accept this as final proof that the entire enclosure was built-up, a true city. If it did not, then the question would remain open.'

The deal was agreed upon, and we picked the south-west corner of square 210, sub-square A, and started digging. Results were startling and exciting indeed! Immediately below the cultivated surface, we began to uncover walls and characteristic Late Bronze pottery. Here also, two layers of the top stratum, equivalent to 1A and 1B, appeared. Below them a floor of stratum 2, together with Late Bronze I pottery, was discovered. And beneath that, as expected, were two strata, 3 and 4, of the Middle Bronze period, with the lower stratum built on virgin soil, exactly as we had found in area C. So the vital problem, and undoubtedly our most important discovery of the first season, was clinched. It was somehow reassuring that even in the confines of this small square and at a distance of a couple of hundred yards from area C, under the floors of the Middle Bronze houses we again found abundant infant burials in jars. The nature of the entire enclosure finally established, let us go back to area C, which in 1955–6 was the scene of further discoveries – one of them most unexpected.

Three phases of area 210: before excavation (top); at the first sign of a house – stratum 1A (centre); and further strata below (bottom)

3 Site of Three Major Discoveries – Area C

One of the aims of the trench opened in area C was to probe into the nature of the earthen rampart. While digging deep into its lower part, we ascertained that it was made of beaten earth and a conglomerate of field stones and earth. However, when we deepened the trench somewhat, we were suddenly confronted by an unusual and alluring find: a headless statue of a seated man and an upturned bowl close by. Because of the nature of the *locus* of the find, we thought that the statue and bowl might not be *in situ*, but had been thrown into the fill of the lower part of the rampart. So we decided to investigate whether or not this was so by enlarging the trench near the statue somewhat to the north. Immediately we struck an upright basalt stone with a curved top. It seemed obvious that we had come upon a promising area, so we decided to enlarge the trench even further. In the course of the following days of very exciting work, we uncovered a row of about ten basalt stelae with curved tops, flat fronts and concave backs – some larger, some smaller – and in front of them a flat basalt slab that obviously served as an offering table.

What we had come upon was a little sanctuary of an unusual type featuring upright stones – *mazzeboth*, to use a biblical expression, stelae, in Greek. It was quite clearly a miniature sanctuary: the statue was small, the stelae were small. But we were so bewildered and excited about the discovery that to us everything looked big, and our attitude was well depicted in a cartoon drawn by a member of the staff. When we deepened the dig just in front of and below the statue, we found the head of the statue, which exactly fitted the torso, lying on the floor at a depth of 86 centimetres. This find taught us two bits of important information: first, that the head was decapitated deliberately by a blow at the small of the neck with a sharp instrument; second, and even more important, that the shape of that part of the sanctuary

A *mazzeboth* (stelae) temple

opposite The trench in the rampart, showing the headless statue, as found, together with an upturned bowl
below, left J. Perrot and the author looking at the small stelae temple during the excavations
below, right The cartoon drawn by a member of our staff expressing our excitement during the excavations

was peculiar, indicated by the fact that the statue's head lay below its torso. Obviously the statue, the row of stelae and the offering table were erected on a high platform – in fact, a semi-circular one – while the floor of the room around it was on a lower level. This conclusion was further strengthened by the fact that in front of the table we found heaps of pottery lying on a diagonal from the table towards the floor. Some of the fragments on this axis could be joined together into complete vessels.

To get a closer view of the finds themselves, let us begin with the statue. Just 40 centimetres high and made of basalt, it depicts a man seated on a low stool holding a cup-like object in one hand while the other hand rests on his knee (it also appears as if holding something, though no object has been depicted by the artist). Such representations of either deity or king, shown seated and holding a cup in one hand and a sceptre in the other, are very common in the ancient Near East. The man in our statue is wearing a long tunic with a pronounced hem falling slightly below the knee; the upper part of the tunic has a curved neckline, from which an inverted crescent is suspended onto the chest. This symbol is known to be the emblem of the moon god. The head is short and round; the brow is low; the nose – which was slightly damaged in antiquity – is long and thick and the eyes are somewhat large. Although the finish of the surface is very good, considering the hardness of the stone, not all the features are equally accentuated, and the execution of some lacks detail. Thus the ears are shown without the cavities, the eyes without pupils and the fingers are hardly noticeable at all. On the one hand, the artist succeeded in creating a harmonious figure with a serene facial expression; while on the other, he obviously did not intend to accentuate the facial details. Was there any special reason for this? We shall explore one possible explanation later on.

Did the statue represent the deity, the king or a priest? Theoretically, all three alternatives are possible, but in the light of later finds I believe it is a statue of the deity itself. When we first published our report and expressed this view, one scholar challenged it on the ground that the emblems of the ancient Near Eastern deities were never depicted on their statues. Later on in the course of our excavations, however, we discovered another statue that was definitely a representation of the deity, and, sure enough, on its breast was its personal emblem, the symbol of the weather god.

While the statue was an intriguing find, the fact is that the more important part of our discovery was the stelae. Except for the one in the centre, none of them bore a relief. Some of them stood to the right and left behind the statue, serving, as it were, to support it. Although the tops of the stelae were more or less on an even level, their bases were found at different depths, due to their varying sizes. The tallest of them was 55 centimetres and the smallest 22 centimetres.

above A close-up of the left side of the stelae, showing the statue and central relief with the hands and the emblem of the moon deity. *left* Front view of the statue, showing the moon deity emblem on its chest. *right* Rear view of the statue

What purpose did the stelae serve? And what did they represent? In the second season of excavations, we enlarged this area to the south, where just adjacent to the temple, on the lower part of the rampart's slope, we discovered another seventeen stelae of various sizes, most of them only roughly worked. Some were found on a higher level and others at the bottom of the slope. Perhaps this indicates that the stelae in the temple were memorial stones to commemorate a dead king or priest, and the unfinished ones stored nearby were worked from time to time, as the need arose, and added to the sanctuary. If we accept

above A close-up of the stelae temple, showing all the stelae, the deity statue and the offering table
below The central stele with the relief

this explanation, then the temple of the moon god may also be defined as a memorial chapel. But whether or not such an interpretation is correct, these stelae are some of the boldest representations of the cult stones mentioned so often in the Bible. The Law of Moses not only forbade the Israelites to make them, but enjoined them to destroy those of their pagan neighbours. It must have been when Hazor was occupied by the Israelites that this chapel met its fate, in fulfilment of the commandment: 'You shall surely destroy all the places where the nations whom you shall dispossess served their gods, upon the high mountains and upon the hills and under every green tree; you shall tear down their altars and dash in pieces their *mazzeboth*. . .' (Deuteronomy 12:2–3). At least we can say that the head of the statue was deliberately chopped off.

The most interesting of the stelae was, of course, the centre one because of the simple but very expressive relief it bore on the upper two-thirds of its surface, which may indicate that it was meant to be sunk into the ground up to nearly a third of its height. The relief depicts two hands stretched upwards in a gesture of supplication and, above them, the symbol of a deity, which is composed of three elements: a crescent, a disc within the crescent and two small tassel-like circles suspended in the centre. There can be no doubt that the symbols are those of the moon god as they represent the moon's two phases: the crescent and the full moon. More difficult, however, is the explanation of the two hands. Is this just, as appears to our modern taste, a simple and expressive way of showing a state of supplication and prayer, or does it have another significance? We were not able to analyze this problem critically until additional finds made in the vicinity shed some light on it.

The discovery of the statue and stelae was made, as will sometimes happen in a dig, during the last two weeks of the season. So in the short time left to us until the end of the season, we could only ascertain a few more details concerning this unique temple. Nonetheless, these extra details were sufficient to indicate that the objects we found in stratum IA, the topmost stratum and last Canaanite occupation in the area, represented only the last phase of the temple's long life. Evidence of earlier phases came to light partly during that first season and partly in the following one, when we enlarged the excavations in this area. The first sign that earlier stages of the temple existed came together with a most surprising and important find.

When we cleared the ground under the stele on the extreme right (from the viewer's perspective), which was found lying slanted, we found a unique slab of basalt buried there. On one side it bore a relief of a crouching lion and on the front the lion's head and forelegs, while the other side of the slab was unworked. This slab, which measured 44 centimetres wide, 33 centimetres high and about 12 centimetres

An earlier phase of the temple

The lion orthostat, discovered under the top level, in secondary use (see next page)

Drawing of the glass cosmetic
bottle found in the sub-layers
under the stelae

thick, was obviously what is called in archaeological terminology
an orthostat. Orthostats (the term is composed of two Greek words
meaning standing upright) usually served as panels or dados for the
lower part of walls. This one was probably a door-jamb orthostat, with
its unworked side built into the jamb and the carved side facing the
entrance. Obviously the orthostat as found was not in its original
position. Either it belonged to a different building and was buried
here deliberately, or, more probably, it was an heirloom left behind
from an earlier phase of the temple, where it likewise did not serve its
original function. Together with this orthostat, in the same sub-layers
under the stelae, quite a number of interesting objects belonging to
earlier phases were discovered under fallen debris. Among them were
a beautiful mace-head, a crude (nearly abstract) basalt figurine and
a most beautiful glass cosmetic bottle, one of the earliest of its kind ever
found in this country. Altogether, we reckoned that there were two
or three sub-phases under the top one, all of them, we believe, belonging
to stratum IB of the fourteenth century.

It is possible that the temple, built as it was at the very foot of the
rampart, was repeatedly destroyed not only by enemies but perhaps
by the elements as well, and some of the objects may thus have been
forgotten and buried under the debris. Be this as it may, it is quite
clear that most of the objects found in the upper stratum originally
belonged to an earlier phase and were salvaged by the people of IA
when they rebuilt the temple. It is even possible that the lion orthostat
originally belonged to a much older building, perhaps of the Late
Bronze I or even the end of the Middle Bronze period. But this problem

will be discussed when we describe another temple adorned by ortho-stats in chapter 6.

The rich discoveries in area C made mainly towards the end of the season whetted our appetite, and we eagerly returned there in the second season, this time enlarging our excavations mainly in the north. Our expectations were not disappointed. In the vicinity of the temple, we found quite a number of complexes structured around central courts, all of them somehow or other connected with the temple, its cult or its function. Let us first turn to room 6225 in the northern part of the excavated area, because this was the room in which a dramatic discovery was made. The room, or rather court, is rectangular, measuring about 7 × 3.5 metres. On its eastern wall was a low bench built of small, undressed stone blocks. Opposite it, on the narrow side of the court, was an installation in the shape of a double wall set at a right angle to the main wall. Between the two walls was a narrow gap filled with earth. As a rule, it is a natural tend-ency for archaeologists to define any strange building as a temple, or at least to say that it has some cultic significance. Had we found in court 6225 only the remains and structures I have just described, we, too, would have regarded it as a temple, taking the double-walled platform to be an altar or cultic platform. Fortunately we found two very in-teresting objects in this platform. I remember vividly the great ex-citement on that day, when Trude Dothan called me on the field telephone to come to her area immediately. There, in the platform, I saw a little clay mask, quite intact. The scales of judgement im-mediately balanced in favour of a temple. But right nearby was

Room 6225 (actually a court), in which dramatic discoveries were made. Note the bench around the walls and the rectangular installation

A dramatic discovery

opposite The mask and potter's wheels as found
left The mask. Note the holes for threading a string to fasten it

above The upper and lower potter's wheels

quite another kind of object – a pair of potter's wheels, upper and lower, made of basalt.

It seemed that we had found a potter's workshop – and perhaps the entire court was a pottery. Additional evidence to this effect was the fragment of a much-worn sherd found nearby. Like similar sherds found in potters' workshops at the famous biblical city of Lachish, in the foothills of Judah, it served to rub and thereby finish the surface of the earthenware. The two wheels were in such perfect condition and so smooth that by slightly lubricating the socket the upper one turned very easily. This discovery also explained why we found single potter's wheels, both uppers and lowers, in other rooms in the vicinity. It seems that the entire area was part of a storeroom and potter's workshop connected with the temple.

But let us return to the clay mask, which was perhaps the more important discovery up to that time in relation to the temple and its cult. The mask was made first as a bowl; then the eyes were cut out, the long eyebrows joined to the upper end of the straight slender nose (which lacks nostrils), the mouth given shape and the ears moulded. Two holes were perforated at the upper end and two more on each side, one above and one below the ear. These were for threading a string to attach the mask either to the head of its wearer or to another object. The mask is rather small – 14 centimetres high – and is beardless.

The clay mask

The 'cruder' mask found in area D
opposite, *left* Part of the rich assortment of vessels found in the potter's storeroom
opposite, *right* A painted chalice (top) and a few of the scores of bowls found in the storeroom (centre). The votive bowl found near the statue (see page 42) is identical in shape. The drawing of one of the typical locally painted jars (bottom) describes two strips of the designs: horned animals and a series of palm-style 'trees of life'

During the first season, while digging in area D several hundred metres further to the north-east, we found a similar – though slightly broken – mask thrown into a cistern. It, too, had first been made as a bowl and then had the eyes, brows, nose and mouth moulded by hand. It is clear that both potters aimed at achieving the same object, but the results were clearly different. The area-D mask is slightly cruder, styled with some naïveté. When we found the second mask, we happened to have had a visitor on the dig who was an art critic, and in his opinion the mask from area D had been made by the better artist. I wonder what the people of Hazor thought about these two masks? And we all wondered what the purpose of the mask was. It was too small to put on the face of an adult; but it could have been attached to the face of a deceased infant or served other functions in the cult. We shall return to this question once we have dealt with the next important discovery, which sheds further light on the cult of this temple.

The potter's storehouse

As mentioned earlier, the whole area near court 6225 and south of it was occupied by structures with central courts. In their rooms, but particularly in the courtyards themselves, we found huge quan-

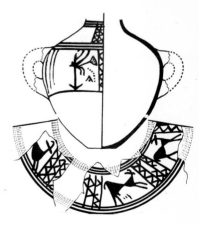

tities of pottery, the most conspicuous pieces being large storage jars or *pithoi* of the 'Ali-Baba' size. Jars of this type had never been found before and have been known since as the 'Hazor *pithoi*'. Then, in one room further to the east of room 6225, we were fortunate to have found what may be defined as the potter's storeroom. Here, too, we found benches along the walls, but in contrast to room 6225, this time the floors and benches were covered with a rich assortment of pottery, including many bowls, chalices, goblets, juglets, lamps – some of them stacked in heaps – and even a stand. It was quite clear that this was a potter's storeroom, because many of the objects showed no sign of use. This was particularly true of the oil lamps, which are usually found in excavations with traces of soot on the nozzle, while here they were brand new. Taken together, we had a very fine collection of typical local pottery of the fourteenth–thirteenth centuries BC, some pieces simply, but impressively, painted.

The biggest discovery of all came when we had almost finished clearing the pottery from the room. While the finds were being removed, three bowls stacked one on top of the other were uncovered,

right The silver-plated bronze
cult standard. Note the crescent
and stylized snake, the two
snakes flanking the figure of
the deity and the stylized snake
at the bottom.
below The heap of bowls
under which the standard
was found. This photograph
was taken at the moment of
discovery

and underneath them was a peculiar jar containing, to our great astonishment, a silver-plated bronze standard. I wish I could reproduce here the gasps and exclamations emitted by members of the team as they watched it emerge from the jar. The standard is rectangular, 12.5 × 7 centimetres, with a tang at one end. The surface is plated with a thin sheet of silver pressed tightly onto it. The details of the depiction on it, made by both relief and incision, are not clear because of the silver plating. But I hope that with the aid of the photograph, it is possible to make out, as we did, the face of a woman holding a snake in either hand and wearing a pendant shaped like a stylized snake. On the upper edge of the standard, above the woman's head, is a crescent, within which the stylized image of the snake is repeated. This depiction is in fact similar to other Near Eastern representations of a snake goddess, the finest of them all being the topless goddess from Crete. But our standard, as such, is unique. One can definitely say that it served a cultic function and, even more specifically, was probably carried on a pole in cultic processions. But its true importance lies in its connection with the stelae temple, for the symbol of the crescent, found on the breast of the headless statue of the deity and on the central stele of the temple, is also represented here. So the woman on this standard must be the goddess of the temple, the consort of the moon god.

Once this connection was established, with the aid of evidence uncovered far from Hazor we were able to make the significance of other finds in the temple area fit into place. Until now, I have been engaged in presenting facts and describing our discoveries: the temple and its stelae, the statue, the potter's workshop, the mask and the silver-plated standard. Now I think we must proceed to indulge in some theories. The following are suggestions that may sound like a complicated puzzle – and one whose pieces are scattered far afield at that. But the complexities of a puzzle, in and of themselves, do not mean that its solution is incredible.

The first clue takes us to a place called Zinjirli in the south-eastern part of Turkey (near the north-west frontier of present-day Syria), where archaeologists discovered a city ruled by a local dynasty of the kings of Samal. Fortunately, these kings left behind many monuments inscribed in Aramaic and in Phoenician, a language very close to Hebrew. Most of their stelae and monuments also bear at the top a series of emblems representing the deities worshipped by them. One emblem repeated on all these monuments is a crescent with a full disc inside it, very similar to the one represented on the central stele in the temple of area C. Several of the deities worshipped by the Samal kings are mentioned in the inscriptions, but, unfortunately, not in relation to a specific emblem; so our first problem was to find out which of the deities was associated with the emblem of the crescent and the disc. For various reasons I thought that these images were related to the

What mean these stones?

An inscribed stele from Zinjirli showing the emblems of the deities worshipped by the local kings. Note the crescent and disc on the right

deity named Ba'al Ḥamman (or Ba'al Ḥammon). Ḥamman may be the ancient name of the Amanus Mountains (in which Zinjirli is located), and Ba'al Ḥamman could therefore mean 'Lord of the Amanus'. If this suggestion is accepted, then the deity of the crescent and disc was the moon god – and like many moon gods was associated with hills.

The second clue leads us to North Africa, specifically the vicinity of Carthage and Sardinia. This area was the centre of the Punic culture, that is, the late Phoenician culture of the fifth–second centuries BC. Here again, we find that the chief, actually the sole, male deity is one called Ba'al Ḥamman, and, interestingly enough, his emblem is also a crescent with a disc inside it, sometimes shown with the ends of the crescent pointed downwards. What struck us most, however, was the fact that in searching for parallels to the two outstretched hands, the only place we could find them was on the hundreds of stelae discovered in the area of Carthage and other places of the Punic Empire, although a span of a thousand years separates them from the stelae of Hazor. What did these hands mean on the Carthage stelae? Did they, too, only represent acts of supplication by the worshippers? I believe that the hands were actually the emblem of Ba'al Ḥamman's consort. The only goddess ever mentioned in all these stelae in conjunction with Ba'al Ḥamman, or sometimes independent of him, is a powerful goddess called Tanit, or Tinnith. When presented in full, she is always shown as a woman with both hands raised upwards and sometimes holding snakes (as on the standard); but she is more often represented in a rather schematic manner – a triangle with a circle on top and the two hands – which has come to be known as the symbol of Tanit. When shown alone, the two hands represent an abbreviated form of the same deity; and I believe that in Hazor, too, these hands are not an expression of a worshipper's reverence, but the emblem of the consort of Hazor's moon god, be her name what it may. On many of the Carthage monuments, Tanit is called 'the face of Ba'al' – her official title, as it were.

Now we come to yet a further clue, admittedly an amazing one. The area of the Punic culture yielded not only the emblems of Ba'al Ḥamman and the two hands depicting Tanit, but also strange masks not unlike the ones discovered at Hazor. There, too, the masks are of a beardless being and sometimes they come outfitted with earrings. Is it possible that the clay masks in Carthage represent Tanit, 'the face of Ba'al'? And, turning back to Hazor, would it be far-fetched to suggest that the small mask devoid of nostrils and opened mouth was really the emblem of the snake goddess, consort of the moon god, and that the mask was actually attached to the face of the moon-god statue, thus representing the 'face of Ba'al'? Such a conclusion certainly would be in keeping with the small size of the mask and may also explain why the face of the statue was crudely executed and so lacking

in detail. A final resemblance between the discoveries of Hazor and those of the Punic culture is the fact that in some of the monuments, the sanctuaries of Baʻal Ḥamman and Tanit are depicted with stelae above a platform, exactly like the ones we found in Hazor. Whether or not this theory is correct, it is quite clear that the Punic culture preserved elements of the Phoenician culture, and the latter was definitely influenced by Canaanite elements similar to the ones uncovered in Hazor.

The finds in area C were fascinating both in themselves and in the context of the cross-cultural analysis they enabled us to explore. But they hardly exhausted the enclosure's potential to yield information on cultic and daily life in Hazor before the Israelite conquest. Much more was awaiting us in the other parts of the lower city.

A Punic stele dedicated to Baʻal Ḥamman and Tanit, showing a representation of their sanctuary with stelae erected above a platform

opposite, above A Punic votive stele showing the emblem of Baʻal Ḥamman (crescent and disc) and his consort, the goddess Tanit, depicted as a woman with raised hands. Note the hand on the left

opposite, below Two hands, symbolizing Tanit, on a Punic stele

4 A Huge Altar and Mysterious Tunnels – Area F

While walking between areas C and D sometime in the first season, our attention was drawn to a huge block of well-dressed stone that protruded just above the surface, about 400 metres east–north-east of area C. The stone resembled an altar, because its upper surface featured two rectangular depressions and several cup marks. Some 25 metres north of the altar, the top of a massive wall of large, undressed stones also projected from the ground. Such bait was too tempting to leave untackled, but during the first season our efforts were already over-extended. So we postponed investigation of this vicinity (designated as area F) to the second season, when Jean Perrot assumed supervision there and Trude Dothan replaced him in area C. Had I known what awaited us deep underground, I might not have begun this venture – certainly not for lack of importance and fascination, but because the work here was extremely difficult technically and required special attention for longer than we planned at the outset. In retrospect, however, I have no complaints. Enough was discovered not only to indicate the high standard of building in the Bronze Age and whet our appetites for the future, but to teach us a valuable lesson about the intricate problems of excavations in this area.

Let us begin with the altar, which, after all, was the item that attracted us to the area in the first place. It is made out of one large ashlar block, 2.5 metres long, 85 centimetres wide and 1.2 metres high, weighing about 5 tons. It has two depressions on its upper surface: one (right, as you look at the picture) is rectangular and shallow, about 10 centimetres deep, with three small hollows known as cup marks; the other (to its left), also rectangular, is deeper (35 centimetres) and forms a sort of basin. The two depressions are separated by a slender partition with a narrow passage to allow the flow of liquids. One of the shorter sides of the deep depression was broken when found; but I believe that it originally had an outlet for the liquids that accumulated there. I have been describing the stone as an 'altar' without really proving it to be one. Actually, no altar of the type had ever been found in this country before. In fact, rarely have any altars for the slaughter and sacrifice of animals been found in archaeological excavations. My opinion, therefore, is based mainly on logical assumptions. It is true that similar installations – though mainly for libation sacrifices – were found by us at Hazor and by Sir Leonard Woolley at Alalakh, in northern Syria. But none of these were anywhere near the size of the stone

The bait

opposite The huge stone altar, looking east, with the Golan Heights in the background
below The same altar photographed at sunrise shows the orientation of the sanctuary towards the sun

we found in area F. I had the privilege of showing a photograph of our altar to the aged Sir Leonard Woolley just before his death. It did not ring any bell. 'This is similar to the one in your book, sir,' I explained. 'Young man,' he rejoined, with a twinkle in his eye, 'I do not read my own books.'

Our own excavations, however, did supply evidence to support the assumption that the huge slab was indeed an altar. We decided to begin our dig, obviously, in the vicinity of the stone. It was surrounded by thickets and thorns, so we burned the area, marked the squares and were ready to excavate. As soon as we began, we uncovered huge quantities of cattle bones around the stone, and particularly east of it – a reassuring sign that the place had been used for slaughtering and sacrifice. The actual cultic nature of the area quickly became clear. The altar was situated on the east side of a large open square. Within its confines we discovered a well-built drain, or canal, leading towards the altar and then disappearing under it into a vast network of canals covered by slabs of stone. Slightly north of the head of the drain, a niche had been built. Unfortunately, it was not intact, but in it we found a lovely, though broken, alabaster incense jar, with many other fragments of alabaster nearby, the most beautiful found in Hazor.

below Some of the bones of sacrificed animals found near the altar

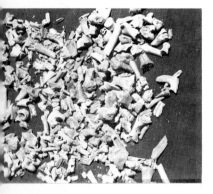

right The altar and the canal leading towards it

The alabaster jar, or goblet, was turned on a lathe, and its two parts fitted each other to perfection. The incense was obviously placed in the top cup, which could be separated from its base.

About 2 metres north of the niche, we found cooking pots, a baking tray and – most important – a bull's skull on an elevated rectangular platform that looked like an open high place, or *bamah*, where the votives and some parts of the sacrificed animals were laid. This find in itself was adequate testimony that we were actually dealing with an open cult area. What strengthened the assumption were the enormous nests of vessels, including typical cult vessels, such as pierced incense cups, so-called cups and saucers, rattles and votive vessels, also found in the vicinity. Such objects were particularly plentiful east of the altar and below it. Indeed, the area looked like a *favissa* (a collection place for discarded cult vessels) and yielded layer upon layer of this type of vessel.

The altar, as we found it, was used during two phases, equivalent to periods of strata IB and IA in the other areas (*i.e.*, the fourteenth and thirteenth centuries). At the end of the fourteenth century, it apparently tilted, either through deliberate action or otherwise, and efforts were made to shore it up with stones.

The two parts of the alabaster incense jar, showing the marks of the lathe (left); and a drawing (right) of the two pieces in their original position

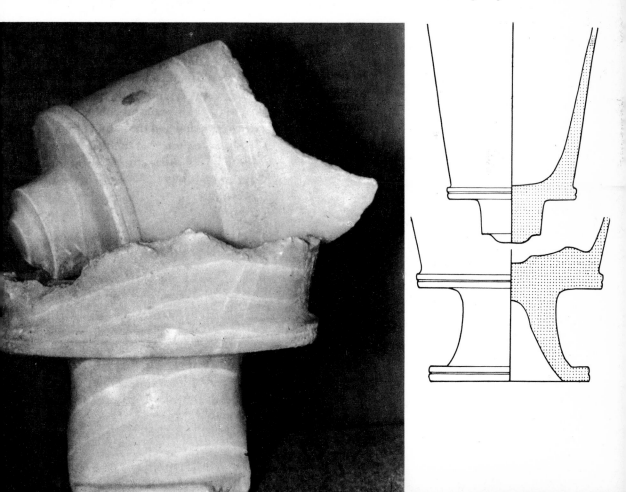

A room near the altar with a fine cobble-stone floor

This bronze lugged axe, found near the altar, was probably used for slaughtering animals

Dwellings of the cult-area servants

A small lion-shaped bronze weight

The entire area north and east of this cult place, up to the boundary of the huge wall in the north, was found to have been occupied by a series of dwellings whose design was typical of the period: a central court surrounded by rooms, some with beautiful cobble-stone floors. The proximity of this quarter to the altar and the nature of some of the finds in the rooms may allow us to assume that it either was occupied by the servants of the cult area or served partly as storerooms and magazines. In and around the room immediately to the north of the altar, we found a quantity of Mycenaean pottery of the IIIA and IIIB periods, a bronze axe (which may have been used for slaughtering animals), a small but impressive bronze weight shaped like a crouching lion and many *pithoi* around a well-built 'table' made of basalt. The dwellings in this area also augmented the knowledge we acquired in area C and provided a good example of the plan and buildings of the Canaanite city in the last two centuries before its destruction.

As a rule, archaeologists find their major caches in graves and tombs because the pottery there is relatively well preserved and far more varied than that found in homes, where only vessels used in daily life are uncovered. We were therefore fortunate to find in area F a number of tombs of the Late Bronze II period (the fourteenth or perhaps early thirteenth century) that yielded enormous quantities of pottery, including not only some beautiful Mycenaean pieces, but vessels imported from Cyprus and their local imitations, as well. Indeed, the full repertoire of pottery of the last 200 years of the Bronze Age in this country was revealed in these tombs, and they gave us another peg on which to fix our absolute chronology. The first tomb (8065) was found right in the middle of the court of a house situated immediately north of the altar. It was just a crevice in which a single man was buried under a slab of basalt. But it also contained a nice array of pottery, of which the prize piece was an exquisite Mycenaean pyriform jar of the IIIA-B type (from the second half of the fourteenth century) found fully intact! The greatest amount of pottery, however, was found in another tomb, which deserves a special description.

While we were busy clearing a structure and debris in the IB stratum near the north-east corner of the huge northern wall, we saw a pit

Caves and burials

A fine Mycenaean pyriform jar (of the Mycenaean IIIA-B type) found in area F

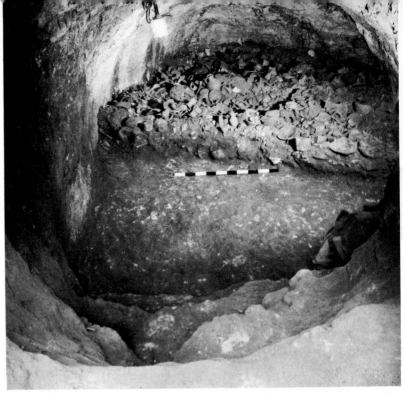

The slabs (above, left) covering
the entrance of the shaft
leading to the burial cave
(above, right) and the plan
of the cave

Three views of the rare
Thutmose IV scarab

covered by two large slabs, and under them we found a shaft with
steps. It soon became obvious that someone had planned to cut a burial
tomb here, and the workers had already finished preparing the steps
when they unexpectedly came up against a huge underground tunnel
of previous strata. Realizing their predicament, they blocked the
opening into the tunnel with well-built walls and began to quarry
another cave (8144, this time in a north-westerly direction) in the
hope of avoiding the tunnel below them. And this time they were
right. The new burial cave was oblong, about 5 metres long and nearly
3 metres wide, with four steps leading into it. It was so well sealed
in antiquity that when we discovered the cave it contained practically
no earth, although it seemed that over the centuries water had seeped
in from time to time, and as a result the bones in it were in a state of
decay and crumbled to the touch. The sheer quantity of bones indicated
that quite a number of people had been buried there.

In the first 2 metres from the entrance, we found practically nothing;
but then, in the inner 3 metres, beyond a sort of low partition wall,
we found over 500 pottery vessels thrown in disarray, some intact,
some broken. Periodic attempts to clear the cave and use it for additional
burials by pushing the bones and the pots inwards must have caused
the utter disorder that reigned within. Clearly the cave was used for
a long time, throughout the period of stratum IB. We were fortunate
to have found objects that enabled us, by post-dating, to indicate
roughly when this cave was first used. One such object was a scarab
bearing the name of Thutmose IV (Men-Kheperu-Re). All Thutmose

left Two Cypriot bucchero juglets

below Three Cypriot tall-necked *bilbils* used for exporting opium

IV scarabs are rare and a boon to archaeologists in this country because we know that they were made exclusively during his reign (the names of some Pharaohs continued to be inscribed on scarabs after their death, but the popularity of Thutmose IV was buried along with him). We can therefore conclude that the cave was first used sometime during his eight-year reign, from 1410 to 1402 BC, or immediately thereafter.

The final period of the cave's use was indicated by the fact that it was discovered under stratum IA, but the clue to its absolute chronology was again its great yield of Mycenaean pottery – indeed, the largest collection found in Hazor – belonging to the IIIA and IIIA-B type of the end of the fourteenth century. This find was also among the best we uncovered in all four seasons of excavations for absolutely dating stratum IB. As mentioned earlier, the cache also included a large amount of imported ware from Cyprus, including the so-called tall-necked *bilbils*, which may have been used for exporting opium, and two rare bucchero juglets. The bulk of the finds was, of course, locally made pottery typical of the period, such as lamps, bowls, jars, juglets and so on. Most interesting were the attempts of the local artists to imitate the imported *bilbils*. The difference between the two lay in the fact that the local variety was made on the wheel, while the Cypriot vessels were hand made; the local clay is light coloured, as compared with the dark-chocolate, metallic effect of the Cypriot ware; and, of course, the painting varies.

Once we began to excavate under the two top strata all around area F, we were entangled in a maze of massive walls that belonged to the

above Locally made pottery, including an imitation of the *bilbil*

top The well-built drainage canal of the Middle Bronze II building, in which a burial of the Late Bronze I period was found

above, right The burial inside the canal, as found

above, left The vessels found in the burial place

opposite The ivory stopper shaped like the head of the Egyptian goddess Hathor (actual height is 4.5 centimetres)

huge earliest buildings of the area. We could discern two complexes on two different strata, the lower of which – consisting of a large building – belonged to the last phase of the Middle Bronze II period and went out of use in the Late Bronze I period. There was very decisive and interesting proof of this. On the floor of the well-built drainage canals belonging to that building, we discovered a burial with pottery typical of the Late Bronze I period, a clear indication that by this time the building was no longer in use. The pictures here show what the grave looked like when we discovered it and some of the pottery found there, including a black Cypriot juglet typical of the fifteenth century BC. A pleasant little surprise awaited us here in the form of an ivory stopper shaped like the head of the Egyptian goddess Hathor. The head is pierced vertically so that the contents of the bottle, presumably perfume, could be poured into the concave sun-disc spoon and then applied by the finger-tip of its owner (who,

Typical designs of Bichrome Ware: 'Union Jack', spiral, fish and bird

by the way, was interred in this grave with her husband). Since the whole area was occupied by a bizarre temple in that period, as we shall see in a moment, the woman may well have been a priestess or the wife or daughter of a member of the temple staff. Another point of interest is the Bichrome Ware found among burials in many of the disused areas of the destroyed Middle Bronze II building. This is a subject that deserves to be expanded upon.

Bichrome Ware is the name given by archaeologists to a very distinct type of pottery decorated in red and black with a design composed mainly of animals, birds, fish and some geometric patterns – such as the Maltese Cross, Union Jack, spirals and so on. It was first found in Philistia, on the Mediterranean coast, by Sir Flinders Petrie, and later a theory evolved that the whole lot was made by one artist, known as the Ajjul painter after the place where the pottery was first discovered. But the distribution of this pottery over an area ranging from the north coast of Syria to Egypt – and even Cyprus to Upper Galilee deep in Canaan, as we now discovered – plus the great quantities and varieties found, indicate clearly that it could not have been made by one man only and was more likely the product of a school of artists. It probably began to make its appearance at the end of the Middle Bronze II period, becoming most prevalent in the sixteenth–fifteenth centuries (the Late Bronze I period). It has recently been suggested that Bichrome Ware was actually made in Cyprus and exported to Canaan, but this has yet to be proved. Whatever the case, the existence of this pottery in burials within the destroyed Middle Bronze II building helped us to fix the outside dates of our next discovery to before 1400 BC (i.e., the approximate establishment of stratum IB) but after 1550 BC (the end of the Middle Bronze II period).

Now we could tackle what had been a great enigma for many years. In the northern part of this section, above the remains of the destroyed Middle Bronze II building, we came upon a square area covered with a thick white-plastered floor and surrounded by very broad (but mostly destroyed or mutilated) walls, with short, undestroyed walls protruding from the centre in all directions. We could not make head or tail of it. The real significance of that structure came to me only recently as the result of another discovery made near Amman, Jordan. In 1955, the very same year in which we began our excavations at Hazor, the Jordanians were preparing a large landing-strip near Amman for their airport when bulldozers uncovered an old building with many interesting finds of the Late Bronze period. Only in 1956, however, did proper excavations – carried out by the Australian archaeologist Basil Hennesy – shed real light on the nature of the building discovered. The Amman building turned out to be a unique temple planned as a perfect square (of about 15 × 15 metres), with a central square court (of about 6 × 6 metres), surrounded by six equal-sized rooms. The entrance to the building was through a corner room, and the central court also

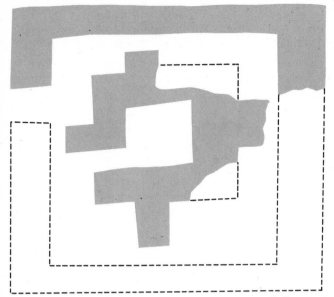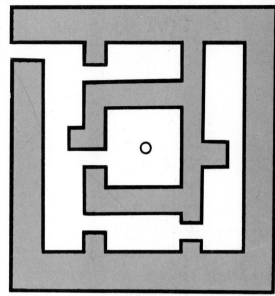

The plan of the square temple of Hazor (left) compared with that of the Amman temple

had only one entrance near a corner. It was this building that provided the key to the reconstruction of our own odd discovery at Hazor, for the two of them turned out to be very similar in design and can be attributed to more or less the same period (the establishment of the Amman building was dated to the end of the fifteenth century).

Our strange building, then, was a temple. But what was the significance of such an odd temple? Two American archaeologists, E. Campbell and G.E. Wright, recently suggested that the temple in Amman, and perhaps a not dissimilar one near Mount Gerizim in Samaria, be regarded as cult centres for people who did not live in their immediate vicinity, meaning people belonging to a single but widespread group or tribe. This is a very attractive suggestion that may apply to the Amman temple, which is rather isolated in an area that lacks signs of occupation even in the past. But the Hazor temple is within the limits of a flourishing Late Bronze I city, and therefore hardly fits the critical characteristic of isolation. Thus it may be assumed that the sole fact that a temple is square is insufficient to classify it as an isolated tribal cult-centre, although it is conceivable that this temple in Hazor is a vestige of an earlier tradition brought over by nomadic people. But even if we could not narrow down the precise significance of this square temple, the very fact that it was a temple indicated that the holy nature of this area went back to at least the Late Bronze I period. In fact, as we were soon to discover, it went back even further. It is rather common in Near Eastern archaeology that once a temple was built on a site, the place was marked by tradition, and people would rebuild temples on the same spot for generations thereafter. With this knowledge in mind, we continued to dig downwards to determine what had come before.

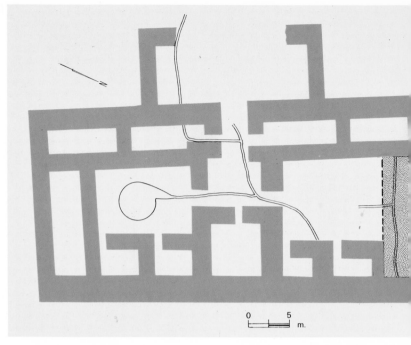

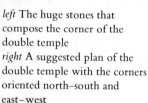

left The huge stones that compose the corner of the double temple
right A suggested plan of the double temple with the corners oriented north–south and east–west

The double temple

The next built-up stratum (3) consisted of a building so large that it occupied almost the entire excavated area! In fact, the stones we had seen protruding from the rugged surface before we began to dig belonged to its northern wall. The structure, when found, was in a very bad state of preservation, and many of its stones had been re-used in the upper strata. Even the altar discussed at the beginning of the chapter may originally have belonged to this stratum, for judging from other stones found in the area, it could well have been part of the building's beautifully dressed corner. Nevertheless, it was possible to reconstruct the main contours and features of this most interesting find. It was a wide building designed in neat 2:1 proportions of 46 × 23 metres. Its external walls were very thick, varying from 2.5 to 3 metres, and the foundations were built of large, coarse field stones trimmed slightly for adjustment. Huge stones measuring up to 1.5 metres were used in the corners. The northern wall is particularly thick (5.5 metres) because of the inner platform attached to it. It was under this platform that we found the well-built drainage canal that led us to the Late Bronze I tomb. A complicated net of drainage canals traversed the building from west to east and south to north. Most of them emanated from the western part of the building, which suggested that a huge open square had been there.

In the preliminary reports, we called this building 'the palace' or the 'palatial building' mainly because of its huge dimensions and thick walls. But later on, further study led me to believe that what we had here was indeed another temple. The building is composed of two identical units – one in the north and one in the south – flanking a series of halls and the entrance, which is preceded by a sort of porch. Each of the twin units has a central court surrounded by rooms on three sides. The reasons for regarding this building as a temple, actually a *double temple*, were both positive and negative. First, a symmetrical plan is not useful in a palace, so there was little reason to believe that this structure with two identical wings was a royal abode. Second, the situation of the building is unsuitable for a palace, as it is not in an easily defended area. Third, remembering that the tradition of building temples and cult places here goes back as far as the Late Bronze I period, one would naturally look for an even earlier (Middle Bronze II) temple on the site. The clinching argument, or at least the one that convinced me, is the building's striking resemblance to the double temple in Asshur – of about the same period – which is dedicated to the sun god Shamash and moon god Sin. It is difficult to determine to which deities the Hazor double temple was dedicated, but its very existence in that period is another indication of the contacts between Hazor and Mesopotamia. Be that as it may, if our assumptions about this being a double temple are indeed correct, then it is the only double temple and largest temple of any kind found in this country. Although it is entirely different in plan and orientation from Solomon's temple, built centuries later, it is interesting to compare the measurements of the two buildings. Solomon's temple (as we shall see later) was a long building, while this was a wide one; but its external measurements, 50 × 25 metres, were nearly the same as those of the double temple and in exactly the same proportions: 2:1.

I mentioned earlier on that this temple had a very ramified drainage system consisting of well-built canals covered over by slabs of stone. We could see quite clearly that the canals originated partly in the west, outside the building. We also noted that all these canals, like arteries, joined into a single main one leading north–north-east. Where to? Well, for us, as you probably suspect by now, they led to the next discovery in this area.

At the end of the first season of excavations here, in 1956, many of us felt like Jean Valjean of *Les Misérables* – sewage sweeps. We were crawling in these drainage canals, trying to clean them (fortunately just of earth and silt) and see where they led to. Towards the end of the season, we suddenly stumbled onto a rock-hewn tunnel just a few metres under the stratum of the huge building. It was 2 metres high and 1 metre wide and beautifully cut and dressed – an amazing feat of engineering. We managed to trace it westwards to a large cave whose collapsed ceiling was entirely covered by debris (cave 8183). We could not dig it up from below, so we started from the very top, only to find that we were not original in this method. There on top we found an ancient robber's trench – now filled with loose earth – that was most probably cut in the Late Bronze period, when the robbers

top An entrance to the temple's drainage system
bottom A rock-hewn tunnel

left Digging down towards the tunnel
right Clearing the tunnels by the light of miners' lamps

Enigmatic underground tunnels

penetrated this cave-tomb and looted it completely. Digging down to nearly 6 metres was not an easy task, but it was well worth the effort, for at least here we had some clue about the function of the tunnel (which we soon discovered was a whole system of interconnected tunnels).

Since the tunnels were cut into the solid rock 7 metres below the surface, it was impossible to excavate them from above. Some of them were filled with silt and earth almost to the brim, but in others the accumulation was only up to half their height. While planning how to proceed, Jean Perrot and I tied ourselves to ropes and started crawling inside. It was quite an adventure, especially in the dark, with very little air and even less information about who or what you might meet up with at any moment – a snake, or scorpion? And the tunnels were so narrow that we were sometimes unable to make a turn and had to crawl in reverse, which, I assure you, is a most unpleasant exercise. But the investigation was too important to leave undone, and we dedicated the whole of the second season, 1956, to these clearing operations.

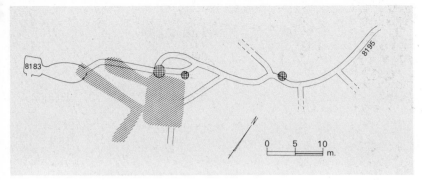

Schematic plan of the ramified system of the tunnels and the huge caverns (see page 75)

Unfortunately, we were not entirely successful. In tunnel 8195 we managed to penetrate 30 metres before the work became too hazardous and had to be abandoned, although we did determine that its inclination was eastwards to a point outside the lower city. In the end, we managed to clear a total of 100 metres of tunnels and began to gather evidence about their function.

The builders of the Middle Bronze period double temple, as well as the population during the Late Bronze period, not only stumbled onto these tunnels while building their own canals, but made very good use of them by having their sewage system join up with them. This was an ideal solution for the disposal of their sewage. Since the original network of the tunnels coming from all directions did not suit them, they occasionally blocked some of the offshoots, which were then used by the later occupants (sometimes even for storage, to judge by the great quantities of pottery of later periods – especially the Late Bronze II – found in them). It is possible that all these tunnels linked a huge, underground necropolis, of which 8183 was but one burial cave. They may have served as approaches to the tombs, as well

left The tunnels, as found, partially blocked
right A 'joint' of tunnels

The Hazor Museum

Drainage system

as to drain the water that accumulated in them. Or strange as this may seem, it is also possible that during the Middle Bronze period the people who established the lower city used the tunnels as one means to drain the entire area when the city itself was still in the planning stage. In fact, we came across an additional find that supports this theory.

.This clue to one of the possible functions of the tunnels turned up much later in a most unexpected place. Several years ago we decided to build a museum to exhibit all the finds of Hazor, and the site we chose was the area of the expedition camp. We were fortunate to receive a very handsome gift from Mr and Mrs Sam Zacks of Toronto, Canada, for this purpose and equally fortunate to have found a very talented architect, Mr D. Reznik, of Jerusalem, to plan the museum, which is now one of the most beautiful and instructive in the country. While the workers were digging the foundations of the museum building, they struck an underground canal 2.3 metres below the surface. Made of slabs of stone, it was very similar to the ones we encountered in area F, which was quite amazing. In the 1968–9 season, we decided to investigate the origin of the canal. It was impossible to excavate the whole area, of course; but we made checking trenches every 20 to 30 metres and discovered that the canal found by the construction workers was an outlet of a larger two-pronged canal of the Middle Bronze period. One prong came from the southern end of the lower city – area P (of which we shall speak later); the other branched off rather abruptly towards area F. We could not follow this second prong further because the entire area it traversed is now covered with a beautiful vineyard and orchard; but the direction is quite clear. So it is possible that the tunnels in area F – or at least 8195, which seems to be their outlet – joined with these underground canals outside the city perimeter. This system of canals found beyond the city limits is unique in the country, and it was probably used not only to drain the city but also to irrigate some of the fields of Hazor.

Yet another clue to the possible function of the tunnels in area F came from the vicinity of the square temple. When we began to clear the debris under its foundations, we detected the top of a large rock-hewn shaft measuring 8 × 6 metres. It was very difficult to dig into the deliberate fill in this shaft, and we did not anticipate that we would have to go down 8 metres from the surface. But when we finally reached the bottom, we found two openings into three huge caverns, the longest of them extending some 15 metres. This complex was definitely planned as a burial place and probably for V.I.P.'s, at that, as the cutting of the shaft and caverns required tremendous labours. It appeared that the caverns had been rifled in antiquity, perhaps by the people who built and filled the shaft when preparing the area for the construction of the double temple. When we entered the caverns they were nearly totally free of debris and silt, as the openings were

above The covered canals, as found, near the museum
left One of the large caverns, as found, with practically no silt inside

An aerial view of area F, looking west, at the end of the excavations. Note the altar (top, right), the square temple (centre, left) and the northern wall of the double temple (bottom)

apparently blocked by earth and stones used to fill the shaft. Practically nothing was found in these caves, except for a few intact Middle Bronze vessels. It is possible, of course, that this huge underground cave was actually never used, and the few vessels found in it had been left there by the workmen. The southern cave was definitely abandoned by the workers before completion (perhaps a change in plans caused the interruption). In any case, at one time the intention was to use the area for burial purposes, and perhaps the enigmatic tunnels were connected with these planned tombs as well. It is also interesting to note that the huge shaft leading to these caverns cut through some of the tunnels, so it must have been hewn later than the system of tunnels but still within the Middle Bronze period. It therefore seems that the tunnels, shaft and caverns were part of the town-planning during its earlier stage in the Middle Bronze period (equivalent to our stratum 4 in the lower city). They may have been used for a while until, in the next phase (Middle Bronze IIC, equivalent to stratum 3),

the huge double temple was erected and the entire area was sealed off and covered. Whatever its purpose, this system is, to the best of my knowledge, the most intricate, vast underground rock-cutting of that period ever found in our part of the world and serves as impressive testimony to the highly developed technical skill of the Middle Bronze population.

Area F, in fact, is still a great challenge to future excavators. If tombs are found intact in the vicinity, they may well prove to be part of the necropolis used by the nobility of the city's early founders. Whoever attempts this work in the future should entertain no illusions that it is an easy task. On the contrary, it is an enormous task requiring much patience and sophisticated mechanical and technical aid. As a matter of fact, I was so taken by the mystery of this underground network that in the third season I was tempted to allocate more labourers to this area. But a sudden and no less interesting discovery elsewhere compelled me to divert both my attention and some of the workers to the new area, so let us now move over there.

A challenge for the future

5 The Last of Four Temples – Area H

A chance discovery

While we were deliberating the excavation of the small square 210 to determine the nature of the enclosure in the 'city-or-camp' debate (discussed in chapter 2), I decided to open another square further to the north. The task was assigned to Claire Epstein, who was not too happy about it. For a while she thought that 'the grass was greener' elsewhere and began to roam about outside her 'boundaries' to the extreme northern part of the enclosure. This area was not ploughed by the Rosh Pinah farmers, partly because it is covered with stones and partly because its distance from the main road is an inconvenience. While roaming around, she caught sight of a few field stones protruding from the ground – in fact the only stones in the area anchored in the earth – so she asked me for two or three workmen to help her investigate them. I must confess that I agreed rather reluctantly, but a few hours later this little probe turned into a major excavation. It transpired that these field stones were the outer facing of a tremendously thick wall – about 2 metres wide – whose inner facing (uncovered only a few inches below the surface) was lined with a row of most beautifully dressed and laid basalt orthostats, each pierced by two holes at the top. We were flabbergasted, to say the least! And I, patently contrite for my earlier reluctance, warmly congratulated Mrs Epstein on her uncanny intuition. For this was the first time that orthostats of that type had been found in this country, and they were decisive evidence of what we had always suspected: northern – particularly Hittite – influence on Bronze Age Hazor.

Orthostats!

As mentioned earlier, the term orthostat (meaning 'standing upright') was coined to describe stone slabs used in the lower part of a building as panels or dados. This was not the first time we had uncovered orthostats in Hazor. But these orthostats with two holes on top were intriguing, because they are most commonly associated with Anatolia, particularly the Hittite capital of Ḥattushash (present-day Bogazköy),

opposite The first view of the orthostats as they emerged from the soil
left A few weeks later, the panel of orthostats

and some northern Syrian sites that were in the sphere under Hittite influence, such as Alalakh. In later periods of the Neo-Hittite era, at the beginning of the first millennium BC, they were abundantly used in sites such as Zinjirli and Carchemish either as a base for the superstructure or to line the inner facing of thick brick walls. Scholars still disagree about the function of the holes on the top of the orthostats. One school of thought believes they were for dowels, by which the beams of the wall's wooden infrastructure were connected to the tops of the orthostats. Another school of thought, championed by Woolley, believed them to be Lewis-holes, which helped the builders hold the orthostats in balance while they were building or to manoeuvre them with pegs as levers to bring them into position. I do not believe that the Hazor orthostats help to decide either theory. But if we remember that basalt is a very hard stone and at that time iron was still unknown, then it obviously took tremendous effort to make these two holes (on our orthostats, for example, the holes were drilled to a diameter and depth of 5 centimetres); and it is hard to believe that so much labour would be expended on just Lewis-holes. After all, even though the dimensions of some of these orthostats range from 40 centimetres to 2 metres in length and 50–60 centimetres in height, they are not all that heavy to move for balance or to manoeuvre slightly back and forth. I believe, therefore, that the dowel-holes theory better explains their function. Be that as it may, the fact that these orthostats bore resemblance to the type found in the northern territories caused quite a stir among us. But we didn't stand around gaping at them for long. Obviously we had come upon an important building just below the unploughed surface, and we immediately decided to begin excavations in this new area, now designated as area H.

An enigma – the absence of pottery

After the removal of the top soil, the excavations became increasingly difficult. The earth felt like hard cement, and we had to resort to quite a new device in archaeological practice: pneumatic drills. We later learned that this cement-like soil was actually composed of the disintegrated mud-bricks of the building's thick walls. Several days passed while we managed to clear a considerable part of a large room with the orthostats lining its walls. Still, we were puzzled, for although we reached a surface of white material that looked like a floor, there were no vessels on it – not even sherds! Moreover, all the earth we had removed up to that point – nearly a metre's worth – did not yield a single sherd – a very unusual phenomenon in excavating cities, where one usually finds more than he needs. The explanation for this phenomenon soon became apparent.

The clue of the charred beams

We decided to cut a probing trench into the white material, and in it we encountered a well-preserved charred beam. So now it was evident that up to that time we had been digging above a fallen roof, where obviously no pottery was to be found. The discovery of the

charred beam and this possible explanation for the sterile soil encouraged us enormously, as we had reason to hope that the fallen roof may have preserved whatever was left under it after the building had been looted by whoever destroyed it. The first object to appear was a basalt offering table lying on its narrow side amidst ashes – further evidence that the building had been burned and also the first indication that what we were digging up was a temple. In fact, we were fortunate to discover the entire floor of the holy of holies with its smashed

left The charred beam found below the fallen roof
right Charred wood, evidence of the final conflagration

A cultic offering table as found

and burned cult objects littered all over it. Although the heavy objects themselves lay more or less in their proper positions, some large fragments of deliberately broken stones were found about 4–5 metres away from them, another sign of the havoc wrought on the holy of holies when it was destroyed. The proximity of the building to the surface and the clear sign of fire left little doubt in my mind about who had caused the destruction, for the vivid evidence closely supported the biblical description in the Book of Joshua: '. . . and he burned Hazor with fire . . . none of the cities that stood on mounds did Joshua burn, except Hazor only; that Joshua burned.' Here, then, was the holy of holies, richly endowed with well-preserved cult objects, of a temple that was used by the last Canaanite inhabitants of the city of Hazor.

In the northern part of the excavated room, we found a well-built niche, which obviously served as the focal point of the holy of holies. At a distance of about 2 metres from it, we found the first of the objects that helped us determine the deity to which the temple had been

The basalt, pillar-like incense altar

dedicated, and when it emerged, it left us gasping. What came up, lying sideways, was a tall, square basalt pillar with a beautifully carved emblem at the top. We immediately recognized it as an incense altar. It is 50 × 50 centimetres square and 1.7 metres high; and two of the deliberately chipped-off corners of its upper surface were found about 4–5 metres away. On the top flat side, remains of burning were still visible. On the upper part of one side, as the picture shows, is a relief of a disc within a square frame and a four-rayed emblem in the centre. Below the emblem are two long, chiselled depressions, giving the front of the altar the appearance of a relief of three columns. The back surface is similarly dressed, except that the dented square frame has no relief. It may originally have had an incrusted design made of wood or other perishable material. The other two sides of the altar each have an oblong depression, giving the impression of two columns.

The most important element of the relief, however, was the emblem itself. This symbol is well known in Near Eastern archaeology as the emblem of the great god, the weather god (sometimes called by the

left Four rays within a disc, the emblem of the weather god
right The back of the altar, with an empty frame for an incrusted design, probably of perishable material. Note the indications of fire

A bull of wrought bronze (originally on a wooden base) that was found near the altar. The bull is associated with the weather god in Near Eastern iconography

Semites Hadad). Occasionally it appears with wings on each side of the disc (also referred to as the solar disc), and it is usually associated with the bull. In fact, quite often in Near Eastern iconography, the weather god is depicted standing on a bull. This suggested identity for the temple deity was immediately strengthened by the discovery nearby of a beautiful little bull of wrought bronze that originally stood on a wooden base (probably a votive brought to the temple). However, the most important object related to the identity of the temple deity was found later on, broken in two, just outside the temple. It was badly damaged (partly deliberately), but enough of it remained to make out a male torso on the back of a bull. The reconstruction of the two pieces explains their positions exactly. Here we have a combi-

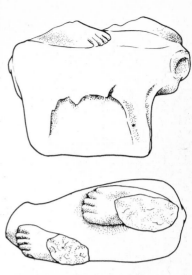

nation of the deity and the bull. Yet even more important, as can be seen from the picture, a pendant comprising the same circle-and-rays emblem found on the incense altar is depicted on the breast of the figure, a clear indication that this is indeed the emblem of the deity. So we can definitely regard this temple as the sanctuary of the weather or storm god, Hadad. The way in which the altar is made to appear as if its top part were supported by pillars may indicate that originally this type of altar actually did stand on wooden legs. In fact, the relief on our altar is strikingly similar to a depiction of an altar of about the same period – again with a bull – discovered in Alacha Huyuk, not far from the capital of the Hittite Empire.

Slightly to the west of the altar, we found a round basalt slab with

above, left The broken pieces of the statue of the temple's deity – the weather god – standing on a bull. Note the disc and rays depicted on the deity's breast

top, right Side and top views of the bull's pedestal showing the deity's feet

centre, right A relief from Alacha Huyuk depicting an altar with a bull, strikingly similar to the one from Hazor

Libation utensils

below A basalt, basin-like, cultic vessel found near the altar
bottom A general view (looking south-east) of the holy of holies with the cult furniture as found

a central circular depression 50 centimetres in diameter. This basin-like object was found lying on its narrow side, again giving the impression that it fell off a wooden stand when the latter was burned. It must have had an important function in the libation ceremonies, for animal sacrifices were never made in the holy of holies but always – for obvious reasons – in the courtyard, as was the custom in the temple of Solomon. The holy of holies here was used mainly for incense burning and libation offerings. This became clear beyond doubt when about 2–3 metres south of the altar and basin we found a set of five objects, all connected with libation and liquid offerings. In the centre of the group were two basalt libation tables (one found upside down), both rectangular, but slightly different in arrangement: one table had a very deep rectangular depression on half of its surface and a shallow depression on the other half, while the other had a deep rectangular depression in one corner and a shallow depression in another. We do not know why one was made one way and the other in a different fashion, but we assume that it all depends on the liquids offered there. These offering tables were no doubt an important element in the temple cult, because we found quite a number of them in open-air libation courts outside the temple and, broken and discarded, in the temple garbage heaps.

left An open-air libation table as found
right, top One of the two libation tables found upside down in the holy of holies. Note the 'negative' impression on the soil after the table was removed
right, centre The other libation table found in the holy of holies

One of the huge earthenware
libation kraters, with the
offering table shown in the
background

These libation tables were flanked by two huge earthenware kraters,
one with four handles, the other without handles but with an outlet
at its bottom. The two kraters were found broken (either by the conquerors or by the collapsed ceiling), but all the pieces were there and
were easily restored. Again, we do not know whether the liquids held
in each of the kraters were wine, oil or perhaps just water. A most
special krater connected with this libation cult, and up till now unique
in the finds of the Near East, lay just to the left of the group, near the
handled krater. It is made of beautifully dressed basalt and its upper
part is decorated with Mycenaean-style spiral carvings. Again I must
stress that considering that iron was still unknown then, it was quite
a feat to carve and dress such basalt. The krater is a masterpiece of the
fourteenth–thirteenth centuries BC and must have been used for special
offerings, either liquid or fruit. The liquids were cupped from the
kraters and poured onto the libation table with the aid of little dipper
juglets, or bowls. In fact the floor of the whole area between these
objects and around them was littered with dippers and bowls.

A beautiful basalt krater with spirals

To this discussion of the vessels used for libations, sacrifices and
other cult operations we must add the offering table found under the
fallen ceiling and the charred beams. This table, found in the south-
east corner of the room, has four round and two elongated depressions
around a central rectangular depression. It is unique in this exact
arrangement, but similar ones were found in great quantities in Egypt,
and many pictures depict them used in conjunction with different
types of offerings. Ours must have originally stood on a wooden stool,
to judge by the ashes in the midst of which it was found.

The offertory table

left The beautiful basalt vessel
in the course of excavations,
shown with a student clearing
the broken remains of an
earthenware libation krater
below The unique basalt vessel
with Mycenaean-style spiral
carvings

right A vessel shaped like a
house (perhaps for holding
holy snakes)
opposite Three photographs of
the beads found in the holy of
holies (restrung): those on the
top left are mainly of brittle
faience; note the blue lapis
lazuli bead in the string on the
top right; those on the bottom
are of carnelian and agate

Beads and a scarab of
Amenophis III as found

Among the multitude of pottery pieces scattered on the floor, one
must be singled out. It is shaped like the entrance to a house, with
sockets for a door hinge, and is not unsimilar to the piece of pottery
found in the moon-god temple. Another like it, bearing the emblem
of a snake, was discovered in Ugarit, on the northern coast of Syria.
I believe these were used to hold the holy snakes of the temple. In
fact, in this temple, too, we found a bronze snake similar to those
found in many parts of the country – the most recent near the Timna
copper mines.

In the vicinity of the altar we also found scores of beads made of
semi-precious stones or of brittle faience, some of which we strung into
graded necklets. They must have been part of the votive offerings
brought to the temple, and among them was a scarab bearing the
name of Amenophis III – Neb-Ma'at-Re (the father of Akhenaten and
son of Thutmose IV, whose scarab was found in area F) – who reigned
between 1402 and 1364 BC. This scarab does not give us the actual
date of the temple but rather its *post-quem* date to after the reign of
Amenophis III, in the thirteenth century, as we also know from the
pottery. Similar scarabs had already been found in many other sites
in Israel, and at first they misled quite a number of archaeologists
(like those who excavated Beth-shan) to date their buildings too
early. We now know that these scarabs of Amenophis III were very
popular even in the thirteenth century, as was the case, for example,
in the temple at Lachish.

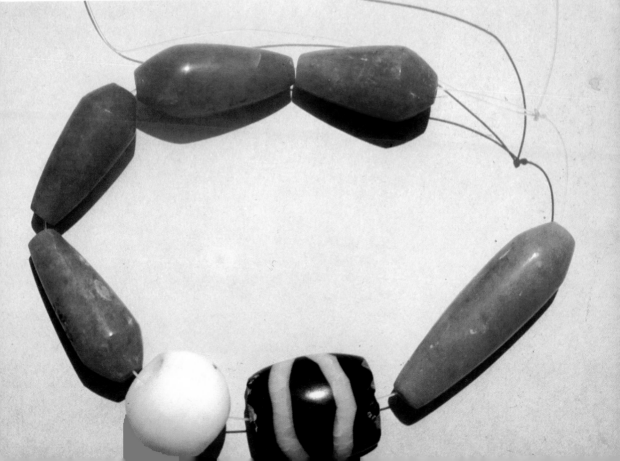

Two cylinder seals, with their
impressions, depicting cult
scenes

A most informative group of objects was the nineteen cylinder
seals of brittle faience found amid the beads in the western part of the
holy of holies. The scenes depicted on them, in a very stylized and
aesthetic manner, seem to be connected with the temple cult, since
they are mainly depictions of animals used for sacrifices. Some of
them show the animals tied to the tree of life; others just show the
animals symmetrically arranged in different ways, sometimes dispersed
between stylized solar-discs. But the direct connection with the cult
is best depicted when these same animals are shown crouching with
their legs tied. This type of cylinder seal, commonly known as popular
Mitannian, originated in the Mitannian Empire in northern Syria and

may have infiltrated into Palestine with the northern elements who settled in the country at that time. They must have been produced in one or two centres, because either identical or very similar ones are found in both Syria and Palestine, like those found in Ugarit and Beth-shan, Megiddo and Lachish of the same period. One seal, though, was different: made from hard hematite, it depicts a deity seated on a chair or throne under a winged sun-disc (similar to the emblem depicted on the altar) being approached by a king offering gifts, with a line of gift-bearers behind him. Above the latter are two facing cherubs (winged sphinxes with human faces). This seal was rather worn when found, and from its style and state of preservation we have

top Four cylinder seals, with their impressions, depicting stylized fish and geometrical designs
centre An enlarged impression of the hematite seal depicting the seated weather god, a pair of cherubs and an offering procession headed by a king

Bronze figurines

reason to believe that it belonged to an earlier period (probably an heirloom from an earlier temple).

In addition to the bronze bull mentioned earlier on, we also found a number of bronze figurines depicting female deities. One was of the so-called 'peg type', normally associated with foundation deposits. Another was made of a very thin bronze sheet and depicted a woman, but only the head and two breasts are emphasized. Near the entrance to the holy of holies, a most dramatic find was made. Here, amidst a thick layer of ashes, lay a little statue of a seated male; his chopped-off head rested nearby, surrounded by a number of broken bowls. The figure bears no emblems on its chest and is identical with another, though cruder, statue found headless on the surface in area F. I believe that they represent a king and demonstrate in a most dramatic way

below A bronze 'peg' figurine (left) and a stylized bronze-sheet figurine of a woman (right)

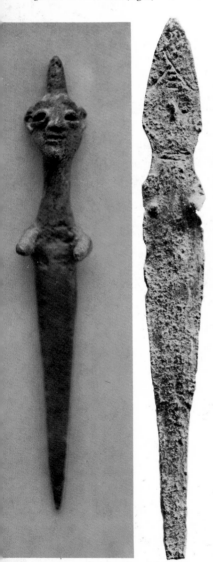

above The statue (shown restored, opposite) as found amidst the ashes and broken bowls

right The headless statue found in area F

opposite The votive statue of the king (?). The fly that was resting on the statue's head when this photograph was taken serves as a guide to its actual size

A general view of the temple (looking north) showing the porch, with the bases of two capitals, in the foreground

the havoc caused by the burning of the last Canaanite city of Hazor.

The holy of holies is a wide room, about 13×9 metres, with a niche in its northern wall. Obviously its large roof required the support of pillars; and indeed, in front of the niche, evidence of two pillars was found. In the east was a metre-high monolith, found still standing, although slightly slanted; only a base slab was found where the other pillar must have stood. It may be assumed that both pillars were made of wood and rested on these stone foundations. The entrance to the holy of holies was through a passage in the south. We found the threshold *in situ*, and on either side of it was a stone door socket, with one basalt door-pivot shoe still in one of the sockets and the other lying nearby in a thick layer of ashes. Obviously these were the lower parts, or shoes, of the wooden doors, which had been burned.

The other parts of the temple

In front (south) of the holy of holies was a hall of the same width that must have had a tower on its west side. On the east side we found a table made of a well-dressed basalt slab, as well as a sort of platform or tiny altar. South of this hall was a porch, somewhat narrower than the other parts of the building, and just in front of its entrance into the hall, two well-dressed, slightly conical, basalt pillar bases were found *in situ*. In this position, the pillars had no structural function and must therefore have had some cultic significance, placed as they were just in front of the entrance to the main building. The porch itself also had orthostats in the lower part of its wall. We found them arranged in a haphazard manner – so much so that an offering table

was found, in secondary use, serving as an orthostat. Why the main hall – between the porch and the holy of holies – was not adorned with orthostats, and the porch so poorly adorned, we learned only later (and will be discussed in the next chapter when we come to deeper strata).

The plan of the temple can therefore be summarized as follows: a building of three rooms – a porch, a main hall and a holy of holies – situated one behind another with all their entrances on the same axis. This layout is unique among the temples of the period found in this country to date, while quite similar to contemporary temples discovered in Alalakh. The main interest of the plan, however, is its basic resemblance to that of Solomon's temple, built about 300 years later. No traces of Solomon's temple will ever be found, because it was razed to the ground, and its area repeatedly cleared for the

A basalt door-pivot shoe found *in situ* amidst ashes

The basalt offering table found, in secondary use, serving as an orthostat

building of the Second Temple and later Roman, Byzantine and Moslem shrines. The only evidence we have of its plan comes from the biblical description, difficult though it is to visualize a building described in words alone. But enough is preserved in the books of I Kings and II Chronicles for scholars to agree about the basic plan of the building, although details are beyond our reach. Indeed, the struggle of archaeologists to visualize the details of Solomon's temple was aptly characterized by W. F. Albright as the 'sufferings of Tantalus'. The basic plan is a porch, with two enigmatic cultic pillars (called 'Jachin' and 'Boaz' in the Bible), leading to the main hall of the temple and beyond that the holy of holies. All of the parts are of the same width, with all their entrances on a single axis. The two pillars devoid of architectural function that we found on the porch of our temple are strikingly reminiscent of Jachin and Boaz.

A prototype of the Solomonic temple

Putting one and one together, it is not difficult to see this Hazor temple as a prototype of Solomon's temple. And the fact that the latter broadly resembles a Canaanite temple – particularly a northern Canaanite one – should not really surprise us, for even the Bible admits that Solomon had to bring Phoenician builders, artists and architects to help him build it. The difference between Solomon's temple and those of the Canaanite pagans was not in the plan, of course, but in concept. In Solomon's sanctuary, no statues of the deity were installed and the only visible religious elements were the Ark and the cherubs. The only parallel to Solomon's temple up to the time of our discovery was a temple discovered at Tell Ta'ayanat in northern Syria, but it is dated to a period 200 years later than Solomon.

left A schematic plan of the IA temple with its three parts: porch (bottom), main hall and holy of holies (top), similar to the plan of Solomon's temple
right A plan of the temple at Tell Ta'ayanat, similar in design but built several hundred years later

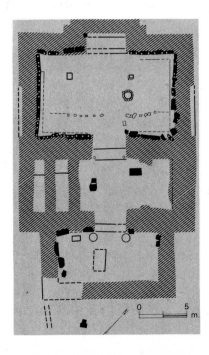

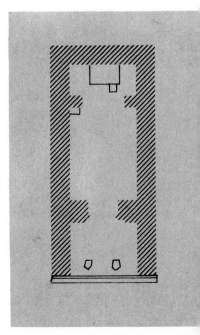

The tiny clay Mycenaean IIIB figurine of a bull (above, left) that was found standing on the floor (above, right)

Our temple was uncovered in the topmost stratum of area H. Nothing was found on top of it, and it lay in ruins, completely burned, several inches below the unploughed surface. This evidence could have permitted us to ascribe it to the same level as stratum IA in the other areas, fix its date in the thirteenth century BC and relate its destruction to the one wrought by Joshua. Fortunately, we also have other evidence: all the pottery found on the floor is identical to that of stratum IA, including vessels typical of the thirteenth century. The decisive piece turned up in the shape of a small clay animal – miraculously found intact, standing on its legs on the floor of the main hall. What sort of animal is it? Some cautious archaeologists described it as a four-legged animal, which it certainly was, though this does not help us much. I believe that the fact that it was found in a temple dedicated to the storm god, whose animal was the bull, allows us to identify this tiny figurine as such; and its shape, though rather stylized, substantiates this assumption. Most important, however, it is clearly a Mycenaean figurine, known from sites all over the Aegean and Syria, of the IIIB type, that is, of the thirteenth century. So no doubt remained that this temple of stratum IA was of the thirteenth century. But that was hardly the end of the story. An inkling of more to come kept our workers glued to area H, and the rewards for their patience were rich indeed.

A Mycenaean animal

below The holy of holies of the orthostat temple with its two phases
opposite A pillar of the IA temple and the protruding pillar base of the IB temple that was used as a platform for the liquid's krater in the later phase of the sanctuary

6 Three More Below!

There were certainly enough reasons to believe that earlier temples existed on this same site. First of all, as we saw in area F, the tradition of a holy place was tenacious, and people built and rebuilt temples on the same sites. Secondly, the arrangement of the orthostats on the porch of the IA temple indicated that they were mainly in secondary use. So we decided to deepen our dig under the floors of the topmost temple, and there, indeed, we found not just one other temple, but three – one under the other! When we removed the sherds of one of the large earthenware kraters found in the holy of holies, we realized that it had been standing on top of a well-dressed basalt column base surrounded by a row of small stones. Finding a column base under the floor of the IA temple in itself indicated the presence of an even older floor. So we dug up the entire floor to see what we could see. And sure enough, at a depth of 50 centimetres under the IA floor, we found a lower floor, made of beaten earth, with two column bases: the one on which the krater had rested and another (to its left), not as beautiful, but also made of basalt. Obviously both had supported wooden pillars, and since they stood in the very centre of the holy of holies, they could very well have supported its roof.

Between the two bases, right in the centre of the room, a pit of about 70 centimetres in diameter was cut to a depth of about 3.5 metres

Two views of the headless statue found in the pit of the holy of holies

(the upper part of it was built of courses of field stones). Very few finds were made there, but one very important object was discovered at the bottom: a basalt statue of a headless man (the head, broken in antiquity, was not found by us). Similar in general lines to the statue found in the stelae temple of area C, it was both larger and devoid of any emblem on its breast. It seemed that this statue had been thrown into the pit by the occupants of temple IB after it had been broken. It may have been an heirloom from a previous temple – perhaps the statue of an earlier king – stored there out of reverence. The nature of the pit was not disclosed by other data, but from its position we may infer that it served as an outlet for the libations performed in that part of the temple. Finding the statue buried or discarded in the pit may sound unusual to some readers, but exactly the same phenomenon occurred in Alalakh, where a statue of its king, Idrimi, was thrown and buried in a pit. Other than this statue, hardly any objects were found on the floor itself, except for a few cylinder seals of cultic nature associated with a solar-disc deity. It seems, as in the stelae temple, that the people of stratum IA salvaged most of the furniture for their temple from this earlier one, which had been destroyed, and then simply raised the floor and built new columns. A few of the sherds here pointed clearly to the fourteenth century, equivalent to stratum

IB in other areas. It was also clear that the orthostats, at least in their present position, originated in this stratum.

In front of the holy of holies was the middle room, or main hall, laid out more or less as the one in temple I A but with one interesting difference. This wide, central room was flanked by two narrow passages on the west and by a single room on the east. The two passages, which

The plan

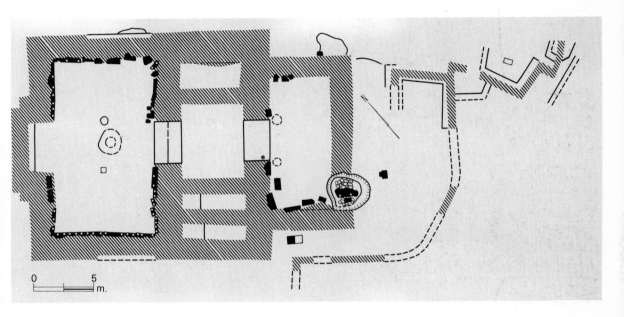

Plan of the IB temple. Note the temple courts at the right

survived in the IA temple, undoubtedly served as a staircase leading to the second floor or roof. The room on the east may have served as part of a tower or storeroom. It should be noted that in stratum IA (compare plans), the wall of that room was destroyed in order to widen the central area. (It was on that destroyed wall that we found the offering table.) The IB temple also had a front porch, which was adopted in the plan of its successor. No columns were found between the porch entrance and the main hall, but it may be assumed that the two bases, or columns, found in IA originally came from this temple. In other words, the entire plan of the temple of IA, with its tripartite division, originated in IB; or, rather, the IA temple is just a reconstruction of the IB temple, a situation similar to that of the temples we found in area C.

Much more of this temple complex was found to the south of the three rooms. Just in front of the entrance to the wall-enclosed court, we came across a basalt obelisk with a flat slab in front of it, obviously a holy stone. It was not far away from there that we discovered the broken statue of the temple's deity with the emblem on its breast. All around were many *favissae* (cult garbage dumps), in which the temple's broken vessels and furniture were disposed of. It is quite clear from the obelisk that some cultic rituals – most probably sacrifices –

were performed outside the temple itself, although we found no altar for animal sacrifice in this area. But on the west side of the porch, we found a well–preserved libation altar, and on it a libation table (still *in situ*) similar to the one found in the holy of holies of temple IA (see photographs on page 87).

The top temple (IA) was excavated mainly during the 1956 season. In 1957 we thought it imperative to continue there, and most of the discoveries in the IB temple and the others I am about to describe were made in 1957 (under the supervision of Trude Dothan). It was a most exciting season indeed! While excavating the porch of the temple, we noticed a gap in the western part of its front wall, as if a bit of wall were missing. As we began to clear this spot, I recorded with my camera the progress made from hour to hour. Some of my pictures are reproduced here so that the reader may become a partner to our excitement and a witness to the step-by-step process of how the find was actually made. They also convey the reason for the difficulties we had in understanding the significance of our discovery. Immediately after removing the top soil, we saw the head of a lion protruding from a heap of stones. As the area was cleared further and we descended

centre A general view of the temple (looking north towards the holy of holies), showing the porch with its two pillars in the foreground. Note the gap in the left side of the front wall

bottom, left The lion's head just emerging from under the heap of stones

bottom, right The lion turns into a huge orthostat. Note the disturbed state of the cobble-stone floor

deeper, it became apparent that the lion lay in a circular pit that seemed to have been carved into an earlier pebble pavement. What emerged was part of a lion orthostat, 1.9 metres long and 90 centimetres high, with two holes drilled into its top like those in the orthostats found in this area earlier. Once the stones were removed, the entire length of the orthostat became visible and what we saw at that point was its back side. It was rather heavy and difficult to move, and we had to resort to a truck's jack to turn it over. Only then did it appear in its full glory.

The piece was clearly a door-jamb orthostat and is similar in style to the smaller lion orthostat found in the stelae temple, but identical in size to some of the uncarved orthostats found in stratum IA here in area H. The sculpting of the orthostat is superb, especially when we remember that it was executed in hard basalt stone before iron tools were known. On one long side was a relief of a crouching lion, while the front, narrow side shows the head and forelegs in the round. The lion's mane is sculpted in a very stylistic manner and ends off at a point. The tail is sculpted so as to show it between the body and the hind leg, a very characteristic feature of these reliefs. It was quite a

centre, left The orthostat found buried on its side. Note the two holes in its top
centre, right The unworked side of the orthostat
bottom, left Using a truck's jack to turn the orthostat over
bottom, right The front and carved sides of the door-jamb orthostat, as it was seen by those who entered the temple. Note the disturbed cobble-stone floors of strata 2–3, respectively
overleaf The lion photographed *in situ*. Note the stylized mane and the tail between its leg and body

Exit lion

problem to move the lion outside the excavation area, and in due course we managed to do so only with the help of a big crane. Today this lion is one of the prize exhibits in the Israel Museum in Jerusalem.

The style of the relief clearly shows the orthostat to be of the northern type. Yet it is interesting that neither in Hittite Anatolia (Bogazköy) nor in Syria (Alalakh) were such beautiful lions found. There is a close parallel to our lion in Alalakh, where Sir Leonard Woolley found crouching-lion orthostats decorating door jambs; but the comparison on artistic grounds definitely comes out in favour of the Hazor lion. Though the concept is the same, one can see how much cruder are the lions from Alalakh. We searched in vain to try and find the lion that must have graced the second door jamb, and it may still be buried somewhere. But another possibility was unwittingly suggested by our

A door-jamb orthostat from Alalakh, which is similar in concept yet distinctly different in execution

predecessor in excavating Hazor. In his first article on Hazor, Garstang recorded a story he had heard from the Arabs of the neighbouring village about 'a black stone with a lion carved upon it'. Perhaps this was the other lion, found on the surface at one time and hidden, removed or broken.

Talking of that lion reminds me of another orthostat we found on the *tell* proper, and thus anticipates some of our discoveries in the upper city. While we were excavating the Late Bronze strata on the mound, we came upon a broken, basalt, animal orthostat with only the forepart of the animal preserved. It proved identical to the first orthostat, except that, judging by the mane, its relief was of a lioness. Both orthostats must have been produced in the very same atelier, if not by the same artist. Here the artist adopted a more refined approach and used very few lines, but even without creating many details he achieved a very expressive head of a lioness. This one, of course, is not the missing orthostat of the temple pair. But it indicates that lion orthostats must have been rather popular in Hazor. A joke current among us back in those days when we were trying desperately to locate the missing part of the orthostat (unsuccessfully to this day) was that both we and the lion of area H would give a great deal to find the hind part of the lioness!

Returning to the lion in the temple, we found that we had quite a difficult problem interpreting the information provided by the find. Obviously the lion had been deliberately buried in a pit cut from the top down and then covered with stones. Our questions were: when was this done, by whom and why? Since the floor of stratum 2 was cut (no doubt in either the IA or IB periods, during the lifetime of the two upper temples), and since the front wall of the porch, too, was cut, the lion must have been buried after the construction of the

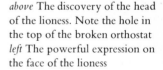

The lioness

above The discovery of the head of the lioness. Note the hole in the top of the broken orthostat
left The powerful expression on the face of the lioness

IB temple. But how long afterwards? After IB was destroyed and before IA was built? Or after the destruction of IA? The stratigraphic evidence is not decisive on this point. The lion may have been buried after the IA temple had been destroyed, either by the conquerors who demolished the temple, then buried the lion and covered it by a heap of stones in a memorial symbolic fashion, or even more likely by survivors of the destruction – maybe members of the temple staff – who fled and later returned to bury the lion out of veneration, hoping one day to retrieve it and reconstruct the temple. There are parallels to this phenomenon in other thirteenth-century finds, as well as those of later periods, although it is difficult to know their motivation. For example, as mentioned earlier, the statue of the king of Alalakh, Idrimi, was found by Woolley broken and deliberately buried in a pit in the top level of the temple. A similar case was noticed by a former student of mine, D. Ussishkin, in Zinjirli, where lion orthostats were also deliberately buried – although at a later period. In all these cases, including our own, the problem of why the objects were buried remains unsolved. Yet we still faced another question, that of the origin of the orthostats. Were they all made for the fourteenth-century IB temple and then used again in the top level? That is what we thought during our excavations. But in the light of some discoveries made on the *tell* in the last season (1968), I believe we must change our opinion and conclude that they originated in an even earlier period. In order to understand why, let me now move to what was found under the top two temples.

Once we began to excavate under the floors of the IB temple, it immediately became apparent that an older building had existed there – another temple. As we did not wish to remove the walls of the upper temples, we were compelled to excavate between them and

Plan of the stratum 2 temple. Note particularly the court (2149) with its cult installations (2534, 2554); the propylaeum (2169); and the drainage installation (2150)

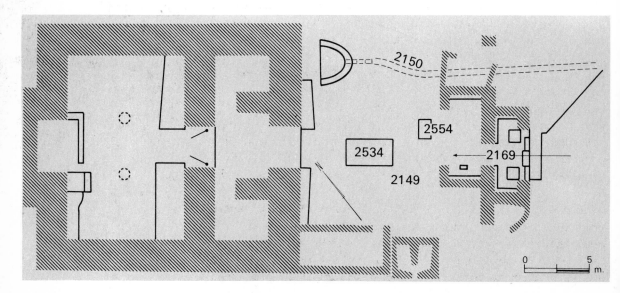

2150

2554

2534

2169

2149

0   5
m.

make some sections and trenches near their foundations. Enough was found to give us not only an exact plan of the stratum 2 temple but also many interesting details. The plan of this building differs from those above it. To facilitate comprehension, let us say that basically the plan of stratum 2 is that of IB without its porch. In other words, it consists of only two main elements: (1) a main room (holy of holies) with a niche, measuring 13.5 metres from west to east and 8.9 metres from north to south, with 2.3–metre-thick walls; (2) a porch with two towers that flank the main entrance to the temple. In addition to the sections against the walls, which revealed the exact plan and thickness of the walls, we also found the temple's floor (made mainly of heavy cobble-stones) and its thresholds and door sockets. These elements were particularly noticeable in the passage between the porch and the holy of holies, where, under the sockets of the IB temple, we found those of stratum 2. The position of the sockets indicates that the entrance to the holy of holies was closed by two winged doors opening inwards. If there were jamb orthostats in this temple, they definitely could not have been at this entrance; therefore they must have belonged to the main entrance to the temple. Unfortunately, there we could not excavate under the top temple, so we do not know whether it had sockets and, if so, where. But when we compare the plan of stratum 2 to that of IB and IA, we can again see the deliberate addition of a third element in the later temples: the original porch had been converted into a main hall. It is this aspect of the later temples that makes them a sort of prototype of the Solomonic temple.

Now let us return to the very important problem of the orthostats. Two things about the position of the orthostats in IB and IA were disturbing and suspicious: (1) that they were not found close to the floors of IB or IA, but high above them, contrary to the normal practice of finding orthostats in the lower parts of the wall foundations; (2) that only the holy of holies and porch in strata IB and IA were adorned with orthostats, while the main hall was not. Furthermore, as we have noticed in the porch, the arrangement of the orthostats was rather haphazard. They did not fit each other too well, and in one case they were replaced by an offering table. At the time of excavation, we lacked clues to determine their age or to explain these strange phenomena. But in 1968, while excavating on the *tell*, we found structures with identical orthostats – seemingly made by the same craftsmen and of the same period – *in situ*! And on the *tell* we found conclusive proof that they originated in at least the Late Bronze I period (sixteenth–fifteenth centuries).

Now we can re-evaluate our discoveries in area H. The orthostats must have originated in stratum 2, at the latest, and been re-used later on in the IB and IA temples. This conclusion, I believe, not only explains the strange phenomena of their placement *vis-à-vis* the floor and disorganized arrangement, but enables us to suggest the position of

The door sockets of stratum 2 seen under those of the IB temple

opposite, left A well-defined
circle in the cobble-stone floor
marked the position of some
cult object
opposite, right The rectangular
platform that appeared to be a
bamah, or high place, found
in the middle of the inner court

the orthostats in their original state. If we assume now that they
belonged originally to at least stratum 2, then the orthostats found
in the holy of holies of IB originally adorned the holy of holies of
stratum 2 (both rooms are practically of the same dimensions). Likewise,
the orthostats that adorned the porch of the IB temple in secondary
use must originally have belonged to the porch of stratum 2. Now
we can understand why the main hall of the IB and IA temples were
unadorned by orthostats. This hall was an addition to the original
temple plan made in the IB period. But the orthostats found by the
IB people sufficed for only two rooms: a holy of holies and a porch.
Therefore the IB people moved the orthostats of the earlier porch
(below their main hall) to the new porch, leaving the new main hall
unadorned. I believe this to be the only explanation for the strange
problem of their placement in the upper-level temples. So our orthostats
are at least of the sixteenth–fifteenth centuries and are thus among the
oldest orthostats known in the Near East!

The temple court

The temples of antiquity were the houses of the deity, not the setting
in which cult sacrifices took place. Therefore, the large square or open
area in front of and around these temples, where the sacrifices were
performed, was a very important element. We were very fortunate
indeed to find in front of the stratum 2 temple considerable parts of
this open court and in it important cult installations (see previous
plan). The court itself consisted of an inner yard near the temple and
an outer one further south separated by a monumental propylaeum
(free-standing entrance gate). The floor of the inner yard is paved with

The court of the stratum 2
temple, looking west. Note the
cult installation (2554) and
the threshold of the
propylaeum

coarse cobble-stones, like those of the building itself, and is built so that its northern half slants southwards and southern half slants north-wards. Thus a sort of shallow trough was created in the centre, further accentuated by a low guiding line, to drain away to the south-east the liquids from the sacrifices and the libations. It appears that the main cult activities took place in this inner yard. Immediately south of the entrance to the temple, the cobble-stones were laid so as to form a well-defined circle 1 metre in diameter, which may have served to mark the position of some cult object. The entire area was littered with animal bones and ashes, further evidence that this was the main sacrifice area. In the middle of the inner court – on the axis of the propylaeum and the porch entrance – we found a large rectangular platform (3.5 metres wide, 2 metres long and 30 centimetres high) built upon the floor. It looked like a *bamah*, or high place, and 2 metres south of it a similar, though smaller, structure was found.

In the eastern part of the inner court, about 5 metres east of the *bamah*, an interesting drainage canal was discovered just beneath the court floor. Its southern part was built of field stones and covered by undressed slabs, but it was the northern part that aroused our interest for it was built of disused incense stands. Only temples could afford

above The temple's drainage canal, made of disused incense stands (right)
below Two of the disused incense stands with triangular 'windows'

such drainage! They were huge, similar to those found on the floor of the temple court, and had triangular holes or 'windows'. The course of the drains southwards is unknown to us, since the area has not been excavated. But it may be assumed that eventually this canal joined the main drainage system of the lower city, which we found in area F. The origin of the drainage was most probably a semi-circular installation found to the right of the temple entrance (see plan) in which two basalt pillar-bases were incorporated in secondary use. This canal seems to have drained the blood and water of the sacrifices.

Above the canal, within a great heap of discarded vessels in the southern part of the court (the *favissa*), we found an unusual object: a small clay model of a cow's liver with omens inscribed on it in cuneiform script. This was used by the temple diviners, and it is the only one found in this country with such inscriptions. Liver divination was very common in Babylon, and this discovery of the fifteenth century BC is further evidence of the links between Hazor and Mesopotamia. The model consists of two broken fragments bearing inscriptions that were pressed into their face and back. These enigmatic inscriptions hardly win grades for precision, as we can see from this partial reading of them by the late Professor B. Landsberger and Professor Haim Tadmor:

above The *favissa*, or dump for discarded cult vessels, in which the object shown below was found

below A unique clay model of a cow's liver, with cuneiform inscriptions, used for divination

One king will bend down another.
An enemy will attack my country

. . . .

Forgiveness [will be granted] by the god to the men.
A servant will rebel against his lord.

On the other fragment we find the inscriptions:

Ištar [?] will eat the land
Nergal will . . .
The gods of the city will come back.

We do not know, of course, when these evil and good omens would
be fulfilled; this was the privileged knowledge of the temple's priests,
who announced these tidings to the king and worshippers, as they saw
fit, according to the livers of the sacrificed animals.

The above temple, like the one in area C, had its own potter, who
produced the votive vessels for sale to the worshippers. We found his
kiln with twenty-two miniature votive bowls still resting on the floor.
This find, like many others, obviously indicates that the temple of
stratum 2 was destroyed by an enemy and the people abandoned it
abruptly.

The temple potter's kiln

above Miniature votive vessels
as found in the kiln of the
temple's potter
left The votive vessels after
cleaning

The magnificent bronze plaque
depicting a Canaanite dignitary
opposite, top A bronze figurine
à la Picasso
opposite, bottom Plan of the
stratum 3 temple

Finally, the stratum 2 temple yielded two metal figurines, quite different from each other yet both of high artistic interest. The first object is the more interesting of the two and – to the best of my knowledge – unique: a tiny figurine of a woman made of a thin bronze sheet, altogether 5 centimetres in height. It depicts schematically a woman's body with only specific features accentuated: one eye, only half a nose and mouth, one breast and the vulva. I know of no similar figurine in the Near East, and it is not likely that it indicates a Picassoesque approach. It more likely represents life and death, or the born and the unborn, and must have been brought to the temple as a votive. I wonder if Hazorites thought of it as unusual; to our modern eyes it seems one of the most original pieces of art of the second millennium BC. The second piece is a bronze plaque of particularly beautiful execution. Found resting on the partition line that separates the inner and outer courts, it is made of a thin bronze sheet, 9.4 centimetres long. The rivets on its back indicate that it was at one time fastened to a wooden panel; and its position suggests that it may have been part of a whole procession. The figure is hammered, and some of its details are further delineated by incisions. It depicts what appears to be a Canaanite dignitary whose right arm is raised in a salute, a pose similar to that so often depicted on Egyptian monuments. He is wearing a long robe with wrappings at the bottom, which is also similar to depictions of Canaanite dignitaries on fifteenth-century Egyptian wall paintings. On top of it he is wearing a poncho-like garment terminating in fringed bands. This piece is also unique in Near Eastern archaeology and is no doubt one of the most beautifully executed bronze figurines of its time. In fact, both these objects, as well as other finds in the stratum 2 temple, demonstrate not only that Hazor at this period reached a very high standard of development, but that stratum 2 must have dated to the period of Thutmose III and was probably destroyed in the first half of the fifteenth century.

Below the stratum 2 temple, which was the third temple from the top, we found the remains of the oldest temple built on virgin soil. Its plan was similar to that of the stratum 2 temple – or rather the opposite, since this stratum 3 temple was the first to be built on the site. Its remains were all beneath the later buildings, and in many cases only the contours of its walls could be detected – with the aid of soundings made at right angles to their courses – or could not be traced at all. It is therefore quite understandable that our knowledge of the temple's plan was incomplete and in some cases conjectural. Enough evidence was uncovered, however, to trace its main features and stratification. The plan is unique in this country, although strikingly similar to the stratum VII temple in Alalakh, to which it is also akin chronologically. It is also a further indication of northern influence on the architecture (and other aspects of the life) of Hazor from the Middle Bronze II period onwards. The only two temples in Palestine

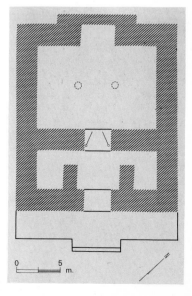

0   5
|__|__| m.

that can be compared to this one are those in Shechem and Megiddo,
dating to the end of the Middle Bronze period or possibly the beginning
of the Late Bronze period. Both have a porch flanked by towers, leading
into the holy of holies. The basic difference, though, is that the Hazor
holy of holies is a wide room, while those of Megiddo and Shechem
are elongated. This point may seem trivial to the reader, but as we
are talking about a basic architectural concept, the difference in
architecture must reflect a deeper, cultural variation as well – either
in religious tradition or, perhaps, in ethnic composition.

In addition to the temple floor, we again found door sockets in
the threshold between the porch and holy of holies, directly under
those of the stratum 2 temple. But here, again, we know more about
this temple's courtyard and its arrangement than about the temple
itself. A most impressive feature is the basalt ashlar steps that constitute
the entrance to the porch and lead to a platform. The steps are
beautifully dressed, which indicates that as early as the Middle Bronze
period – more precisely, at the end of the Middle Bronze II (roughly
the seventeenth–sixteenth centuries) – the people of Hazor had
achieved high technical standards. It may also suggest that the orthostats
originated then (although this is certainly not conclusive). As in the
stratum 2 temple, here too the entire area south of the temple was
occupied by a large open court, this time paved with a very fine
pebble floor, almost like a mosaic. We also know from the technical
evidence that this temple was built after the earthen rampart, for in
order to build it the labourers flattened the lower section of
the rampart in order to turn it into a sort of platform for the
sanctuary.

Now that we have surveyed the various temples discovered in the
lower city – from the Middle Bronze down to the end of the Late
Bronze period – it is appropriate to say a few words about some
aspects of temples in general. First of all, the most striking feature of
our discoveries is that although contemporary temples existed in
various areas of Hazor, not one of them resembles another. (I am not
referring here to temples built one on top of another in the same area,
but, for example, to a temple in area C as compared to one in area H, or

above The mosaic-like cobble-
stone floor of the stratum 3
temple's court
right The fine basalt ashlar steps
leading to the temple

both as compared to one in area F.) Since strong conservatism pervades temple plans, the most reasonable explanation for the difference in layout emanates from the different deities worshipped in the temples, each one having its own temple tradition. Or perhaps it suggests that the population of the vast city of Hazor was composed of various ethnic elements that merged into a pluralistic unit, with each group retaining its own tradition. But the first explanation seems more plausible to me.

Another interesting aspect of the temples we found is their orientation – a term to describe the position of the entrance vis-à-vis the holy of holies, like south to north or west to east. The orientation is, of course, very important because it indicates certain aspects of the cult of a particular deity, particularly the east–west orientation, which has a direct bearing on the importance of the sun in the cult. Sometimes orientations are connected with the original provenance of a people, for they pray facing, as it were, their original holy places or mountains (compare the Moslems praying towards Mecca and the Jews towards Jerusalem to this day). In this aspect, the Hazor temples have various orientations. The stelae temple is basically oriented east–west; the orthostat temples are, on the whole, south–north; the double temple, in a way, is west–east; and another temple of orthostats – found on the *tell* proper – is also oriented east–west. However, we discovered in Hazor yet another aspect of orientation that is of importance. It became apparent that all the temples – irrespective of the orientation of their entrance vis-à-vis the holy of holies – were so built that the *corners* of the buildings were on the points of the compass, a definite Mesopotamian or northern trait. In contrast, some temples of other Palestinian sites, like Lachish, Megiddo, Beth-shan and so forth, show wall orientation, meaning that if they are oriented south–north then the walls too are south–north and east–west. This may show perhaps more of an Egyptian influence.

Finally, since most of our discoveries concern temples, the reader may come away with the impression that the whole lower city was composed of temples. Nothing could be more wrong! I have dwelt on the subject of temples because in one case we were fortunate to discover a temple by chance (area C) and were drawn to the others (in areas F and H) because some of their relics protruded from the soil. On the other hand, there is no reason to believe that the temples we excavated were the only ones in the area of the 'enclosure'. After all, this lower city could have had a population of 30,000 people, requiring quite a number of sanctuaries to serve the various deities worshipped. And since only a small fraction of the nearly 200 acres of the lower city were excavated, it is very possible that more temples will be found in the future. In areas D and E of the lower city, however, we excavated residential neighbourhoods, and the finds there helped us visualize aspects of daily life in pre-Israelite Hazor.

7 Cisterns and Dwellings –
Areas D and E

It was while working in area C in the lower city that we also looked for other areas to be excavated there. One spot several hundred metres north-east of area C attracted our attention because many vertically scarped and dressed rocks were visible on its surface, and it occurred to us that here, far away from the city centre, we might expect to find tombs. Claire Epstein was entrusted with this excavation, which turned out to be most difficult from a stratigraphic viewpoint because a great part of the remains on the rocks had been washed away by the elements or destroyed by local farmers. Moreover, the area was terraced, and it was difficult to find direct connections between the strata of one terrace and those of another. Nevertheless, the excavations here proved most rewarding indeed, and the finds were so numerous that they occupied thirty-nine plates of the first volume of our official publication reporting the first season's results.

The first and most important discovery had to do with the nature of the enclosure, which we had just then begun to regard as a veritable city. The entire area was covered with remains of structures, and their sequence of occupation was identical to that already found in area C: five strata of occupation, the two bottom ones (4 and 3) pertaining to the Middle Bronze II period, the middle one (2) to the Late Bronze I period, and the top two (IB and IA) to the Late Bronze II period (that is, the fourteenth and thirteenth centuries, respectively).

In the southern part of the area, we clearly discerned a well-dressed rock face even before we began excavating. As soon as the excavations began, we came upon a family of porcupines who made their home in the cave located under this rock, so we named it the 'porcupine cave'. The cave itself was well cut and had a vaulted entrance leading to a narrow passage and a room, of which we dug only the east side. The ceiling of the cave had collapsed completely. Caves of this type are found over a wide area in and around Hazor and appear to be burial places. Several skulls were found in this one and some smaller caves nearby, which looked more like natural caves. The hewn caves were evidence of the earliest human activity in the area. Subsequently, the entire area in front of the caves was covered with residential buildings, of which, as I said, five strata were uncovered.

Of the earliest dwellings, only some wall remnants were found. These ran parallel to one another and enabled us to reconstruct the general layout of the stratum. The originally open courtyard in front

Area D

The 'porcupine cave'

Area D on the first day of excavations, with vertically scarped rocks visible on the surface

The 'porcupine cave' in the course of excavations

of the cave had been converted into a residential area and divided into a number of rooms. The entrance to the 'porcupine' and adjacent caves was partially visible to the inhabitants of this stratum, and it is possible that they used the caves. In stratum 3 a new set of dwellings was found. Although they were still of the Middle Bronze II period, the plan of the rooms was entirely different from that prevailing in stratum 4. In this stratum the visible entrance into the 'porcupine cave' was reduced to a height of 1.3 metres, and a door sill of undressed stones was laid over that of the preceding period. On the whole, the pottery – so-called typical Hyksos pottery – indicated that this stratum, like its parallel in area C, belonged to the last century of the Middle Bronze II period. In the settlement above (stratum 2), the plan of the entire area was again changed, and the pottery indicated that it had been occupied mainly in the Late Bronze I period. The last occupation was in the Late Bronze II period and probably consisted of two phases. Of the upper (later) one, very little remained after the plough and the elements had wrought havoc, but the varieties of pottery (including a number of Mycenaean pottery fragments) indicated quite clearly that it corresponded to the last occupation in area C. This sequence of occupation was visible in all the terraces, and it would be pointless to go into details here; but I would like to describe an unusual find made slightly to the north of the 'porcupine cave'.

Kilns or furnaces   Just under the surface here, we found two kilns or furnaces – one circular and the other oblong — with very interesting ventilation systems. The circular one was made of undressed stones that showed ample traces of burning on the inside. Its ventilation arrangements were located in the north, undoubtedly to exploit the constant wind from that direction. A large horizontal stone that formed part of the kiln's wall was located above an air duct that extended to a point outside the kiln; and a large field stone with four natural holes, through which the air filtered from above, had been placed on it. Surrounding this stone on three sides, we found the remains of a wall of undressed blocks of stone that formed a kind of chimney. In the neighbouring oblong furnace, the ventilation systems were somewhat different. Its northern, tapered part was covered with large stones, thus forming a channel with a vertical opening at the end. As it had deep foundations, a vertical chimney may have been built over it. It is difficult to determine exactly the purpose of these two kilns. Obviously they were intended for different purposes, as they had different plans and arrangements. In the circular one we found some pieces of copper slag, which may indicate that it served to smelt copper; the other may have been used to make pottery. Since the kilns were very close to the surface, it was difficult to date them exactly to either the Middle Bronze or Late Bronze period. A few sherds of the latest occupation were found nearby, and if they are indicative of the date, then the evidence points to the Late Bronze period. But there is always a chance that they may just have filtered in. Whatever the case, the two kilns are most interesting from a technical viewpoint and as testimony to the activities of Hazor's inhabitants. If they actually belong to the Middle Bronze period, then we have confirmation of the production of bronze in the area, as mentioned in some of the Mari letters.

The most exciting aspect of the excavations in this area was the many bottle-shaped, rock-cut cisterns (some up to 9 metres deep) that were scattered all over it. Excavating them was very difficult, a real underground operation — so that sometimes on approaching the area the only signs of life were the many tripods erected above the entrances to the cisterns, ever ready to haul up the finds. These consisted of hundreds of vessels of all periods — one of the richest repertories we have of Hazor pottery. Originally, some of the cisterns were created for water storage, some for burials. In one cistern the upper, more porous parts of the rock were even plastered! This one went out of use for water storage as early as the Late Bronze I period. It is one of the earliest examples of its kind known in the country and disproves the allegation that plastered cisterns were first introduced by the Israelites in the twelfth and eleventh centuries BC.

How were these cisterns filled with water? Because of the rocky ground around them and the absence of any large channels leading to them, we cannot assume that rainwater collected on the ground could have filled the cisterns. The next logical assumption is that they

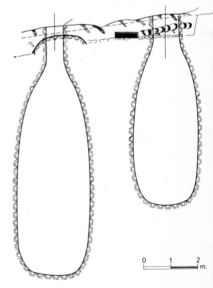

top The circular and oblong kilns
centre A few of the hundreds of vessels found in the cisterns
bottom Sections of the two cisterns

0   1   2
m.

were filled by water drained off the roofs of the dwellings built over or near them. If the average annual rainfall was then about 600 millimetres – as it is today – a roof surface of about 25–30 square metres would suffice to fill most of the cisterns. As it turns out, the remains of structures in the vicinity of the cisterns indicate that the built-up area of some houses was of those dimensions. It seems, though, that this original scheme was abandoned either because of lack of rain or because the cisterns did not function well enough, since all cisterns we dug were eventually converted into burial or storage pits. In one of them (9024) we found a large quantity of skeletons, accompanied by an abundance of burial furniture and scarabs, just above a layer of silt. Some of the dead were buried in successive layers over a fairly short period. Most of the scarabs found in this cistern belong to the very beginning of the Middle Bronze II occupation. Above them we found a layer that

below Scarabs found at Hazor shown from two sides

contained mainly Late Bronze I pottery, including the distinct type called Bichrome Ware, which was described in chapter 4. In the very top layer of silt, many fragments of Late Bronze II pottery were found, including the crude clay mask mentioned in chapter 3.

In a neighbouring cistern (9027), the one that was plastered, we encountered a most pathetic sight. Below the top debris, at a depth of about 5 metres from the mouth of the cistern, was a skeleton of a young woman lying in an east–west direction with her hands crossed on her breast and her head leaning against a stone. Near the skeleton we found vessels that disclosed its date, such as two Mycenaean *pyxides* a 'milk bowl' and a decorated jug, all typical of the end of the four-teenth to the thirteenth century. This young woman must have been buried in the cistern several decades before the final fall of Hazor. The last cistern to be mentioned here (9017) yielded the richest store of pottery belonging to the last two centuries of the lower city, particularly the thirteenth century. High above the bottom, but still about 5 metres

above Two Middle Bronze II jugs found in cisterns in area D

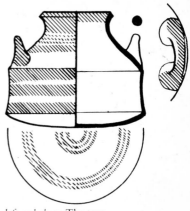

left and above The two Mycenaean IIIB *pyxides* found with the woman's skeleton

top The sherd bearing two
Proto-Canaanite letters
centre A votive ewer from
Lachish bearing a Proto-
Canaanite inscription
bottom The ancestors of A and K

A	✶	🐂
K	y	🖐

from the top, several scores of vessels were found nearly intact in a level about 70 centimetres thick. The quantity of objects found in such a condensed area indicates that in that phase the cistern must have been used as a storage pit. The vessels were mainly household pottery, such as bowls and cooking pots, juglets, jugs and storage jars, but there were also quite a number of decorative pieces.

Before leaving area D, so rich in pottery, I should like to mention another object found right on the surface: a tiny sherd of a locally made Late Bronze II pot whose importance is in inverse proportion to its size. To our amazement, the sherd bore two letters inscribed in the so-called Proto-Canaanite script. The letters of this script – which is a forebear of our modern alphabet – retain some of the original pictorial elements evolved from its predecessor, Proto-Sinaitic script. Both Proto-Sinaitic and Proto-Canaanite were acrophonic, which means that the first consonant of the word represented in the picture served as a letter. Thus, the ox, (*aluph* in Canaanite-Hebrew) was used for the letter *aleph*, ✶ (or later *alpha* and then 'A'); the palm of the hand, (*kaph* in Canaanite-Hebrew) was used for the letter *kaph*, y (or later *kappa* and 'K') and so on. The two letters on our sherd were painted in dark brown and read: . . . *lt*. This inscription is the only one in that script found to date in northern Palestine and may be compared to the one discovered on a thirteenth-century ewer from Lachish, which ends with the word *'elt*, that is, goddess.

A few words should also be said about the small area E because of the similarity between its levels of occupation and those of area D and the abundant discoveries belonging to one period that we made there. Area E is in the south-central part of the lower Canaanite city, just north of the *tell* proper. As it was not too far from area C, we decided to have Jean Perrot, who supervised the latter, look into this extension of his domain, as it were. Two things prompted us to dig there: first, Garstang's report that he found tombs with Iron Age pottery there, which seemed rather strange since no occupation of the Iron Age proper had been found in the lower city; second, the intuition that tombs might exist in the worked, scarped rock. I shall not go into a detailed description of this small area, and suffice it to say that here, as in area D, the caves we found were first cut in the Middle Bronze II period. But one of the cisterns, which had also been made during the final phase of the Middle Bronze period, was 'sandwiched' stratigraphically between the Middle Bronze II and Late Bronze II levels and was of extreme importance. No Middle Bronze II pottery was found in it, as the later occupants cleared it completely. On the other hand, the people of the latest two strata of the Late Bronze II period (the fourteenth and thirteenth centuries BC) built their houses over its sealed mouth, so whatever had been in it was archaeologically 'trapped'. In the lower part of that cistern, we found literally hundreds of vessels, and from the amount of the silt

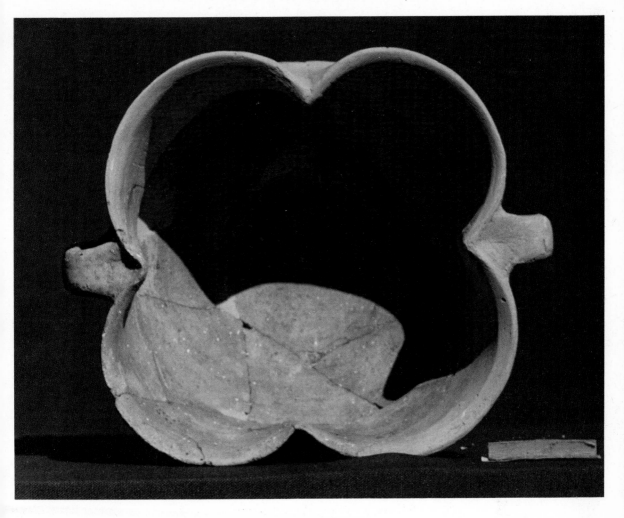

deposit and incrustations on them we could infer that they were thrown, or had fallen, into the cistern. All these vessels belonged to a single period, the Late Bronze I. This was invaluable to us, for the Late Bronze I was the period of Thutmose III, in whose documents Hazor is mentioned. The array of pottery found here is the best of Hazor for this period, though its main contribution is a very beautiful type of pottery – as can be seen from the quatrefoil bowl (of which we have samples with and without handles) – found nowhere else in the country. The closest parallels, though not identical, come from Anatolia, which may indicate relations between Hazor and the Hittite sphere of influence in that period. Since no tombs with Iron Age pottery came our way – and we could not be sure about what Garstang found – we decided to discontinue the dig here, despite the existence of remains of quite a number of well-built walls with polygonal stones. Perhaps future excavations will reveal more about its nature.

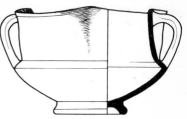

Two views of a unique quatrefoil bowl of the 15th century BC

8 The Lower City's Fortifications

Once the nature of the enclosure was clarified as a vast city surrounded by huge earthen-rampart fortifications, it became imperative to probe into these defences, particularly their technical aspects. But before I begin to describe the results of these probes, it will be helpful to say a few words about the general aspect of fortifications in the Middle Bronze II period. Let us deal first with the fortifications of cities perched only on small *tells*, whose built-up areas averaged 10 to 15 acres, such as Lachish, Shechem, Megiddo and others. A very characteristic, albeit enigmatic, way of fortifying cities in the Middle Bronze II period was discovered by archaeologists in the early stages of excavations in this part of the world and was described by the French words *glacis* or *terre pisée* (beaten earth) fortifications. These terms refer to two different features of these same fortifications. *Glacis* relates to their form – that is, to the slant or slope of the forti-fications below the walls – and is borrowed from medieval French, in which the term described the defensive slopes in front of fortifica-tions. *Terre pisée* refers to the unique way in which these slopes were built of beaten earth, crushed stones and, quite often, alternating layers of different types of earth. Some archaeologists refer to this method as the 'sandwich *glacis*'.

Since these fortifications were common in the period in which Palestine and Egypt were dominated by the so-called Hyksos – an Asiatic people considered to be horse and chariot masters – it was for long an accepted view that the defences were actually against the onslaught of chariots. But this explanation is quite untenable simply because one does not attack a city with chariots. The ancient chariot – unlike the modern tank – was a light vehicle, and its power of penetra-tion was only as strong as the forehead of its horse, no more. Many years ago I suggested that these fortifications were developed against the battering ram, which began to be employed in strength at the time, as we know from documents and monuments. This ex-

The Middle Bronze fortifications

opposite The huge Middle Bronze revetment wall below the city gate
below A wall painting from Beni Hassan, in Egypt, showing the earliest depiction of a battering ram (*c.* 1900 BC)

A fine example of 'dove-tailing' the earth layers of a *glacis* (Gezer, 17th century BC)

planation, I am gratified to say, is now accepted by many archaeologists. In order to understand it better, one should remember that the *glacis* of cities built on top of existing mounds protected the *slopes* of the mound; only on top of the *glacis* were the cities further protected by walls. The reason for this double caution is clear: since the slopes were composed of debris of earlier cities and were therefore quite soft, an attacking enemy could, without much difficulty, batter and undermine the walls built on top. It was imperative, therefore, to defend the slopes with some kind of sheath – a crust of hard and beaten earth – that would make penetration under the walls difficult. Different layers of earth were used, for this method better held the huge mass of earth on the slope and also helped drain the water. Sometimes the lower parts of an earthen *glacis* were further strengthened by stones, and sometimes a stone *glacis*, which was certainly an improvement, altogether replaced an earthen one.

The phenomenon of the lower city

Now let us turn back to the lower city itself. Once it became apparent that the enclosure was truly a city that was contemporary with the *glacis* of the *tell*, two questions came to mind: why was this lower city built; and why was it defended in such a manner? These questions were pressing not only because of the discoveries at Hazor itself, but also because of the similar type of cities found in Syria (like Qatna, Charchemish and Tell Mardikh) and even, although to a lesser degree, in Canaan (Hazor's neighbour, the smaller city of Dan). Why was it necessary to erect a lower city in an obviously disadvantaged area,

from the defence point of view, when it is far preferable to build a city atop the *tell*, where it could be easily defended? I believe the answer can be found in the large-scale migration in that period of groups bound together by tribal or ethnic traditions. If a group of about 20–30,000 people migrated to northern Palestine at that time and wished to remain together in one city, then, naturally, difficulties arose. The existing *tells* – which were built near water sources – were too small to absorb them; a *tell* could accommodate 5–6,000 people, no more. So the only alternative was to build an adjacent, lower city and try and fortify it. In the case of Hazor, for example, the population group chose the only area possible, north of the *tell*, where a plateau existed. One side of the plateau, the eastern one, had natural slopes, which only required further protection by means of a *glacis*. But on the other sides of the plateau, where there was no natural feature of defence, it had to be created artificially. On the west, the inhabitants had to start by dividing the plateau, earmarked for the city, from the rest of the terrain, and they therefore cut a huge fosse, or moat. Thus, by amassing earth towards the inside of the city, they shot two birds with one stone and created a double defence line: the moat and the rampart.

The first task that confronted us, therefore, was to probe into the nature of these ramparts. Were they just heaps of earth, or were they – like the *glacis* – deliberately built up? In other words, was the earth taken from the fosse and other sources piled up in a haphazard way or was

The southern end of the huge earthen rampart and moat (bottom) and the 'bottle-shaped' *tell* (above)

The ramparts

it fashioned in a deliberate and planned manner that made the slopes of the plateau impregnable to penetration efforts, on the one hand, and strong enough to withstand the pressures of the torrential rains and other effects of the elements, on the other? Probing into the nature of the earthen ramparts was one of our main objectives as early as the first season, when we selected area C, very close to their widest part, for excavation. It was when we made a trench into the earthen rampart that we discovered the stelae temple, which diverted our attention from the probe. Nevertheless, even in area C, the little we excavated into the rampart indicated that it consisted of a conglomerate of beaten earth and basalt stones, the material scooped out of the fosse, thrown here and then compressed. The evidence provided by this section confirmed what we might have expected: that the earthen ramparts were built up in a manner more or less similar to the *glacis* of the *tell* proper. This was an important discovery in and of itself because it showed that the inhabitants of the *tell* and those of the enclosure used the same technique to build their respective means of defence: the *glacis* and the earthen rampart. In fact it could be argued – and seems rather probable to me – that the whole idea of protecting *tells* with *glacis* in this peculiar sandwich manner dawned on the defenders because of their experience in building these huge earthen ramparts. However, the section in area C was inconclusive, as we only penetrated a couple of metres into the earthen rampart.

Then later on, while we were digging the orthostat temple in area H, we managed to get a glimpse of the layered, inner parts of the rampart on which the earliest temple had been built. But since here in the north the plateau has a natural slope leading down to a deep *wadi*, or gully, it was unnecessary to cut a fosse or erect a full-scale rampart. The maximum height of the rampart there was 8 metres above the virgin soil of the city, and its top was about 6 metres wide. Furthermore, it became evident that the rampart extended to a distance of at least 30 metres down the slope. These facts indicated clearly that here the plateau was protected by a combination rampart-*glacis*. Here the rampart was made of layers of yellowish, chalky material whose outer face was covered by a layer of small, basalt field stones. Also, the inner slope of the rampart is somewhat steeper than the outer one. But even the evidence culled from these sections was unsatisfactory because we did not penetrate to the very core of the fortification.

The opportunity to do just that presented itself in 1965, eight years after we concluded the fourth season of excavations, when Kibbutz Ayelet Hashaḥar decided to construct a public building near the northern slope of the eastern spur of the enclosure. On our recommendation, permission was granted by the Department of Antiquities on condition that before construction began a trench be dug on the spot to ascertain its nature. This investigation took three days and

The eastern spur with section AA cut into its ramparts (looking south)

provided important data concerning the nature of the fortifications. We learned that, at least in this area, the earthen ramparts were erected in a much more sophisticated manner than we had assumed up to then. In fact, we dug two trenches, 140 metres apart. First let me discuss the eastern section, marked section AA. With the aid of mechanical equipment, our trench was extended to a depth of 5.5 metres, and another 2 metres were dug up by hand; but even then we did not reach the bottom of the rampart, as that proved too dangerous. At first it appeared that the rampart here – as in areas H and C – was made of beaten earth only. However, because we managed to make such a deep incision into this section, for the first time we were also

A close view of section AA at the start of excavations (looking south)

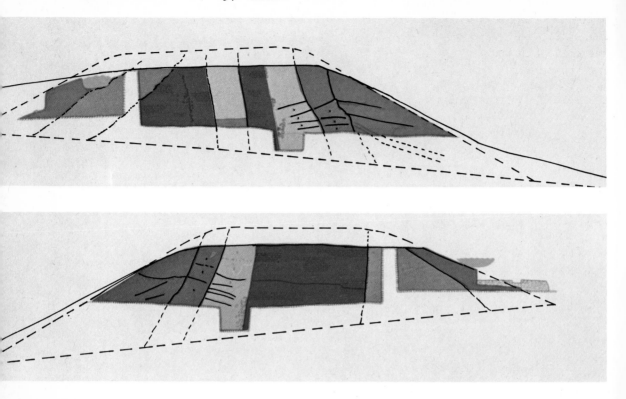

A schematic diagram of section AA, showing the brick core and earthen layers, looking west (top) and east (bottom)

able to examine its insides, as it were. While reading the following description, it will be helpful to refer to the colour diagram given above. The section on top shows the rampart as one looks westwards, towards the *tell*; the one below is a view towards the east, looking away from the city.

The trench revealed that at the centre of the rampart was a brick-built core (red in the diagram), 8 metres wide at the top and between 11 and 16 metres wide at the base. This core consisted of a structural casemate (the ochre colour), about 3 metres wide and 5 metres deep, filled with pebbles of basalt and other stones and beaten earth. This technique of beginning with a casemate core is used when building a huge mass of bricks and there is danger of collapse. By first creating and then filling a hollow space inside the core, the final structure proves to be much stronger. The core was built of sun-baked bricks (measuring 40 × 30 × 15 centimetres) whose colour varied from very dark to very light. Its northern, or outer, face was nearly vertical and was occasionally covered by plaster. However, our main interest lay in the technique by which the rampart itself was built. We found that it was thrust against the core in three more or less vertical blocks (indicated by various colours) made of different types of earth. But the two blocks nearest the core (blue and mauve, respectively) were thrown against it and inclined inwards, that is, in the direction opposite the natural slope. The thrusting of the layers of both these blocks of earth was done in immediate succession, thus identical materials were found in the same order in their various layers (marked in thin lines). As soon as a layer was completed, its outer face was plastered. Finally the outer block (marked green), which also consisted of layers, was thrown along the direction of the slope. Its outer face was then covered with a layer of a beaten chalky substance, some 15 centimetres thick, and the present surface of the rampart's outer slope was achieved. On the inner side of the ramparts – that is, facing the city – we could discern only two layered blocks thrown against the core to form an inner slope of 35–45 degrees (marked beige and green, respectively). Looking at the cross-section eastwards (lower scheme in the diagram), we can see the outer facing of the slope on the left and the inner one on the right. This section differs from the top one in that it does not penetrate as far as the casemate and cuts only up to the brick core. But the structure of the rampart itself is the same regardless of the direction from which one views a cross-section.

In contrast to the picture arrived at here, in section BB (made about 140 metres to the west) the rampart was apparently devoid of the brick-built core and consisted mainly of a beaten-earth core that was reinforced by the addition of several layers. Its proximity to the gate (which I shall soon describe) may explain the change in the method of construction. Amidst the debris of beaten earth, we found huge quantities of Early Bronze and Middle Bronze II pottery, which indicates that the earth was taken from previously occupied parts of the *tell*. It also helps us date the construction of the rampart to the latter part of the Middle Bronze II period. Most of all, it leaves us overwhelmingly impressed by the phenomenal amount of hard work invested in protecting this 1-kilometre-long, 700-metre-wide lower city with 3–4 kilometres of earthen ramparts. As always, man's main efforts are dedicated to defending his home, and no outlay of energy seemed too great for this purpose. The existence of this immense and technically sophisticated defence line also testifies that the people of Hazor – like those of other 'lower cities' – were governed by a strong ruler who could organize them into building such stupendous fortifications.

The lower-city gates

The most interesting aspect of fortifications in ancient cities is their gates. The gate is, by its very nature, the soft spot in any system of fortifications, and much ingenuity was always dedicated to devising its structure. The subject of gates is particularly interesting in these enclosure-like lower cities, for very little was known of them. I wanted to examine the nature of the gates from the very outset, but was always compelled to put this off in favour of more urgent, or more promising, sites. But in the last season of the four-year cycle (1958), I decided to probe into one area – marked K – which looked as if it might have a gate, and placed Moshe Dothan in charge.

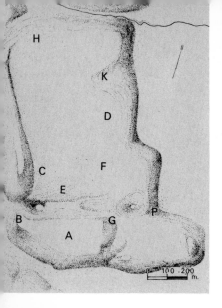

Area K (see map above, left) is located on the north-eastern edge
of the lower city, not far from its northernmost corner. From aerial
photographs and a careful examination of the entire enclosure, we were
convinced that one of the gates must have been located in the north-
eastern part of the city, a deduction made long ago by Garstang
himself. We started to excavate at what looked like the gate jamb –
huge ashlar stones protruding from the ground. It was a difficult dig,
because the area is far from the *tell*, where our main activities took
place, and also because we had to excavate on the slope. But we per-
severed, and since it is difficult to date gates and fortifications without
ascertaining their relation to the strata of the city itself, we also intended
to excavate part of the lower city near the gate. At the same time, we
did not wish to destroy all the evidence, so we decided to excavate
only the southern half of the gate proper, thus leaving the northern
half for future archaeologists to double check our finds. This is not a
question of doing only half a job, as gatehouses are anyway symmetrical, and we could easily reconstruct one half by verifying the plan
and stratigraphy of the other.

Five gates   In the early hours of excavations, just after the top earth was removed,
we found two huge basalt slabs that formed the outer threshold of the

Two huge basalt slabs of the
outer threshold, as found

gate. By the time the excavations were concluded, we had remains of five gates, built one on top of the other, representing the five main occupational strata of the lower city: two of strata 4–3 of the Middle Bronze II period; one of stratum 2 of the Late Bronze I period; and two of strata IB and IA, respectively – striking confirmation of the results of our excavations within the lower city. This time, let me begin the description from bottom to top, that is, from the earliest to the latest gate.

We unearthed very little of the gate of stratum 4, which belonged to the beginning of the lower city and was built on virgin soil, as it lay partially under the succeeding gates. However, enough was uncovered to indicate a general plan: the simple gate passage was flanked on either side by a solid brick-style tower built on stone foundations that averaged about 8 metres square. Some of the stones of the foundations, which were roughly trimmed field stones, measure 60 centimetres in height! The gate itself was located some 22 metres away from the slope and was approached via a gentle beaten-earth incline made of alternate layers of basalt flakes mixed with clay and crushed yellow chalk mixed with brown-brick muds. The method by which the gate was connected to the earthen rampart was very interesting indeed, since the gate was built in a gully, while the earthen ramparts formed the shoulders of the area. The connection was achieved by a bridging wall that consisted of two parallel walls, each just over 1.5 metres thick. This was not a true casemate wall (meaning a double wall divided into rooms) because the space between the walls was filled deliberately with beaten earth – similar to the core of the rampart in section AA. More important than the technical information gleaned here was the very discovery of the gate built simultaneously with the earthen rampart.

The next gate, built partially over the original and destroyed one, differed from its predecessor in plan, construction and location. Its pattern (see plan) is exactly like the 'classical' gates of the period discovered in most of the Palestinian cities built on *tells* and also in the enclosure-like cities (such as Qatna and, since our excavations, Tell Mardikh). Within the gate passage were three pairs of pilasters,

The earliest gate

The second gate

left The earliest gate (black) showing the position of the gate above it (white)
right The gate of stratum 3. Note the casemate wall

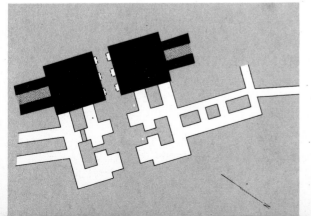

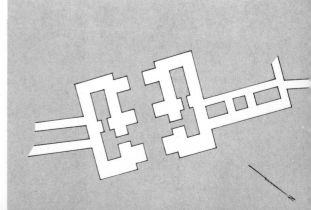

Part of the huge basalt
revetment wall in area K

The revetment wall

An artist's view of the gate in
area K

the outer and inner sets of pilasters with doors (which, of course, made the gatehouse easier to defend). These pilasters narrowed down the actual passage (from 7.5 to 3 metres) from the enemy's point of view, yet left enough room for the defenders' chariots to enter in peacetime. Moreover, the area of the passage between the pilasters could be used by the defenders as guard chambers or for assembling a greater number of troops to prevent enemy penetration. They also served an architectural function by spanning the width of the gate and making it possible to construct the second storey and towers, which were very important elements. On either side of the passage stood a large tower, 16 × 6.5 metres. The southern tower – the only one excavated in its entirety – was divided into two interconnected chambers. The total length and width of the gatehouse were 20 and 16 metres, respectively. This plan for a gatehouse is extremely clever from both the tactical and architectural points of view, and its basic principles were followed again in subsequent periods, including the Iron Age. Finally, the gatehouse was connected with the 'shoulders' of the rampart by a different method: a huge, real casemate wall, which is indeed the earliest of this type found in Palestine.

Perhaps the most impressive architectural achievement of the Middle Bronze II period was discovered about 10 metres down the slope. Here was found a huge revetment or retaining-wall constructed of large basalt boulders built up in a polygonal manner. The wall supported the causeway built along the slope and leading to the gate from both north and south. In front of the gate was a large artificial platform that enabled the chariots to enter after making a 90-degree turn off the causeway. The revetment wall was preserved to a height of over 5 metres and to a length of 50 metres, and it is one of the finest examples of Middle Bronze II fortifications. The reconstruction of the gate shown here is, of course, schematic; but I believe it offers an accurate

The left side of the stratum 2
(Late Bronze I) gate. Note
the fine ashlar stones

impression of the magnitude and layout of the gate as viewed from
the outside.

The gate of stratum 2 is identical in plan to that of the previous
phase but is constructed of huge and well-dressed ashlar blocks,
further testimony to the high culture and skill of Hazor in the Late
Bronze I period. The last two gates (of strata 1B and 1A) are also
identical in plan to their predecessor, but here and there one can detect
minor repairs and additions. Among the latter are the two huge basalt
slabs forming the gate's outer threshold (mentioned before) and the
raised floor in the passage, now built of cobble-stones. However, an
important change took place in the bridging wall: the casemate wall
(at least in the southern part of the excavations) was replaced by a new
brick wall 3 metres thick. In the last phase of occupation (stratum 1A),
we found – in addition to the minor floor repairs – evidence of the

The third gate – stratum 2

The last two gates

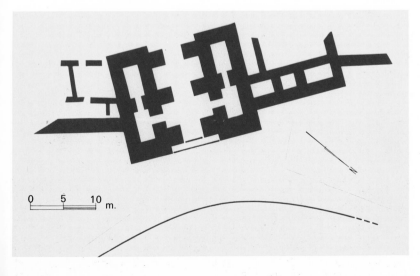

Plan of the stratum 2 gate

0 5 10 m.

A layer of ashes and brick debris on the floor of the last gate in area K

Another gate – area P

gate's final fate. The floor was covered by a thick layer of ashes and rubble containing brick-work of the gate and towers. This was an obvious sign of the final destruction of the city gate by violent conflagration, similar to the fate of the temple in stratum 1A of area H.

From studying the aerial photographs and surveying the terrain, we were convinced from the outset that another gate of the lower city may have existed in the corner between the east and north side of the eastern spur (see map on page 136). Today's highway passes at this point, and in the course of its construction in the 1920s large structures (remnants of which can still be seen in the ditch along the roadside) were destroyed. When we resumed excavations in 1968, ten years after the excavation of the gate in area K, the Public Works Department was planning to widen this road, and we were asked by the Department of Antiquities to 'clear' the area by excavating it. The excavations, under Amichai Mazar, were particularly difficult technically, due to the proximity of the road. But there was another difficulty: the existence of a recently planted memorial forest that we were reluctant to uproot. Nevertheless, we managed to uncover fragments of a gate here, to grasp its plan and to discover additional technical data about the joint that connected the gate (built, as in area K, in the natural depression) and the 'shoulders' of the earthen ramparts. The western tower of this gate had been built west of the new road, but, unfortunately, most of the gate-passage area and the eastern tower were destroyed completely when the road was constructed. Nevertheless, here too we discovered remains of five successive gates from periods that corresponded exactly to the gates in area K. The plan of the earliest gate could not be verified because,

The gate of area P, with the road (bottom) and memorial forest. Note the two chambers of the tower, the cobble-stone floor of the gate passage and the threshold (left)

as before, the gate itself lay deep under the later remains. Yet enough is visible in the section to confirm its existence. The plans of the subsequent gates are generally clear and are identical to those of area K: a gatehouse with 3 pairs of pilasters and two large, double-chambered towers on either side. The gates proper were built of brick on stone foundations, and one can see that the upper part of the foundations was levelled and paved to serve as a base for a brick wall.

Of the gate of stratum IB (belonging to the fourteenth century, as attested by the discovery of Mycenaean pottery), we found a well-preserved threshold of basalt slabs near the inner pair of pilasters. Nearby, the socket of a door was found, suggesting that in gates of this type doors were put up by both the outer and inner pilasters, as was the case in the newly discovered gates in Tell Mardikh. Unlike area K, where the IA gate was just the same as the IB gate with only minor adjustments, here a new gate – or at least a new threshold near and above the IB gate – was built of crude, white boulders in the IA period. Other changes were apparent in the inner part of the gatehouse. It is interesting to note that in the top layers of the later gates, we discovered a considerable amount of broken basalt orthostats. This would indicate that the lower parts of the earlier (Late Bronze I) gate were adorned by orthostats, and when the gate was destroyed these broken orthostats were converted into building material.

The most important results of this dig were uncovered east of the road, where we found the joint between the gate and the eastern rampart, which met at right angles. The technique used here differed from that of area K because it had to take account of the terrain. The difficulty in constructing these joints was twofold because the gate was lower than the rampart and because of the technical difference between the construction of the gate and that of the rampart. Here in area P, the excavations proved that the joint was created by a number of stone-built terraces that gradually rose from the gate level to the top of the rampart and served as a foundation for a thick and impressive brick wall.

All the evidence elicited from the trenches cut through the ramparts and the excavations of the gates shows that the people of the Middle Bronze II period achieved high standards of engineering techniques. They never used a single, stereotyped method but adapted their methods to the requirements of the topography and terrain, using all sorts of sophisticated and ingenious construction devices. With all that, I have a feeling that we still do not know enough about the technique used to build the ramparts. This is a challenge for future excavators and the most appropriate place to dig is near area C, where the rampart is widest and highest. It will be a difficult task to cut through the rampart and the moat on its west; but it will definitely be most rewarding to cast new light on the construction of the remarkable fortifications of the lower city.

top A door socket near the inner threshold
centre The terraced foundation for the 'joint' wall of the gate

Summing up

9 The Rise and Downfall of the Lower City

Now that we have looked at the most important aspects of the lower city as revealed by the spade, I think it worthwhile to dwell upon certain general aspects of our discoveries whose implications reach far beyond the confines of Hazor itself. The first and foremost discovery of the excavations – as emphasized repeatedly in the foregoing pages – was that the so-called enclosure (or fortified camp, or chariots' parking-lot, as this site was sometimes called in the past) was indeed a full-fledged city with huge, strong fortifications and all the trimmings – such as public buildings, private dwellings and temples. The area of the lower city, including its eastern spur, is 200 acres, ten or twenty times the size of the largest of the *tells*, which are the common location of ancient cities in this country. If we assume a ratio of 250 people per acre – as argued by Garstang – then the lower city would have had a population of 50,000. And even if we reduce the ratio by half, the number would still be astounding, as there are very few cities of this size in the whole of the Fertile Crescent! The biblical description of Hazor as the 'head of all those kingdoms' is therefore not only historically correct but very apt. It was not by chance that Hazor is mentioned in the Mari documents together with Qatna, Babylon and other cities of the same size. However, another important fact emanates from our discovery, and that is the date of Hazor's foundation. Indeed, this aspect of our finds touches upon one of the most important and still very debatable problems of Near Eastern chronology.

As I have said, Hazor is not only mentioned in the Mari documents, it is the only city in Palestine mentioned in them *often*, implying its importance. (Once or twice, the Mari documents refer to the city of Dan, north of Hazor, which was also a city with earthen ramparts, although built on a smaller scale). I believe that this fact can be explained only if we assume that the Hazor cited in the Mari documents included the lower city, for only in such a case is Hazor comparably important. In other words, by the time of the Mari documents, the lower city of Hazor must already have existed. This conclusion has a direct bearing on the problem of what are called the high, middle and low chronologies of the Near East, since all these chronologies depend on the fixing of the dates of Shamshi-Adad 1 and the great Hammurabi, in whose days the Mari letters mentioning Hazor were written. It should also be remembered that for a short while, during

Far-reaching implications

Hazor and chronology

An aerial view of the upper and lower cities (looking north) with Kibbutz Ayelet Hashaḥar on the right

the last years of his reign, Shamshi-Adad I was contemporary with Hammurabi. Our excavations show that nowhere in the lower city were there any remains of the Middle Bronze IIA period (usually dated between 1900 and 1750 BC); in other words, it was quite clear that the city was established and flourished in the so-called Middle Bronze IIB period. This dating was further supported by a quantity of sherds extricated from the core and earthen blocks of the ramparts. The main dates assigned to Hammurabi, according to the different schools of thought, are given in the following chart:

	BC	
ultra high chronology	1900	Middle Bronze IIA 1900–1750
high chronology	1848–1806	
middle chronology	1792–1750	
low chronology	1728–1686	Middle Bronze IIB 1750–1650
very low chronology	1704–1662	

If we follow the normally accepted date for the beginning of the Middle Bronze IIB – 1750 BC – then obviously the ultra-high, high and middle chronologies must be abandoned. If, on the other hand, we raise the date of the beginning of the Middle Bronze IIB to 1800 – as some scholars do – then the middle chronology can be maintained (albeit with great difficulty because Hazor is already mentioned in the days of Shamshi-Adad I). Furthermore, a certain time must be allowed for such a city not only to be built, but to establish itself and become known. I believe, therefore, that the new evidence tends to support the low chronology advocated by William F. Albright. One thing is quite clear: one can no longer simultaneously follow the middle chronology, on the one hand, and the 1750 date for the beginning of the Middle Bronze IIB, on the other, as is done in quite a number of recent scholarly publications. Thus the importance of discoveries at Hazor extend far beyond the actual finds themselves, and studies concerning Hazor and Near Eastern chronology will certainly not be out of place in the future.

Ties with the north   The other important point revealed in the excavations is the strong influence of the Hittite-Mittanian culture on Hazor during the Late Bronze period. Our finds are the first concrete evidence that prior to the Israelite conquest the population of Canaan was composed of various ethnic groups. Such findings were not unexpected as they confirm facts often repeated in the Bible and documented by the el-Amarna letters, in which the various 'kings' or 'city mayors' of Canaan bore Hurrian or Mitannian names. As a matter of fact, so did the ruler of Hazor, Adbi-Tirshi.

Ramses II with vanquished Hittites at the Battle of Kadesh. Hazor was conquered by Joshua most probably during the latter part of this Pharaoh's long reign

Last, but not least in importance, is the evidence that this huge city with a population of thousands came to an abrupt end by fire in the second half of the thirteenth century, never to be rebuilt. The discovery of the Mycenaean IIIB fragments in the topmost stratum shows that the city existed while such pottery was still extant, namely until 1230 BC. Most probably the city was destroyed sometime in the second third of the thirteenth century (*i.e.*, during the reign of Ramses II). We can also assume that the IB city, that of the el-Amarna period, was destroyed by Pharaoh Seti I, or at any rate while Mycenaean IIIA–B was still in use, around 1303–1290. The striking similarity between the size of Hazor as revealed by the excavations and its description in the Bible as 'the head of all those kingdoms', plus the insistence of the biblical narrator that Hazor – and only Hazor – had been destroyed by Joshua and burned, leave little doubt, it seems, that we actually found the Canaanite city of Jabin that was destroyed by Joshua. In that case, the excavations at Hazor provided, for the first time, decisive archaeological data for fixing both Joshua's dates and, indirectly, the date of the Exodus from Egypt.

Hazor's destruction and Joshua

But what about Hazor in the times of Deborah (who most probably lived in the twelfth century, about 100 years after the destruction of the lower city)? How are the events described in the Deborah narrative related to the description in the Book of Joshua? Indeed, where is the city of Hazor that the Bible claims Solomon rebuilt? No traces of these are to be found in the lower city. In order to answer these questions, we must now move up the *tell* – the upper city – where further discoveries in the course of excavations finally resolved these pressing problems.

Deborah and Solomon

above The row of pillars of stratum VIII as excavated by Garstang. *below* The parallel row of pillars begins to appear (right) among buildings of later strata

10 Hazor after Solomon – Ahab to Pekah

In our description of excavations on the *tell*, as in the lower city, we must begin at the beginning, which – from the excavator's point of view – means the top. The top stratum of the lower city was the last Canaanite occupation of Hazor. As we move up to the *tell*, we find ourselves simultaneously leaping forward 500 years to the period of the divided Israelite kingdom and then working our way down in strata and back in time. From the very outset, I decided to excavate two areas on the *tell* because Garstang's activities were more extensive there, the remains of his discoveries were partially evident on the surface and the meagre descriptions of his results were more generous.

The first and more inviting area was right in the centre of the mound, where Garstang discovered a row of monolithic pillars in a deep, narrow trench. He believed that they belonged to 'a building, supported by a row of square stone monoliths, possible stable', and he dated the structure to Solomon, obviously, because of the biblical verse stating that Solomon rebuilt Hazor and Solomon's association with horses. At the start, there was no reason to doubt his conclusions. We marked the area near the row of pillars A (under Y. Aharoni's supervision), cleared the debris and fallen stones accumulated there since Garstang's excavations and uncovered the row of beautifully preserved monoliths. Then we decided to excavate mainly south of the area, and while looking at the side of the trench we could see quite clearly that when Garstang dug for the bases of these monoliths, he cut through several strata. This discovery restrained our haste, and we began to dig slowly and systematically from the top down.

At first we had to remove remains of an Arab tower. Soon we found out that the area had served as a cemetery in the Persian era (538–332 BC), a point that became particularly obvious when we enlarged the area in 1968. Several of the graves were covered with stone slabs, and the skeletons in them lay on their backs accompanied by a little juglet, sometimes by even a glass vessel. Coins found there indicated that the corpses were buried mainly in the fourth century BC. Remains of the Persian period were found more extensively in other areas under a later stratum of occupation of the Hellenistic period, which we marked stratum I; the Persian period was marked stratum II. Immediately after removing the graves, we came upon a thoroughly destroyed level covered by thick layers of ashes and pottery ascribing it to the latter part of the eighth century. There was

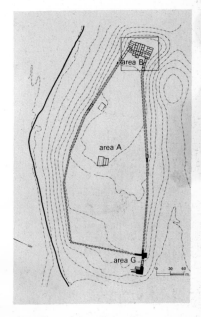

above Plan of the *tell* showing areas A, B and G
below A Persian period glass bottle found in a grave

above The two faces of a silver *stater* of Tyre from the Persian period (fourth century BC)
top, left A grave of the Persian period as found
top, right Another grave of the same period with the covering slabs removed
right A fallen roof and loom weights, evidence of the destruction by Tiglath-pileser III found in stratum V in area A

The destruction by Tiglath-pileser III

no reason to doubt that these were remains of the city destroyed by the Assyrian king Tiglath-pileser III in 732 BC, as recorded in the Bible. The results of the destruction were indeed striking here and even more conspicuous in other areas (to be described later). The discovery served as a milestone because it helped us to absolutely date this stratum, which we later marked stratum V from the top (strata III and IV, found in other areas, were not discovered here).

Once we began to uncover the remains of the days of Pekah son of Remaliah in stratum V, we noticed that the pillared building had,

as expected, a parallel row of pillars slightly south of the first. It also became clear that the building belonged to a much older stratum, and the people of stratum V incorporated its pillars in their walls whenever a wall crossed one, decapitated them when they interfered with the building's new plan or re-used them in any other way that suited their needs. The northern row of pillars, that discovered by Garstang, had apparently remained untouched and served to support the roof of the newly built court. We also discovered that the houses of the last Israelite fortified city of stratum V were often reconstructions

Garstang's row of monolithic pillars (right) with a parallel row (left) embedded within the walls of stratum VI–V (looking west)

left Testimony of an earthquake: a tilted wall in stratum VI
right Jars under a fallen roof in stratum VI

City VI destroyed by an earthquake

of houses built in the preceding stratum, for in many of them two layers of floors were uncovered in conjunction with the same walls. As such a find is uncommon, we found ourselves asking why.

When we removed the accumulation of debris and the floors of stratum V and continued descending towards the floors of the earlier strata, we were struck by two facts: (1) that many of the walls of the lower stratum were tilted, as if shaken by a terrible earth tremor, and (2) that the floors of many of the houses were covered by fragments of the ceilings that had fallen suddenly, another unusual phenomenon in archaeological excavations. Since this stratum was below the stratum of Pekah son of Remaliah and its pottery was still typical of the eighth century, it was easy and logical to ascribe this destruction to an earthquake, which is indeed referred to in the Bible: 'And the valley of my mountains shall be stopped up, for the valley of the mountains shall touch the side of it; and you shall flee as you fled from the earthquake in the days of Uzziah king of Judah' (Zechariah 14:5). This earthquake must have been a total catastrophe that seared

its mark on the entire period, because it was used to reckon the years by, as we learn from the opening lines of the Book of Amos: 'The words of Amos, who was among the shepherds of Tekoa, which he saw concerning Israel in the days of Uzziah king of Judah and in the days of Jeroboam the son of Joash, king of Israel, two years before the earthquake.' Thus we could ascribe this stratum (VI) to the days of Jeroboam II, whose reign in Israel (789–748 BC) was basically contemporary to that of Uzziah, king of Judah (785–733). This was a fortunate discovery for us – tragic as it must have been for the people of Israel at the time – for it enabled us to date this stratum absolutely to within a few years earlier than the one above it.

Judging by the standard of its buildings, during the times of Jeroboam II the city of Hazor enjoyed an era of great prosperity, as did the whole of Israel during the long reign of this great king. The buildings themselves are among the finest of the entire Israelite period found to date and had a row of shops and workshops adjacent to them. Two of the houses found in area A deserve special mention, because of both

above The fallen roof of Ya'el's house

below Fragment of a ceiling with reed impressions

Ya'el's house

their unusual plan and the interesting objects discovered in them. Ya'el's house (named after the student who happened to supervise excavations there) is located south-west of the older pillared building and is the most beautifully planned and preserved of the Israelite structures at Hazor. We were drawn to its site upon first seeing the tops of stone pillars protruding from the ground, and these soon proved to be a row of pillars in a court of a house. The pillars were found tilted, first evidence of the earthquake. The house itself consisted of a large court (measuring 9 × 8 metres) with a series of rooms on two of its sides. The eastern part of the court was covered by a roof supported by six well-dressed, square, stone pillars, three of which were still found *in situ*. The entrance to the house was from the south, through

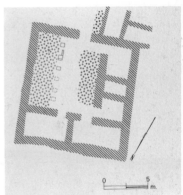

left Ya'el's house, a fine example of an Israelite residence (looking south-east)
below Plan of Ya'el's house

its court, whence one proceeded into the rooms: two large ones in the north and three smaller ones in the west. Of particular interest was the small room on the western side, which had no entrance and yielded an abundance of vessels, including many storage jars. It must have been a storeroom, and access to it may have been from a higher level, not preserved. The house with the corner court is typical of many Israelite residential structures and is known as the 'cornered-court, pillared house'. Its plan and location at an 'exclusive address', right in the heart of the city, indicate – I believe – that the house was owned by one of the wealthier citizens. As it was destroyed by the terrible earthquake, not only were the pillars and walls found askance, but all the floors were littered with hundreds of pieces of ceiling plaster.

right Olive stones, as found, are the remains of someone's last meal
below The jar of Makhbiram

Madame Makhbiram's boudoir

There was evidence that the 'last supper' of the residents, eaten just before the quake, consisted, among other things, of olives, if the many olive stones found on the floor are any indication.

The other house was nicknamed by us 'the house of Makhbiram' after the inscription 'belonging to Makhbiram' incised on a storage jar we found inside. It lies immediately east of Ya'el's house and faces an alley. In fact, it is a partial restoration of its predecessor in stratum VII. Facing the alley were two shops; behind them was a court paved with cobble-stones that led to the house's only two rooms, built one behind the other. The hoard of vessels and objects in the various parts of the rooms indicates their function. In the yard, as expected, we found cooking pots, a basin, a basalt bowl and six basalt millstones. Obviously the daily cooking was done in the yard, just as today in many oriental homes. The richest collection of finds was in the two rooms of the house, where most of the household utensils and personal belongings were found. In the outer room, facing the court, we found an oven (made of the upper part of an upturned storage jar encircled by small stones), deep bowls, kraters, juglets, a decanter, flasks, a lamp and many storage jars, some of them small and slender (for liquids) and some ovoid (one of these bore the inscription mentioned above). This room seems to have served as the main or living room.

The inner room must have been the family bedroom, although here, too, we found storage jars and cooking pots. But the main discovery was a beautiful ivory cosmetic spoon uncovered in a heap by the doorway together with three juglets and some iron tools. Although, generally speaking, it falls within a well-known category, the ivory cosmetic spoon is nevertheless an unusual piece without exact parallel. Madame Makhbiram must have gone to great trouble to acquire it. The spoon is composed of a handle and bowl, taking up three-quarters and one-quarter, respectively, of its total length. The handle is decorated with inverted palmets that curve upwards. This type of palmet, well known from the hoard found in Ahab's ivory house in Samaria and also from ivories found in Syria and Mesopotamia, may represent a stylized tree of life. The back of the bowl is carved in the shape of a woman's head, and a dove on each side of the bowl appears to be caught up in her locks. The depiction may be of the fertility goddess, rather than a portrait of Madame Makhbiram. Although the Makhbiram family does not necessarily represent the Israelite aristocracy of the northern kingdom, this spoon is certainly an indication of their prosperity, and it makes us more understanding of the prophet Amos' strong and scorching reproaches: 'Woe to those who lie upon beds of ivory and stretch themselves upon their couches' (6:4).

While Madame Makhbiram may have boasted of her ivory cosmetic

Front (left) and rear views of the ivory spoon

The mirror of Madame Makhbiram's neighbour

spoon, her next-door neighbour had another object to brag about; and while not of ivory but of bone, it was just as beautifully carved. It was probably a mirror handle with a relief (on the convex face) of a hybrid creature with four extended wings (two on each side) and hands outstretched sideways to clasp the open volutes of the tree of life (carved on the flat face of the bone). These carvings also show the influence of the pagan Phoenician or Canaanite art on the northern Israelites.

The fact that many valuable objects, as well as innumerable objects of daily use, were found on the floors covered by the fallen ceiling indicates the profound effect of this earthquake, which occurred in 763 BC. How apt and forceful (and how illuminated by our archaeological discoveries) are the words of the prophet Amos describing the punishment that the earthquake will bring upon the people:

> 'Shall not the land tremble on this
>   account,
>   and every one mourn who dwells in
>   it,
>   and all of it rise like the Nile,
>   and be tossed about and sink
>   again, like the Nile of Egypt?'
> 'And on that day,' says the Lord
>   God,
>   'I will make the sun go down at
>   noon,
>   and darken the earth in broad daylight.
> I will turn your feasts into mourning,
>   and all your songs into lamentation;
> I will bring sackcloth upon all loins,
>   and baldness on every head;
> I will make it like the mourning for an
>   only son,
>   and the end of it like a bitter day' (8:8–10).

We were now certain that we had discovered the city of Jeroboam II, thus bringing us to the beginning of the eighth century BC. The next stratum below it must therefore belong to the ninth century BC.

Digging below the floors and foundations of stratum VI, we came across remains of another stratum (which we labelled VII), this one utterly demolished by fire. Judging from the pottery and the sequence of stratigraphy, the stratum must have belonged to the end of the ninth century BC and this latest holocaust was therefore caused by the Aramaeans, as biblical narratives relate that during this period the Aramaeans from Damascus were very active in attacking northern Israel. The yield of the stratum is insignificant and only provides testimony to a period of decline. But the stratum is important in and of itself for it revealed that the pillared building belonged to an even earlier level, pushing back its date to about the middle of the ninth century – an invaluable chronological fact for dating the sequence of the Hazor strata.

Three views of the bone mirror handle (opposite) and a drawing (above) of the scene

Ahab's grandeur

above The pillared building
(looking south–east) exposed
in stratum VIII, Ahab's period
below 'Belonging to Je[zebel?]'

Once the floors of stratum VII were removed, the pillared building
emerged as a skeleton of its former splendour, destroyed in the course
of time. Based on the stratigraphy and pottery, it was possible to date
it to the reign of Omri, or more probably to that of his son Ahab
(of Jezebel fame), who reigned from 873 to 852 BC. (On the floor
of this stratum, we found four fragmentary Hebrew inscriptions
of jars, and although not much of them can be read, they are highly
valuable from a paleographic viewpoint because of their early date.
On a particularly intriguing one, only the first three Hebrew letters are preserved: לאי. It is very tempting to decipher this as לאיזבל,
'belonging to Jezebel', but other interpretations are of course possible.)
Later on, many more discoveries of Ahab's period were made in
other places in Hazor, so I shall reserve the description of his activities
and my re-evaluation of his historical role for a more appropriate
place. But the pillared building constructed at this period deserves
further attention because of its inherent importance and its bearing
on other similar buildings.

The structure was composed of two elements: a large rectangular hall (about 20 × 13 metres), extending from west to east, which was characterized by two rows of monolithic pillars, and an adjacent structure that was composed of two halls. The northern row of nine pillars was the one already discovered by Garstang. Of the southern row, six pillars, as well as a fragment of one fallen pillar, were still *in situ*. Counting other fragments and the spaces between pillars, we could reckon that the southern row originally numbered ten pillars. These were square and roughly dressed and averaged about 2 metres in height. Their foundations were sunk about half a metre below ground, and the burned layer of yet an earlier stratum (IX) ran under them. Between the pillars we found what might be described as little cells formed by two rows of rubble stones, and inside the cells were storage jars and kraters. As mentioned above, Garstang thought that the pillars were part of a stable. His conclusion made sense because the building closely resembled the famous stables discovered in Megiddo (of which we shall have more to say in chapter 14); but our excavations found no evidence to support this conclusion. On the contrary, the nature of the vessels found in the building indicated that it served as a storehouse. The pavement of the halls in the north of the building suggests that this area may have been used to store grain in bags or similar containers. It may be assumed, therefore, that the pillared building at the very centre of Ahab's city was a royal storehouse for the supply of the army garrison posted in this strategic city to guard the routes from Damascus and the north to the heart of Israel.

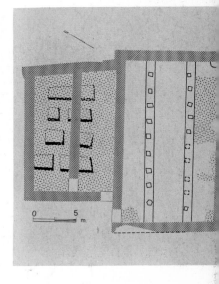

Plan of the pillared building with two adjacent halls. Note the rectangular depressions in the cobble-stone floor (see next chapter)

The pillars definitely supported a ceiling and perhaps even a second storey. Similar, though smaller, buildings were found both before and after excavations in various parts of Israel – like Beth-shemesh and Beersheba in the south and Tell abu Hawam in the north – and just on the other side of the Jordan in Tell e-Saidiyeh. The discovery of that type of building at Hazor later on caused a heated discussion among archaeologists concerning the real nature of similar buildings in Megiddo that had been defined by their excavators as stables. We shall discuss this most important problem in chapter 14, where we deal with the situation in Megiddo. Meanwhile, it is sufficient to say that in our opinion the architectural plan of the building, as such, was not enough to indicate its function. The pillars are only a means to support the roof of a large rectangular building, while the nature of the building itself depends on the other installations found in it. One thing was clear: Israelite Hazor reached its peak, with such a splendidly built storehouse, during the reign of Ahab in the second quarter of the ninth century. Our ability to date the building accurately to Ahab's era and the nature of the pavement of the two northern halls were decisive in our excavations and later played a key role in our search for Solomon.

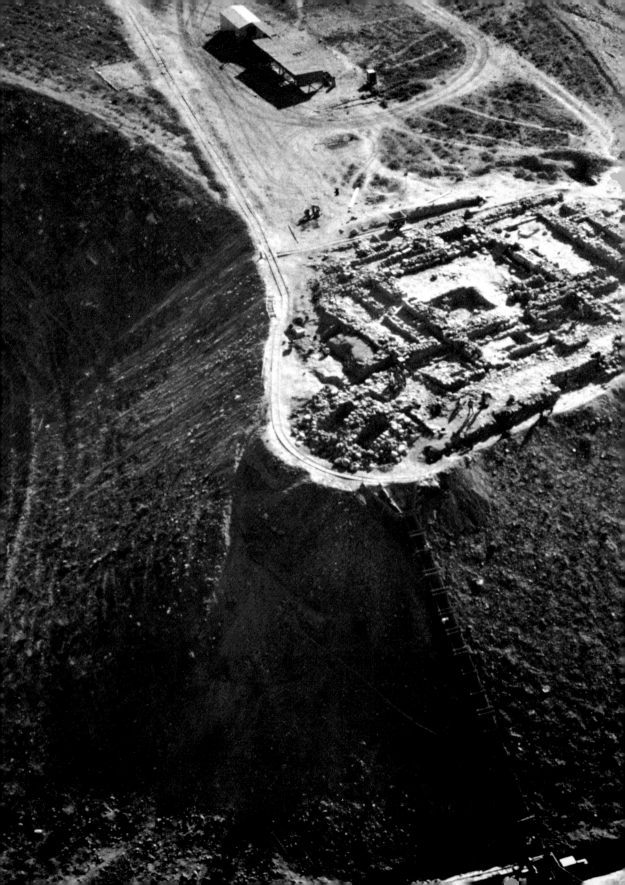

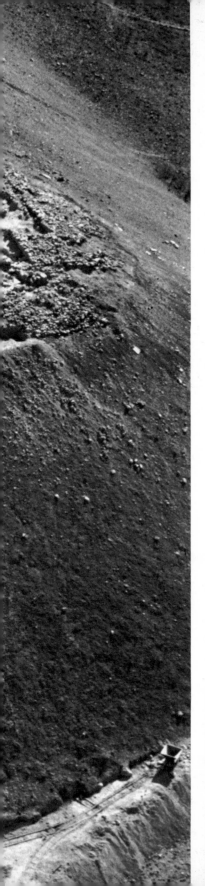

II More of Israelite Hazor

Until now I have described the results of the excavations in area A as they were revealed to us, from top to bottom. But as I explained before, this is the reverse of the actual chronological order of events. I have resorted to this course because I wanted to unfold precisely how these discoveries were made and how we reached the chronological structure. Now that we have the chronological frame of Hazor from Ahab (*i.e.*, post-Solomon) to the final destruction of the city, it is worthwhile to survey results in the other areas of excavations on the *tell* proper according to the true sequence of events, that is, working from stratum VIII upwards, so that we may develop a clearer picture of each period.

From the outset of excavations, two areas on the *tell* attracted our attention: one was area A (discussed in the previous chapter); the other was on the very tip of the western end of the *tell*, the neck, so to say, of the bottle-shaped mound. This area had also been explored by Garstang, and in the brief description of his results he wrote: 'On the west end of the Tell stood a palatial building or temple, the origin of which could not be determined; but it seems to have been in use in E.I.A.II [Early Iron Age II] and to have lasted on until the Hellenistic times.' Remains of some of the walls of these structures were visible on the surface when we arrived in 1955. As a rule, archaeologists dislike re-excavating areas tackled by previous excavators, who may

opposite The steep slopes of the 'neck' of the *tell*, with the citadel of area B (looking south-east)
below Area B as Garstang left it

well have disturbed the strata sequence. But sometimes one is compelled to do so, as was the case with the row of pillars in area A and here on the western side (subsequently marked area B). Another reason that prompted us to excavate here – and a highly important one from a technical viewpoint – was that the intriguing structure was so placed that it dominated the western tip of the mound and the entire area south-west and north-west of it. In fact, even before we started the excavations I visited the site accompanied by the farmer from the neighbouring settlement of Rosh Pinah who owned the land of Tell Hazor. While walking on the mound, he asked me what we were looking for, and I replied that, among other things, we would like to find the city's fort or palace. 'Where would you build your palace,' I asked him, 'had you been the ruler of Hazor?' Without hesitation he said, 'Right here,' pointing at the western tip of the mound. When I asked him why, assuming he would reply that this was the most strategic spot on the mound, his reasoning proved to be quite different: 'Having lived here for many years,' he said, 'I know that this is the only spot where, even on the most scorching days of summer, there is a pleasant breeze from the west. I would *definitely* build my palace here.'

From Ahab to Colonel Teggart

Whether the inhabitants of Hazor were motivated by considerations of tactics or comfort, our excavations showed this area to have been continuously occupied by palatial buildings or large citadels. We found a sequence of nine citadels – one on top of the other – not counting the topmost stratum of the 'British period', when, during the riots of 1936–9, Colonel Teggart erected a pill-box to guard the area against Arab marauders. If area A proved useful for fixing the chronology of the Israelite strata, area B (under Ruth Amiran's supervision) yielded important evidence about the nature of life from Ahab to the downfall of Hazor – and even after the Israelite city had been destroyed. In addition to area B, we later excavated another area on the extreme east of the mound, which we called area G. This area yielded useful information concerning the fortifications of the city, but we also found important evidence about the material culture of Hazor; and in the following description of area B, from Ahab forward, we shall occasionally refer to the discoveries made in area G.

The other end of Hazor – area G

During the reign of Ahab, the whole of area B was occupied by a large citadel, or fort, with its ancillary buildings reaching to the very edge of the mound and its walls there also serving as the city's defences. The slope here is very steep, and no additional city wall was deemed necessary. The fort itself is a 25 × 21-metre rectangular building of symmetrical plan, with its central wall extending from west to east and serving as the axis. The characteristic feature of the fort is its method of construction: extremely thick walls (up to 2 metres thick) and some slimmer ones took up about 40 per cent of the total area of the fort – or rather, as we now know, of the basement of the fort and the deep foundations below its floor. The corners of the struc-

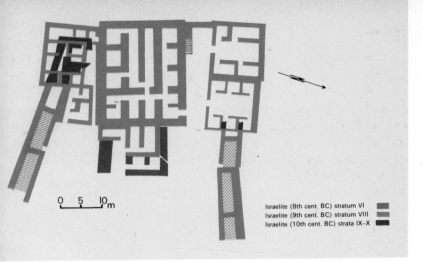

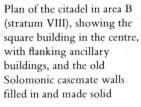

Israelite (8th cent. BC) stratum VI
Israelite (9th cent. BC) stratum VIII
Israelite (10th cent. BC) strata IX–X

0 5 10 m

Plan of the citadel in area B
(stratum VIII), showing the
square building in the centre,
with flanking ancillary
buildings, and the old
Solomonic casemate walls
filled in and made solid

The entrance passage between
the citadel (left) and the
ancillary buildings (right).
Note the ashlar stones laid
in typical Israelite fashion –
headers and stretchers

The heavy ashlar stones at the
corner of the citadel

above The thick walls of the citadel (looking west)
opposite, above The citadel staircase to the main floor

ture were built of imposing, well-dressed ashlar stones, some of them about 1.5 metres long, all dressed in the typical Israelite fashion of slanting, pick-made strokes. The plan of the basement is also quite interesting, as the arrangement of the inside doorways divides it into two uneven parts: a closed block in the south-west corner, with only a doorway between the room and the hall leading into it; and a row of interconnected rooms north and east of the block. All the doorways were made very economically of just wall-ends with only one built door jamb.

Outside the north-west corner of the building, we found a staircase leading to the upper floor. If we assume that the slim walls mentioned earlier were merely partitions dividing the basement into units and did not continue upwards to the top floor, then what we get is a plan based on the thick walls only, known to archaeologists as the 'four-roomed house', comprising three long, parallel halls and one wide hall. It is likely that in these buildings – which are very typical of the Israelite house (as we shall also see later) – the central, long hall was open and served as a sort of patio. In other words, the upper part of the citadel consisted of an enclosed courtyard, surrounded on three sides by a row of rooms. The main entrance to the citadel was through a long passage in the north that led directly to the staircase. The passage is flanked on the south by the northern wall of the citadel, but on its north, and up to the edge of the mound, were two similar administrative buildings (3100C and 3235 on the plan on page 170). These, together with a similar building (3208) south of the citadel, must have housed the governor's family and staff. The layout is simple but indicative of the practical planning of the Israelite house: a square building (about 13 × 13 metres) with two rows of rooms flanking a middle court. These buildings excel not only in symmetry, but also in other features. All the walls are of equal thickness (about 1 metre), all the corners and door jambs are built of ashlar stones and, as in the citadel, the doorways are all placed at the end of the walls with only one door jamb. The series of these buildings in the citadel of stratum VIII and its ancillaries shows a high standard of architecture and grandeur equalled only by the contemporary buildings at Megiddo and Samaria, the capital of Israel. The similarity between these three sites was further strengthened by an unexpected discovery related to the architecture of the citadel.

The true magnificence of Ahab's architecture in this area was not uncovered in the citadel's original stage in stratum VIII, but rather in the following one, stratum VII, which (as we have already seen in area A) was an interim period of decline. There could be no better evidence of this decline – though not yet the fall – of Israelite Hazor than our unexpected discovery in stratum VII just above the plastered floor of the open area in front of the main entrance to the citadel. To our

Plan and axonometric reconstruction of the citadel's main floor (in stratum VIII) with defence walls of stratum (VA)

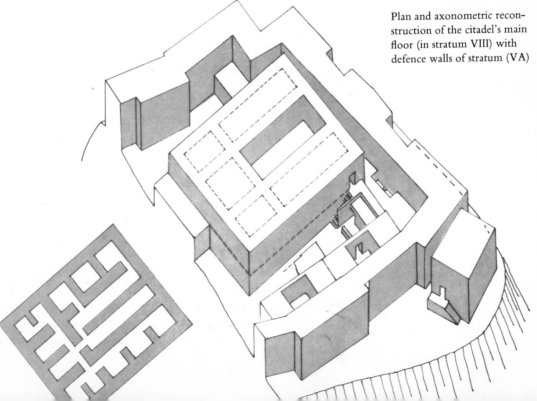

great surprise – and delight – we found two beautiful Proto-Aeolic,
or Proto-Ionic, capitals lying on the floor, one upside down and the
other with its carved face upwards. At first we did not understand what
they were doing there, but after clearing the area somewhat we saw
that they formed a right angle harbouring a clay oven. Obviously
these beautifully carved capitals were not made for that purpose but
must have belonged to the earlier period (stratum VIII), when they
adorned the entrance to the citadel just 2 metres to the west.

This type of capital is the most characteristic architectural element
of the public buildings in the times of the kings of Israel, and some
have been discovered in Megiddo, Samaria and, recently, in Jerusalem
and nearby Ramat Raḥel – all belonging to the tenth and ninth centuries BC. They are known as Proto-Aeolic or Proto-Ionic because
it is certain that the classical Ionic capitals developed from this much
earlier type representing a stylized palm-tree. As a rule, these capitals
bear a relief of the palm-tree on one side only, and we were therefore
delighted to find that one of our capitals bore reliefs on both sides,
indicating – or so we believed – that it was intended to crown a real
column, not just a pilaster. Our suspicions were confirmed when we
found two bases at the entrance to the citadel: one attached to the wall,
which must have been the base of a pilaster; the other free standing,
probably the base of the free-standing column with the two-faced
capital. We were also fortunate to discover nearby a huge monolithic
lintel that had originally rested on top of the capitals, supporting the

left The monolithic lintel, as found, in secondary use
right Reconstruction showing the position of the capitals and the lintel in the entrance to the citadel (for the entrance, see page 163, centre)

wall above it. This was the first time in Palestinian archaeology that such capitals had been found almost *in situ*, enabling us to reconstruct their original position *vis-á-vis* the building. The discovery of the capitals here not only confirmed the date of the citadel to the reign of Ahab, but also indicated the rare nature of this building and the importance of Hazor in Ahab's time. The sight of these capitals in front of the formerly magnificent citadel that had declined to the state of a shelter for squatters or labourers (as evidenced by the discovery of the oven) was a striking example of the temporary downfall of the previously flourishing city.

Ahab's fortifications

Earlier I mentioned that the entire western tip of the mound had no city wall, for the complex of the citadel was considered adequate defence. Further to the east, however, we found remains of the city fortifications butting on the ancillary buildings. Indeed, they were the older casemates (that is, the double-wall fortifications), now filled with rubble and earth, making them into a base for a solid wall. The traces of this solid wall built by Ahab were found all around the mound, and particularly in area G. In each case it was apparent that a change in the system of fortifications had taken place during the reign of Omri and Ahab. Instead of the earlier, flimsier, double walls, a solid wall was built. I believe it will be more appropriate to discuss the reason for this change when we deal with the plan of Hazor in the Solomonic era (in chapter 12). In the meanwhile, the huge storehouse

The filled Solomonic casemates serving as Ahab's fortifications

A fine ashlar in Ahab's own addition to the city's fortifications in area A, the magnificent citadel with its ancillary buildings in area B and finds from stratum VIII made in other areas all indicated the grandeur of the city in Ahab's times, the mid-ninth century. But this was not the end of the story of the citadel.

Stratum VI – Jeroboam II

The period of decline evidenced in stratum VII in area B (as in area A) was not of very long duration, for in the early part of the eighth century the area was again thriving and flourishing. The citadel was again used as such after repairs were made and walls added to enhance its splendour. Even the ancillary buildings to both the north and the south were restored with improvements. The basic plan of the buildings remained unchanged. In fact, the very buildings themselves remained, but new features were inserted, floors were raised, walls were repaired

left The twin ancillary buildings north of the citadel in stratum VIII
right The same in stratum VI. Note the addition of rows of pillars in the building's courts

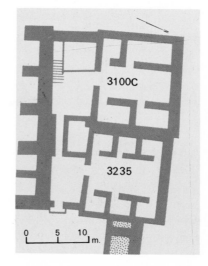
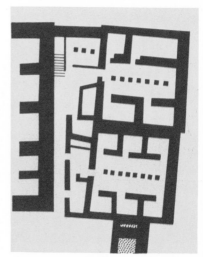

and one important novelty was introduced (particularly noticeable in the twin administrative buildings to the north): the central courts were further divided by a row of monolithic pillars, turning one part of the court into a shaded, or covered, area while the other remained exposed. This style was noted by us in Ya'el's house in area A, where the corner court was further divided by a row of monolithic pillars.

A two-storey house

A similar building – which may have housed one of the administrative or military officials of Hazor – was discovered in area G and is a good example of the high architectural standard of the period. It also indicates that many of these houses, of which we found the foundations only, had upper storeys. This house is located in the corner of a forward bastion in area G and is also of the four-room type, with pillars providing ceiling support. However, here we were fortunate to discover along the northern wall of the house the stone-built staircase, still intact – a flight of well-dressed stone steps, ten of which were found *in situ*. It can be calculated that the entire flight originally consisted of sixteen steps. Since the height of each step was 15 centimetres, we can calculate that the total height of the room (*i.e.*, the height of the stairs minus the thickness of the ceiling) was about 1.6 metres, a number that tallies with the height of the pillars plus the horizontal beams. This is a rather low room, and it may therefore be assumed that the ground floor was used for cattle, while the actual living quarters, built of bricks, were on the second floor. Like many buildings of Hazor, this one was constructed over the ruins of the strata VIII–VII houses; but it far surpassed its predecessors in architectural design. All told, in the first half of the eighth century, mainly during the reign of Jeroboam II, Hazor – like the rest of Israel – was flourishing. But the fate of this thriving city awaited it in the form of the tremendous quake, mentioned earlier.

The decades of the fifties and forties of the eighth century BC were the most critical for the existence of Israelite Hazor. At first, immediately after the reconstruction of the buildings partially destroyed by the earthquake, life went on quite normally – at least from the archaeological viewpoint. The citadel continued to be used, though some changes were noticeable in the ancillary buildings north and south; a few doorways were narrowed; and the original large court between the two rows of flanking rooms was further divided into two unequal parts by a row of pillars set in a low wall. Wherever we dug, it was quite clear that at the beginning of this period (which we called stratum VB) life went on actively all over Hazor.

Then, tremendous changes suddenly took place in the buildings and fortifications of Hazor, as if the king of Israel had anxiously sensed that the existing tranquillity might not last, that danger was looming from the north and current fortifications were inadequate. We know from historical documents that a threat from Assyria was on the horizon;

The calm before the storm

The beginning of the end

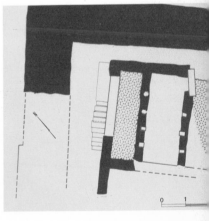

above Plan of the building on the left
left A two-storey Israelite building found in area G

the great Tiglath-pileser III was militarily active. The most noticeable changes were in area B. One should remember that up to that time, the area of the citadel was – paradoxically – the only place in the entire city that lacked a defence wall, because the natural steep slopes protected it and the walls of the citadel itself were thick. One must also remember that the walls of the ancillary buildings were much flimsier than the main walls of the citadel. Now, as the enemy's threat apparently increased, it became imperative to strengthen the fortifications in this area by adding a city wall and tower, for the complex of buildings in the north and south was an insufficient defence barrier. But there was no place to build a city wall here! The entire western tip of the mound was taken up by buildings, right up to the very edge. There was no alternative but to sacrifice part of the ancillary buildings.

The new city wall was built as a solid wall with offsets and insets and a drainage system. Some of the corner offsets looked like real bastions capable of providing a good base for flanking fire. The average thickness of the walls in the offsets is 5 metres and in the insets 3.5 metres. Part of the ancillary buildings had to be partially destroyed to make room for this wall, and in the end some 40 per cent or more of their area was sacrificed by totally eliminating the building in the south and reducing by one-third the building in the north. This method of destroying houses to provide more room for better fortifications was, of course, a very painful operation, but it was not uncommon in those days. What we found in Hazor was a vivid illustration of Isaiah's record of later preparations (these in Jerusalem) to face the Assyrian threat: when Sennacherib (several decades after Tiglath-pileser)

left Plan of the citadel in stratum VA. Note the solid wall with offsets and insets and the tower
right A drainage outlet in one of the insets (looking east)

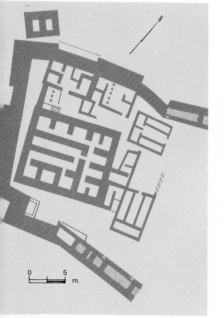

reached the city, 'you counted the houses of Jerusalem and you broke down the houses to fortify the wall' (22:10).

A particularly interesting element in the new fortifications is an isolated tower that was built on the most strategic spot in the area, its north-western tip. It is a rectangular structure (10 × 7 metres) consisting of two chambers. The purpose of the tower and its isolated position may be explained by the topography of this corner of the mound. The bluff here was too narrow for the city walls to be built on the limits of its slope; but due to the tactical importance of this position – which dominated both the western and northern approaches – the building of the tower here was imperative. In addition, the reduction of the area of the administrative buildings near the citadel in the north and south necessitated the building of new structures for administration and stores, and east of the citadel we found two new buildings constructed for this purpose. Both these buildings are of the 'four-room' type. One was built just a few metres east of the main entrance to the citadel, and its own entrance was in the east; the other, similar in plan, was built in front of the south-east corner of the citadel, with its entrance in the north. One could actually feel the anxiety of the commander

Aerial view of the citadel, defence wall and tower (looking south-east)

The forward bastion in area G (looking south-west)

A corner of a deep silo in area G

of Hazor: these two houses were built directly in front of the citadel in what had previously been an open area that may have been used for parades and other ceremonies. There was no other place to construct these buildings, and they were indispensable!

Similar, and in the light of history pathetic, changes took place at the other end of the city, on the eastern side of the *tell*, in what we called area G. There we discovered a sort of forward bastion guarding the gate and the city approaches. In the north there was a very strong wall with a well-built postern gate whose jambs were made of ashlar blocks. The gate's position and size indicate that it was meant to be used when the main gate was closed, probably in times of danger, enabling the city to receive supplies and maintain its commercial and diplomatic relations. In fact, just within this forward bastion we found a huge rectangular silo, with stone-lined walls cut deep into the ground, and it must have been the main granary of the garrison. Then we saw that suddenly in the later phase of VA, the postern gate was cunningly blocked, and clearly the intention was to camouflage its existence. The main blocking in its inner face was of bricks, while the outer facing of the block was of stone made to look like part of the city wall. This tactic may well have been successful, because when the city was destroyed the blocking remained untouched; on the other hand, the onslaught may simply have come from another direction. Be that as it may, once the fortifications were ready the city was sealed. When the approaching Assyrians were beginning to surround it and install their battering ram, the city was 'shut up from within and from without', to quote a biblical expression; 'none went out and none came in'.

In 732 BC Hazor fell to Tiglath-pileser III and was destroyed. The Bible (II Kings 15:29) describes this tragedy very laconically: 'In the days of Pekah king of Israel, Tilgath-pileser king of Assyria came and captured Ijon, Abel-beth-maacah, Janoah, Kedesh, Hazor, Gilead,

left The outer blocking, with stones, of the camouflaged gate
right The inner blocking with bricks

left Broken vessels and ashes, evidence of the Assyrian destruction
right A battering ram of Tiglath-pileser III shown on a relief now in the British Museum

and Galilee, all the land of Naphtali; and he carried the people captive to Assyria.' It is only through the archaeological excavations that we now know the meaning of the words 'came and captured'. Tilglath-pileser razed to the very ground the city of Hazor, once a key stronghold of the northern kingdom of Israel. The sight we encountered in area B is worse than any I can remember in archaeological excavations. The entire area was covered by a layer of ashes 1 metre thick and still black! Everything in sight was broken and scattered on the floors of the houses. We could visualize the Assyrian soldiers roaming about the houses, looting whatever they could and destroying the rest. The fire was so violent that even the stones were black, and numerous charred beams and pieces of burned plaster from the ceilings were strewn all over. The eastern side of the citadel, from which the fort had been attacked, was destroyed so thoroughly that in some places only the

The walls of the citadel in area B razed to the ground (looking south-west)

foundations below the floor level were visible. Here again we had visual evidence of the methods of destruction so vividly described by the Bible: 'Rase it, rase it! Down to its foundations!' (Psalms 137:7).

Callous as it may seem, the sudden destruction of Israelite Hazor by the Assyrians was again a boon to us. After all, the remains of ancient cities are our bread and butter; and if a city is deserted when its inhabitants are not under pressure and they have time to carry away their valuables, not much is left behind. But a sudden or relatively unexpected destruction is the ideal situation for archaeologists. The most valued objects may have been taken away by the Assyrian soldiers, but what was left as unworthy is still a treasure for us. Strewn among ashes or resting on the floors of the citadel and its ancillary buildings, as well as in other parts of the mound, were many objects that indicated more than just wealth in Israelite Hazor before this destruction. They also provided an interesting picture of the material culture of the time and of the strong pagan influence on the daily life of the northern Israelites (a carry over from the previous period in stratum VI).

The *pièce de résistance* of finds in the citadel is no doubt a carved ivory box that could have belonged to the wife of the commander. Four of its broken fragments were found in the passage leading to the citadel from the ancillary buildings in the north. It may have broken when it was removed from the room and was therefore left behind. The ivory box (*pyxis* in Greek) is similar to objects found in the Assyrian palaces in Nimrud, where complete specimens show that they were composed of two parts: a cylindrical body and a flat lid attached to the box by means of a string that passed from a hole in the lid through another in the upper part of the body. Ours is cylindrical, about 70 millimetres high and 56 millimetres in diameter. The upper part has a small diagonal hole for the lid attachment. The outside bears a carved scene enclosed by a simple frame at the bottom and a more elaborate one at the top. Based on the fragments and the comparative material, one can reconstruct the scene as a composition of two heraldic themes, each showing the 'tree of life' with a kneeling human figure on one side and a cherub on the other. (The same theme was also depicted in a seal impression on the rim of a krater.) These carvings covered the entire circumference of the box. In style and subject, the ivory *pyxis* belongs to the so-called Phoenician school of ivories represented not only in Nimrud, but also among the fine ivories discovered in Samaria, the capital of northern Israel. This object cannot be dated later than 732 BC, the date of the destruction of Hazor, but it could have been made many years earlier. Generally speaking, it is typical of the eighth-century Phoenician ivory that adorned the homes of the royal and wealthy throughout the ancient Near East. This box and the ivory cosmetic spoon uncovered in the previous stratum of area A are the only ivories found in Hazor. If we consider that ivories were not very common in ancient Israel, these finds em-

below An ivory box. Note the hind part of the cherub (left) and the kneeling figure (see also next page)
bottom A seal impression of a kneeling figure in a position of submission
overleaf The ivory box enlarged (actual height 70 millimetres)

phasize all the more the high standard of living of Hazor's population.

Another exquisite object salvaged from the citadel is a cult incense ladle that bears on its back a beautifully carved hand whose fingers grasp the 'cup' of the ladle. (One must bear in mind that the Hebrew word for palm, *kaph*, likewise means spoon or ladle). This type of ladle has been found in many Syrian cities, but it is one of the most beautiful ever uncovered in this country. Another, similar ladle – but this one of rather poor execution – was found in this area.

Whether or not the women of Hazor were beautiful we cannot say; but we can say that they were definitely beauty-conscious and took great pains to embellish themselves, because we found many so-called cosmetic palettes. These were made of stone, with a concave depression in the centre in which to grind the mascara, and most are adorned by

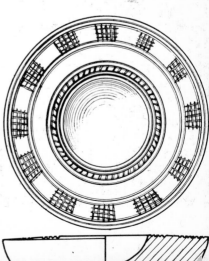

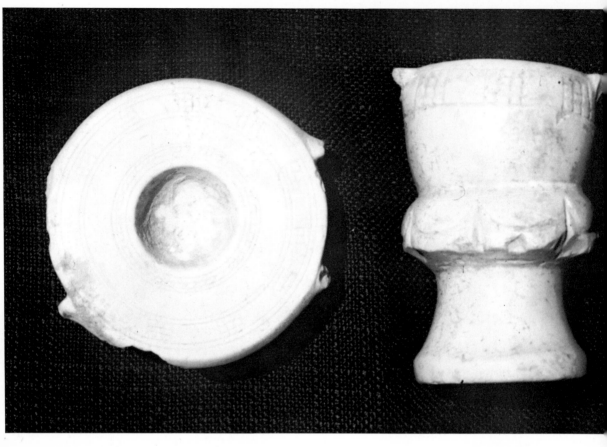

simple patterns, either circles or squares. Woman's nature appears to have remained constant throughout history, for not one of these Hazor women wanted her cosmetic palette to resemble that of her friend, and therefore each bears a somewhat different decoration. On the other hand, like today, they wanted their sets of cosmetic objects to bear identical decoration, and thus we found a cosmetic palette and a cosmetic jar decorated with the same pattern.

Although the official religion of northern Israel was that of Yahweh – the god of Israel – we know from both biblical verses and archaeological discoveries that the cult of Ba'al and Astarte strongly influenced the local population in the form of folk or popular beliefs – for double insurance, as it were. Indeed, we discovered quite a number of clay figurines representing Astarte, the fertility goddess, and of what may be called the holy prostitutes connected with the Ba'al and Astarte cult. A most interesting, albeit unexpected, find, just south of the citadel, was a skeleton lying on the floor. At first, not being a zoologist, I thought it was a lamb, and so identified it in our preliminary report. However, when later examined by the late S. Angress, the expedition's palaeontologist, it turned out to be none other than a pig – a surprising find indeed in an Israelite citadel! We were reminded of the harsh words of Isaiah (65:1–4):

I said, 'Here am I, here am I,'
    to a nation that did not call on my
        name.
I spread out my hands all the day
    to a rebellious people,
who walk in a way that is not
        good,
    following their own devices;
a people who provoke me
    to my face continually,
sacrificing in gardens,
    and burning incense upon bricks;
who sit in tombs,
    and spend the night in secret
        places;
who eat swine's flesh
    and broth of abominable things is
    in their vessels.

Or, further on (66:17):

Those who sanctify and purify themselves to go into the gardens, following one in the midst, eating swine's flesh and the abomination and mice, shall come to an end together, says the Lord.

One could, of course, give the Israelites of Hazor the benefit of the doubt by suggesting that the carcass of the pig was left by the victorious

right A pig's skeleton

The word *qodesh* (holy) incised on the side of a bowl (centre) and repeated on the rim (bottom)

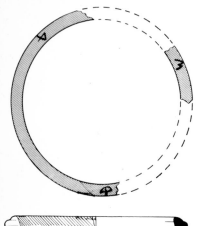

Assyrians celebrating their triumph. Whatever the case, not all the pig's flesh was consumed by the last occupants of the citadel. The study by Angress shows that the successive parts of the backbone were found in their natural position with some vertebrae still connected, indicating that the main trunk, with the flesh on it, was still intact when abandoned. Not only are the limb-bones missing, but the girdles, the sacrum and the tail vertebrae as well. It seems that after partaking of only the most easily carved parts and removing those richest in meat (ham, shoulders, etc.), the participants in the feast left the remainder of the carcass to rot. This may have happened at the moment of destruction. Quite a lot was also learned about eighth-century pigs in northern Israel from the skeletal remains. They were of a domestic kind of pig (which shows that Isaiah had a point) with cranial proportions exhibiting a peculiar combination of features typical of intensive domestication, on the one hand, and of a character approaching the wild type, on the other. The former features resulted from the severe conditions of keeping; the latter were a result of the genetic proximity of the Hazor pig to the wild animal from which it was derived. This ancestral form, which gave rise to or was interbred with the pig stock of Hazor, was probably the indigenous wild boar.

There was no doubt in our minds that the last occupants of the citadel were Israelites. Nevertheless, it was gratifying to find some Hebrew inscriptions to bear us out. The most interesting of these – the word *qodesh* (holy) incised twice – was on the rim of a bowl found in the citadel. The same word, preceded by an undecipherable one, was also incised on the outer face. This, of course, does not indicate that the area had been a temple; but it points out that this particular vessel was either dedicated to the priest or contained holy food (I hope not the flesh of the pig!). Indeed, it was refreshing to discover that some inhabitants of the citadel did follow the religion of Yahweh. On the shoulder of one of the cylindrical store jars, we found a deep inscription reading (in old Hebrew script) לדליו (*ldlyw* = belonging to Delayo). This name occurs several times in the Bible, and the last element in it, *yo*, is an abbreviation of Yahweh.

Perhaps the most important inscription was one scratched, after firing, on the shoulder of an ovoid store jar (found broken on the floor). The first four letters are לפקח (*lpqḥ* = 'belonging to Pekah'). It could be just a coincidence that this was the very name of the king of Israel, Pekah son of Remaliah, in whose days Hazor was captured, as the name was fairly common at the time, in both Israel and Judah, and is an abbreviation of Pekahyahu, a full Yahwistic name. The second word is סמדר (*smdr*, pronounced *semadar*). This word occurs only three times in the Bible, always in the Song of Songs (2:13, 2:15 and 7:12); and although its meaning is slightly obscure, it is certainly connected with the blossoming of the vines or the tender grapes.

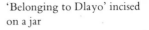

'Belonging to Dlayo' incised on a jar

'Belonging to Pekah, *semadar*' incised on a wine jar

Most probably it means the tender grapes themselves, and the jar must have contained wine made from them. This meaning of *semadar*, is, by the way, preserved in the Mishnah (Orlah 1:17).

These fragments were only a minute portion of the grim evidence of the total destruction of the royal city of Hazor twelve years before Samaria, the capital of northern Israel, was likewise conquered by the Assyrians, the whole of northern Israel taken into captivity and the ten tribes lost. Yet it was not the end of activities on the site of Hazor. Some time must have passed before the ruined Hazor was re-occupied; but then – perhaps still at the end of the eighth or beginning of the seventh century – people returned to settle there. They were most probably Israelite squatters. In many places, particularly above the ruined citadel in area B and in the bastions of area G, we discovered

Not the end of Hazor

very poor structures built on top of the ruined earlier walls. The pottery associated with this stratum (IV) is to all intents and purposes identical with that of the previous layer.

Another citadel

This settlement of squatters did not last long either. Sometime during the Assyrian occupation, or perhaps in the early part of the Babylonian occupation at the beginning of the sixth century, the strategic importance of Hazor was grasped by the foreign troops, and sure enough, a new citadel grew above the squatters' buildings. (We marked this level stratum III.) It was a large isolated building erected to guard the main routes of the north, and it occupied the whole of the western bluff. The citadel was rectangular with a square central courtyard enclosed on three sides by a row of rooms and halls and on the fourth (south) side by a double row of rooms. Adjacent to the north-west corner we found the remains of a tower, consisting of two long rooms partially built above the tower of stratum V. Although there is no relationship between the two towers in either plan or orientation, both were erected for the same tactical reasons. East of the citadel was a large court nearly the size of the citadel itself.

This citadel was abandoned probably just before the country was occupied by the Persians in the sixth century. Then, sometime in the fifth century, Hazor and its surroundings again came to life in the shape of an unplanned city of scattered farmhouses. The citadel was re-occupied, and the newcomers introduced many changes into the building by dividing it into two blocks of residential units: some of the entrances were reduced in size; some of the large halls around the central court were turned into smaller units by means of partition walls; occasionally small chambers were added. But the main changes occurred in the long northern hall. Here a wall with 'enclosures' and niches was added, dividing the hall lengthwise into two long narrow rooms with a passage in between. There were five of these 'enclosures' with three niches between them, and in every niche a few vessels – either juglets, loom weights or broken jars – were found. The building lost much of its military nature and looked more like a large farmhouse. On the other hand, we cannot exclude the possibility that it may now have been occupied by soldiers with their families. We dated this stratum (II) within the Persian period with the help of a silver coin (a silver *stater* of Tyre) to between 400 and 332 BC. Two Attic lamps of the first half of the fourth century were also found in the building. In summing up one can say that the building existed and was still occupied in the latter part of the fourth century, or until the occupation of the country by Alexander the Great in 333 BC.

A silver *stater* of Tyre from the Persian period

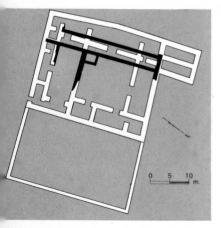

Plan of the last two – Persian (white) and Hellenistic – citadels

This citadel was destroyed and the site lay in ruin until sometime in the second century BC a completely new citadel was built on top of it. This poorly preserved building in stratum I is, in fact, the one excavated by Garstang. The pottery leaves no doubt that it was the fort of the Hellenistic period and may have been the very building that existed here during the Maccabean period. The last historical reference to Hazor is found in the First Book of Maccabees, which mentions the plain of Hazor in an account of the battles between Jonathan the Macca-bee and Demetrius. Finally, nearly 2,000 years after the Hellenistic fort was destroyed, one more fort was erected atop the ruins – this time during the British occupation.

Having surveyed the strata of Israelite Hazor from the times of Ahab up to the last citadel in the Hellenistic period (strata VIII–I), and even up to modern times, we are now ready to return to the period that pre-dates Ahab and embark on the description of our fascinating search for Solomon.

Aerial view (looking south) of the citadel and ancillary buildings in stratum VA

12 The Search for Solomon

The name of King Solomon evokes different associations in different people. For those who like horses – some of us – he is one of the greatest horse breeders of biblical times; for those who admire women – most of us – he was the greatest lover of all times, with his thousand wives; for those who seek wisdom – all of us – he was the wisest of men. And yet, for the archaeologist of the Holy Land, the name Solomon is associated with the greatest builders among the kings of Israel. It was he who was privileged to build the house of the Lord in Jerusalem, and he, too – as we have learned – who built Hazor, Megiddo, Gezer and other cities. Yet, with all that, Solomon remains one of the most elusive builders in the country, archaeologically speaking. Nothing remains today of the temple he built in Jerusalem; it was first destroyed by the Babylonians in 586, then razed completely in subsequent centuries. The reconstruction of the temple's plan – referred to earlier in discussing the temples of the lower city of Hazor – is one of the most difficult tasks of biblical scholars. It is therefore easy to understand why one of the main aims of our excavations in Hazor was to discover Solomon's city. As we dug deeper and deeper and reached stratum VIII – dated to the times of Ahab in the first half of the ninth century BC, barely several score years after Solomon – the tension in our expedition increased considerably. It so happened that we not only found the city and fortifications built by Solomon, but with the help of our discoveries at Hazor, we also managed to discover the Solomonic gates and fortifications at Gezer and Solomon's fortifications at Megiddo. Here I shall try, step by step, to unfold our discoveries at Hazor itself and the further deductions that led to parallel discoveries elsewhere. Some of what I am about to relate may sound like a detective story, but the truth is that our great guide was the Bible; and as an archaeologist I cannot imagine a greater thrill than working with the Bible in one hand and the spade in the other. This was the true secret of our discoveries of the Solomonic period.

As the starting point in our search for the Solomonic city, let us go back to the pillared building of the times of Ahab in stratum VIII. We mentioned that north of the pillared hall, there were two rectangular halls (see plan on page 170). These were well paved with cobblestone floors, and we noticed that in several places the floor had rectangular depressions, which baffled us. Were these depressions made deliberately? Such a conclusion did not make much sense, and one does

The elusive Solomon

The Bible as an archaeological guide

A stylized animal head, with a sun disc and cross on its forehead, of the Solomonic period (for actual height, 80 millimetres, see page 189)

A view of Ahab's storehouse (looking south) with depressions in the cobble-stone floor

opposite, above Solomon's garrison building under the cobble-stone floor. Its plan matches the rectangular depressions
opposite, below The clay animal head with sun disc and cross on its forehead shown in its actual size

not have to be a genius, or even an archaeologist (if this is a superlative), to conclude that the paving on top of the ruins of earlier strata had sunk in at those places which corresponded to the spaces between the walls of the previous stratum. We therefore decided to remove the floors carefully. Look now at the photograph taken from the same angle after the cobble-stone floors had been removed. One can clearly see the outline of structures of earlier strata, with rooms that are identical in layout to the sunken rectangulars. Here was a perfect case of strat-ification, because the buildings we discovered were clearly sealed off by the cobble-stone floors of Ahab's times. There was a good chance that we were now getting close to Solomon's city, if, indeed, he built Hazor as the Bible indicates. We discovered, in fact, that this garrison-like building existed through two strata, labelled from top to bottom IX and X, respectively. The lower one, containing objects from the second half of the tenth century (the end of Solomon's reign), must have been part of the city rebuilt by Solomon, while stratum IX would have belonged to one of the kings of Israel who reigned between Solomon and Ahab.

Incidentally, in one of the rooms of this building we discovered a

very interesting object: a small terracotta head of a stylized animal with the sun disc and cross on its forehead. The similarity between this emblem and the one found on the incense altar of the orthostat temple in the lower city is striking, and it led us to assume that the head represents (in stylized manner) a bull. The triangular object on its forehead is rather common on bull depictions in ancient Near Eastern art, signifying the triangular white-haired spot on the forehead of some of these beasts. On the other hand, it is possible – as I thought when the head was first found – that the head was of a horse, in which case the figurine represented the sun cult, often associated with the chariot and horses.

Back to the building itself, had we been digging a site whose history was unknown from other sources, we would, of course, not be in a position to ascribe stratum X so precisely to the times of Solomon. The relative date based on the stratigraphy, and the absolute date based on the pottery, were sound; but these two factors did not decisively exclude the possibility of dating the building to the end of the tenth century, or perhaps even to the very beginning of the ninth century. Important as the discovery of this building may have been, it did not completely certify the identification of stratum X with Solomon. But further discoveries helped to resolve this important issue.

The casemate wall

Just east of the pillared building, Garstang had already made a narrow trench, which we proceeded to clear. At the bottom two parallel walls came into view, but without further excavation it was impossible to fix their relative or absolute dates. We therefore enlarged an area of our excavations east of the pillared building and the newly discovered garrison-like building of stratum X, where the *tell* has a terrace. While excavating the terrace edge we found a well-built casemate wall; in fact, it was the casemate wall that created the terrace. A casemate wall, as you will remember, is a double wall divided into rooms by right-angled partition walls. This type of construction has its drawbacks, as it is weaker than a solid wall; but its advantage is that the rooms can be used to store food or station soldiers. The discovery of the wall, in itself, was not indisputable testimony that the stratum was Solomonic, although it was an important corroboration. Before our dig, for example, casemate walls had been found in two other sites in the south, Tell Beit-Mirsim and Beth-shemesh, where they were attrib-

A section east of the pillared building, showing the inner wall of the Solomonic casemate wall (bottom)

uted by their excavators to King David. But before I proceed to describe the final discovery that absolutely decided the issue, let me describe the casemate wall itself.

We excavated four casemates completely and two partially. The line of the wall (as the plan on page 197 shows) runs generally north to south, apart from two obtuse angles (one shown) to fit the line of the wall to the topography. The casemates are long rooms, normally between 8 and 10 metres. The outer wall is about 1.5 metres thick and the inner wall just above 1 metre thick; the partitions between casemates are 1 metre thick; and the space between the walls (*i.e.*, the inner width of the casemates) is 2.5 metres. Each casemate had an entrance in the corner, near one of the partition walls, and an earthen floor. Remains of bricks found in the debris indicate that the upper part of the walls was made of bricks, a fact corroborated by the horizontal finish of the top of the stone foundations. Similar casemates were also found in area B and two other areas, all of them west of the wall discovered in area A. Between the inner wall of the casemate wall and the building further to the west, we found a beautifully paved street, with a drainage

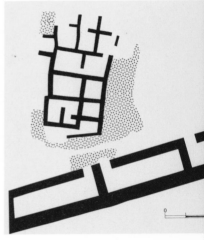

Plan of the casemates, pavement and garrison building (see also page 199)

The pavement and drainage between the garrison building (right) and the casemate wall (looking south-east)

channel running close and parallel to the wall. The pavement was raised several times here, a repair that corresponded almost exactly to the main phases observed in other buildings nearby. All the pavements were built up to the casemate wall.

In order to understand better the situation in front of the wall and towards the east, we began by cutting a deep trench perpendicular

The large trench east of
the Solomonic fortifications
(looking west)

A trapped tortoise

A *shofar* blower with the conch

to the line of the wall in an easterly direction. This trench was also important for gathering knowledge on strata that pre-dated the Israelite period. But as far as the wall was concerned, it showed that the Solomonic casemate wall made use of an earlier Bronze Age wall for its base and that in front of the fortifications there was a huge fosse, which heightened the strength of the fortifications. Thus the entire area of the mound west of the casemate wall was actually detached and severed from the eastern terrace.

Before leaving the wall itself for a while, I would like to mention two small finds uncovered in its rooms – not so much for their scientific importance as for their piquant aspect.

In one of the rooms we found an intact tortoise shell that must have been trapped when the wall was destroyed, or perhaps it was brought there as a pet by one of the soldiers living in the casemate. The other object was also found in the re-used casemate room and may have originally belonged to the Solomonic period. It was a big Red Sea conch, which was obviously used as a trumpet. One hole was drilled through its length for blowing, another at its end for attaching a string. After nearly 3,000 years – the time that elapsed since its last use – it was still in working order. One of our elderly labourers, who was a professional *shofar* blower in his synagogue, took it to his lips and

managed to bring forth all sorts of sounds! Efforts by amateur blowers, however, produced less startling results. Similar conches are occasionally found in excavations, and it may be assumed that this one was used by the soldiers near the wall for alarm signals. Even today some primitive societies in Africa and South America use conches of this sort in the same manner.

Further north along the excavations of the casemate wall, we came up against a large structure connected with it but built mainly inside the city. We immediately realized that we had discovered the gate connected with the casemate fortifications. Furthermore, it was soon evident that the gate's plan – comprising six chambers and two towers – as well as its dimensions were identical to those of the gate discovered

The 'clincher'

earlier at Megiddo and ascribed by its excavators to the city of Solomon. Excitement in our camp intensified. This was the real proof! Not only were our deductions in ascribing this stratum to Solomon correct, but the gate was also confirmation of the authenticity of the biblical verse describing Solomon's activity in these two cities. Our elation was paramount. I even remember vividly the gimmick we used to impress our labourers even before the contours and plan of the gate became clear. We traced the plan of the Megiddo gate on the ground, marking it with pegs to denote corners and walls, and then instructed our labourers to dig according to the marking, promising: 'here you will find a wall,' or 'there you will find a chamber.' When our 'proph-

Solomon's gate and casemate wall (looking south)

ecies' proved correct, our prestige went up tremendously, and we were regarded as wizards. But our workers, mostly elderly Jews who had recently immigrated from North Africa, were well versed in the Old Testament; so when we read them the biblical verse about Solomon's activities in Hazor, Megiddo and Gezer, our prestige took a dive, but that of the Bible rose sky-high! (Incidentally, one of the means we used to increase the interest of our workers in the dig was to assemble them occasionally and explain what we had found and how we had come to our conclusions. This gave them a feeling of involvement and made them part of the team, which was very helpful.)

The gatehouse consisted of six chambers, three on either side of the passage, with a square tower on each side of the entrance. The total outer length of the gatehouse was 20.3 metres, and its width was 18.2 metres; the actual passage between the chambers was 4.2 metres. Most of the gatehouse was built in towards the city, and only the two towers protruded outwards from the casemate wall. The chambers had a dual function: they could be used as guardrooms, and at the same time their structure also supported the ceiling – and perhaps even the second storey, with its walls and crenellations. Such a structure is well known from depictions of cities in the ancient Near East where the gatehouse was actually a fort in itself. Of the actual gate, we discovered only the foundations up to the level of the crushed-chalk

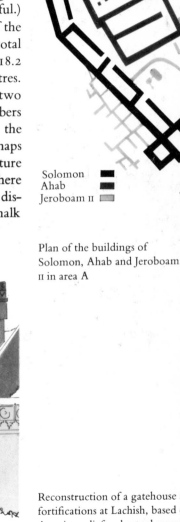

Solomon ▬
Ahab ▬
Jeroboam II ▭

Plan of the buildings of Solomon, Ahab and Jeroboam II in area A

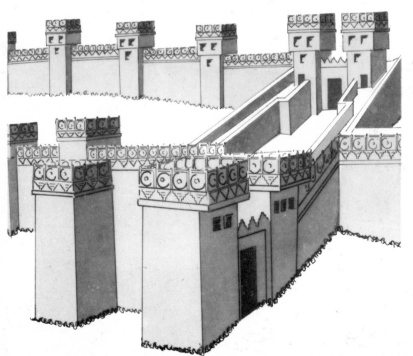

Reconstruction of a gatehouse and fortifications at Lachish, based on an Assyrian relief and actual remains

opposite A vertical air view showing Solomon's gate and casemate wall, as well as buildings of other strata (compare plan above)

paving in the passage. It may be assumed that the gatehouse itself was built of bricks. We also found the inner threshold, which was made of broken, re-used orthostats of the Bronze Age, while the actual slanting approach to the east was cobbled. The position of the gate in the area between the upper and lower terrace made the passage slant outwards from the city, and later we discovered that in order to minimize the steep slope of the approach, the builders carried out enormous levelling operations. Unfortunately, they eliminated most of the Late Bronze period strata and sometimes even the Middle Bronze strata, just under and west of the gate, in the process. We therefore found huge quantities of artefacts belonging to earlier periods in the fill under the gate, including two fragments of beautiful sculptures, definitely of Egyptian origin. One is the middle part of a torso, most probably of a Pharoah, sent as a gift to one of the earlier kings of Hazor – perhaps of the period just before Joshua or in the fourteenth century, the el-Amarna period. The other was just the remains of toes, but exquisitely sculpted ones, and, again, may have been part of a sculpture of an Egyptian king. It is a pity that only these pieces survived. We promised our workers barrels of wine as a reward for finding the other parts of these statues, but unfortunately it was not necessary to come through on the pledge.

top A statue of Amenophis II (1436–1410 BC), similar to the fragment found at Hazor
above and right Fragments of exquisite Egyptian statues found in debris under Solomon's gate

A glance at the map shows clearly that the casemate wall and the gate are built right in the middle of the *tell* in the south–north direction, which means that the Solomonic city occupied only the western half of the *tell* and the eastern half was uninhabited – or at least not within the city's fortifications. This situation stood in contrast to Ahab's period in stratum VIII, where we found remains of a solid wall in the eastern part of the city as well (particularly in area G). Our first conclusion, therefore, was that from the ninth century onwards, the city expanded until its area had nearly doubled. But our discovery was open to other interpretations. The fact that the Solomonic wall was right in the centre of the mound led some scholars, and particularly Dr K. M. Kenyon, to suggest that perhaps it was not a proper city wall but rather the wall of an acropolis or royal quarter. The suggestion was logical, and the question could not be left unanswered. In 1968, therefore, when we resumed excavations after a ten-year interval, I decided to probe into the problem and try to find a solution.

We opened up a new area (called M) on the north side of the *tell* (north of the Solomonic gate), just near the edge of the mound. The site was fixed at the theoretical meeting point of the city-wall line on the northern edge of the *tell* and the estimated prolongation of the casemate wall, about 55 metres north of the gate. When we started

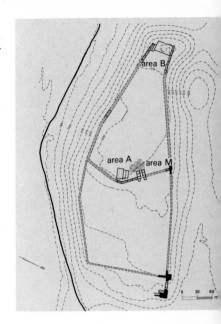

Plan of Solomon's fortifications showing the joint with Ahab's wall (right)

Fixing the theoretical position of the joint of the walls before excavations

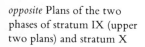

An offset of Ahab's solid wall in the joint

digging – and, indeed, were still debating where to dig – nothing could be seen on the surface. We hoped to turn up conclusive results as to whether the casemate wall of area A turned west upon reaching the northern side of the *tell* – in keeping with the perimeter of Solomon's city as we had previously conceived it – or whether it turned both west *and* east, forming a T-shaped casemate wall – which would indicate that it continued up to the city gate in the east and the western extension enclosed an acropolis. We began by cutting a trench from west to east in order to find the continuation of the north–south wall. It was indeed found along the straight line we conjectured (according to the direction of the casemate wall in the area A). As the casemate wall found here had precisely the same dimensions as the one in area A, there was no doubt that it was one and the same wall. Parts of the wall had been uprooted in antiquity, most probably after the city had expanded eastwards in stratum VIII and thereby made it redundant. Once the direction of the wall had been clearly established, we cut a wide north–south trench perpendicular to the former one and up to the conjectured northern city wall. The results here were decisive and provided an indisputable answer to our main query: the casemate wall turned to the west *only*. Moreover, east of the corner of the casemate wall we discovered a solid offsets-insets wall of stratum VIII built onto the corner of the casemate wall. This little dig provided us with a clear clue that the Solomonic city was indeed confined to only the western portion of the *tell*, and its total area reached some 26,000 square metres (that is 6.5 acres). Although we disproved Dr Kenyon's suggestion, I am grateful to her for raising it, because she compelled us to find solid archaeological evidence to support our conjecture.

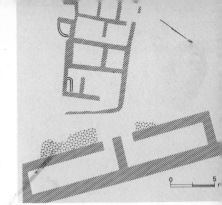

Throughout this description, we have been referring to the main strata discovered: stratum X of Solomon, where the casemate wall and other fortification elements were actually built; and stratum IX, an intermediate level between Solomon and Ahab. In reality each of these strata had two phases, which we labelled IXA (the latest, as we worked from the top down) and IXB, XA and XB, respectively. We could discern these phases very clearly in the history of the rectangular rooms found under the cobble-stone floors of Ahab's pillared building, as well as in the cobbled pavements between that building and the city walls. From time to time, after destructions, changes were made in the rooms or in the houses; doors were blocked, rooms were added and occasionally even the cobbled pavements were raised. A glance at the plans of these four phases will enable even the lay reader to distinguish between them. Four phases within such a short time, perhaps three- or four-score years, are of the utmost importance to archaeologists, for they enable us to follow the history of the city closely and date more precisely the pottery found in each phase.

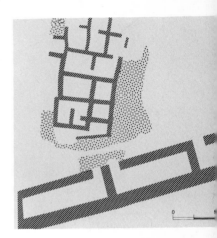

More difficult than identifying the phases, however, is establishing the causes of these frequent destructions. The latter phase of stratum IX was covered by a thick layer of ashes, indicating that the city was sacked and destroyed by an enemy. We may ascribe this destruction to the campaign of the Aramaean king Ben-hadad in 885 BC. This campaign occurred in the days of Baasha, king of Israel. Although the destruction of Hazor is not explicitly mentioned, it can be deduced from the account of the campaign in I Kings 15:20: 'And Ben-hadad ... conquered Ijon, Dan, Abel-beth-maacah, and all Chinneroth, with all the land of Naphtali', and the parallel verses in II Chronicles 16:4: 'And Ben-hadad ... sent the commanders of his armies against the cities of Israel, and they conquered Ijon ... and all the store cities of Naphtali.' It seems that only the northern frontier cities were specifically mentioned. But as the greater part of the land of Naphtali, with all its store-cities, was occupied and Ben-hadad's army reached the Kinneret district, it is hardly to be supposed that Hazor remained untouched; and chronologically the destruction of stratum IX fits Ben-hadad's campaign perfectly. In the final analysis, however, our thoughts were merely speculations about the various layers filling the well-established 'sandwich' of the Solomonic stratum X, below, and Ahab's stratum VIII, above. All told, this is a classic case in which stratigraphy, pottery, historical documents and, above all, the biblical narrative enabled us to date the various cities in an absolute chronology.

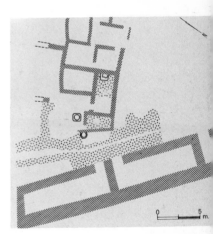

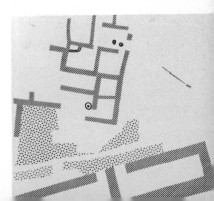

13 Gezer – Excavations in a Book

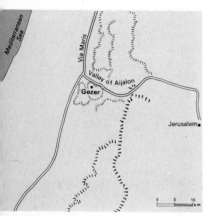

above The position of Gezer in the Valley of Aijalon, dominating an offshoot of the Via Maris

below 'The boundary of Gezer', as published by Macalister

The discovery of identical gates in Hazor and Megiddo, and the fact that the biblical verse mentions that Solomon built the city of Gezer as well, prompted me to investigate the problem of the Solomonic city and fortifications at the latter site. The following description will prove that one must sometimes investigate and 'excavate' not only *tells* themselves, but reports of previous excavations conducted when archaeology was still in its infancy and comparative material that aids excavators was still meagre.

Tell Gezer, the site of the biblical city, is a large and impressive mound situated in a highly strategic spot between Jerusalem and the Mediterranean coast, where it dominated an important offshoot of the highway between Egypt and the north (the Via Maris). In fact, it completely dominates the extensive Valley of Aijalon, the site where the 'sun stood still' during the famous battle between Joshua and the Canaanite kings. It is among the few ancient sites in Israel whose identification with the biblical name is absolutely certain, since several inscriptions found incised into the rock around the *tell* bear the Hebrew words תחום גזר ('the boundary of Gezer'), together with a Greek name in genitive, *alkiou* (meaning 'belongs to Alkios'). The name of the ancient city has not been preserved in the name of the present Arab village nearby, but apparently it was still known in the sixteenth century AD. In 1870 Charles Clermont-Ganneau, the well-known French archaeologist, who was French consul in Jerusalem at that time, identified the *tell* as ancient Gezer in a brilliant piece of detective work. While reading the writings of a sixteenth-century Arab chronicler recounting a skirmish between troops of the Governor of Jerusalem and a band of Bedouin that occurred in the Ramle area in about 1525, Clermont-Ganneau noticed that the cries of the protagonists had been heard at the village of Khuldeh and at Tell el-Jazar. He

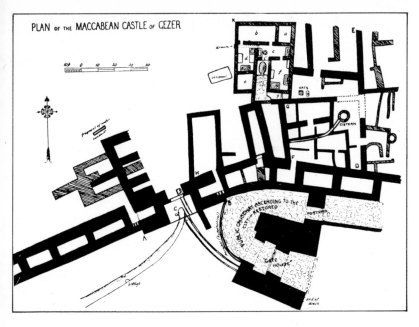

left Solomon's gate and casemate wall are discernible (solid block) within what Macalister called 'The Maccabean Castle of Gezer'. Reproduced from Macalister's publication on Gezer
below Solomon's fortifications at Hazor (top), Megiddo (centre) and Gezer (bottom), as published by the author before the recent excavations at Gezer

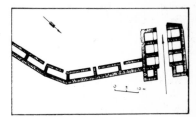

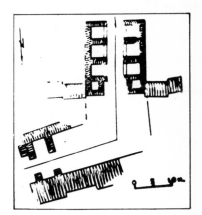

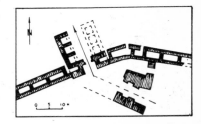

was struck by the similarity between Jazar and the Hebrew word Gezer and so made enquiries that finally led him to the identification of the site.

In due course, one of the first major excavations in Palestine was conducted on this site by a young Irish archaeologist, R.A.S. Macalister, in long campaigns between 1902 and 1905 and then 1907 and 1909. Not only was archaeology in its infancy at the time, but worse, Macalister's own zeal and ambition caused much of the ensuing stratigraphic and chronological confusion about the many things he discovered on that site. He worked alone in the capacity of director, architect and supervisor. Yet to his credit, one must say that, unlike more competent archaeologists of later periods, he published his finds soon after termination of his excavations (in 1912). These are in three sumptuous volumes, written in the enthusiastic and – to my taste – beautiful style of the Victorian age and accompanied by photos and drawings.

Although neither Macalister nor the scholars who perused his three-volume account detected at Gezer anything that could be ascribed to Solomon, the discoveries at Hazor and the famous passage in 1 Kings led me to a fresh examination of Macalister's report in the hope of locating a gate. One can well imagine my astonishment and unbound excitement when, on page 217 of volume 1, I came across a layout (reproduced here) of one of the sections of Macalister's excavations entitled 'Plan of the Maccabean Castle of Gezer'. As one looks at the plan of the structure marked in bold lines, he can easily detect a casemate wall, an outer gatehouse and even more important (on the left side) what looks like half of a city gate, exactly like those found in Megiddo and Hazor. Macalister had marked this structure

right The author's table of comparative measurements, as given in the *Israel Exploration Journal*

Detail	Megiddo	Hazor	Gezer
Length of gate	20.3 m.	20.3 m.	19.0 m.
Width of gate	17.5 m.	18.0 m.	16.2 m.
Space between towers	6.5 m.	6.1 m.	5.5 m.
Width of entrance passage	4.2 m.	4.2 m.	3.1 m.
Width of walls	1.6 m.	1.6 m.	1.6 m.
Total width of the casemate wall	———	5.4 m.	5.4 m.

below Headers and stretchers in Solomon's gate at Gezer

'Maccabean castle' mainly because of the Hellenistic pottery and a Greek inscription discovered in the area. As only the western part of the gate had been discovered and, to be fair, the gates of Megiddo and Hazor were unknown at that time, he failed to realize the true nature and full significance of this complex of fortifications. The remains of this half-gate were curiously called by him 'stall-like spaces'.

In 1958, I ventured to publish an article (in the *Israel Exploration Journal*) entitled 'Solomon's City Wall and Gate at Gezer', in which I suggested that the Maccabean castle at Gezer was actually the remains of the Solomonic fortifications and gatehouse, just like those of Hazor. Reconstructing the plan in hatched lines (as reproduced here), I noted striking similarities with Hazor and Megiddo not only in the plan of the fortifications, but also in their dimensions, as if all 'were in fact built by Solomon's architect from identical blueprints, with minor changes in each case, made necessary by the terrain', as I then wrote. I even calculated a table of comparative measurements. There was other circumstantial evidence to support this identification, notably that the gatehouse jambs here and at Megiddo were built in an identical fashion: each course consists of what we call 'headers and stretchers'. Moreover, even the dressing of the ashlar stones is identical to that of other Israelite buildings from the tenth and ninth centuries. Although my suggestion was nearly universally approved by biblical archaeologists, it was tempting to re-open Macalister's excavation area in order to uncover the eastern half of the gatehouse and to ascertain, with the help of the pottery, the exact date of its construction. I say that it was tempting, although personally I had no doubt about the results. The biblical verse, on the one hand, and the plan's correspondence to that of Hazor and Megiddo, on the other, were striking enough. I kept postponing the excavations, perhaps because I was subconsciously afraid to 'destroy' with my own hands what I deemed to be a brilliant theory.

Fortunately, we need no more rely on the resemblance of outward features only or on the detective work that led to the identification of the Solomonic fortifications at Gezer. The site of Gezer is now being excavated by the Jerusalem branch of the Hebrew Union College. For several seasons, many of the areas excavated by Macalister were re-opened and re-excavated from 1965 to 1973, using the most modern scientific methods. These excavations were directed by Dr William G. Dever, assisted by a very able staff, and one of the objectives was to check and verify my theory. At first they were cautious and non-commital and did not refer to the Solomonic gate or the Maccabean castle but to 'the Yadin gate'. Sure enough, not only did Dever's team find the other half of the gate, but the stratigraphy and pottery demonstrated conclusively that the complex had been built in Solomon's times. In one of his reports, Dever became so excited about the finds that he wrote the following passage: 'The sealed pottery from the floors and the makeup below was characteristic red-burnished ware of the late tenth century BC. Solomon did indeed re-build Gezer!'

'Solomon did indeed re-build Gezer!'

These excavations revealed the gate in its entirety and made it possible to trace its later development (for it was rebuilt several times) through the period of the Divided Kingdom to the time of the Maccabees. The results even proved that the resemblance in measurements between the gate of Gezer and those of Megiddo and Hazor was greater than we had thought. In the table reproduced here, I indicated that the width of the entrance passage was 4.2 metres at Megiddo and Hazor, as against 3.1 metres at Gezer. This calculation was, of course, based on Macalister's plan. However, when the Hebrew Union College team examined the door jambs, they noted the following (to quote one of their interim reports):

The second surprise was that the fine ashlar jamb on the west, unlike that on the east, turned out to be founded very shallowly in a trench cutting an Iron II destruction level; it was thus a superficially skillful rebuild of the Maccabean period, probably using original stones to attempt to match the surviving Solomonic jamb on the opposite side. The discovery of this deception cleared up the mystery we had long since noted, i.e. that the entrance way was quite asymmetrical and that it was only 3.10 meters in width, when compared with the 4.2 of the Hazor and Megiddo gates. Fortunately some dismantling revealed the probable line of the original

Solomon's gate at Gezer (looking south) as revealed by recent excavations. Note the drainage under the floor of the gate

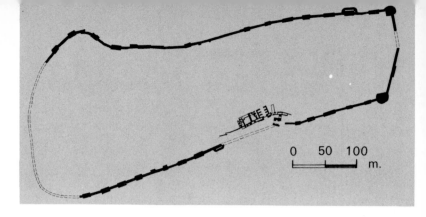

Gezer's fortifications, showing the position of Solomon's gate and city wall, which close the gap in the older and destroyed city wall

threshold, and when measured, it yielded just 4.20 meters, identical to the measurements of the other gates. So Solomon did indeed re-build Gezer!

This is not yet the end of the story of the quest for Solomon. We can now understand precisely what Solomon did in Gezer. After stating that Solomon built Hazor, Megiddo and Gezer, 1 Kings 9 adds parenthetically: 'Pharaoh king of Egypt had gone up and captured Gezer and burnt it with fire, and had slain the Canaanites who dwelt in the city, and had given it as dowry to his daughter, Solomon's wife; so Solomon rebuilt Gezer.' A glance at the plan here shows that what Solomon actually did was bridge the gap in the ancient fortifications

A drawing of a relief (the original is lost) depicting Tiglath-pileser III capturing Gezer

with his new casemate wall and gatehouse. The recent excavations also revealed the burned layer of Gezer destroyed by Solomon's 'father-in-law' and thus clarifies the historical development in Gezer. In fact, these same excavations succeeded in finding the remains of Israelite Gezer after Solomon's days and proving its existence into the eighth century BC. Thus a very famous relief found in the palace of Tiglath-pileser III (the same monarch who destroyed Hazor) depicting his assault on the city of Gazru can now safely be identified with Gezer. That relief, incidentally, depicts not only the plan of the Israelite fortifications, but also their elevation.

A fly in the ointment

When the problem of Solomon's gate and his fortifications was finally solved at Gezer, I wrote (referring to the verse in 1 Kings 9:15): 'Hardly ever in the history of archaeological digging has such a short verse in the Bible helped so much in identifying and dating actual remains found by the spade.' But there was one fly in the ointment – a big, black, ugly fly at that: the city wall associated with the Solomonic gate at Megiddo (by the excavators of that *tell*) was not a casemate wall! This anomaly had to be examined. It could not be explained, as one scholar tried, on the basis of the different character of the three cities. It is axiomatic that the strength and nature of a wall are determined by the tactics, weapons and siegecraft of the enemy against whom it is erected. Gezer in the south and Hazor in the north could, theoretically, have been fortified against different potential enemies; yet both had the same type of fortifications. There was no reason why Megiddo, in the centre of the country, should be protected by a different type of wall, and one which was stronger at that. The only way to get to the bottom of this mystery was to adjourn to the site of Megiddo and undertake some checking excavations there.

Following the archaeological trail

In following the archaeological trail, I caution the reader who wants to learn more about Hazor against grumblings of discontent over this 'tour of the *tells* of Israel'. As we have seen many times in the course of this book, no site ever existed in a vacuum, and sometimes the only way an archaeologist can understand his finds is by turning to comparative evidence found elsewhere – and sometimes far away indeed. In addition, as we have learned in the case of Macalister's assumptions, the discovery of later finds sometimes leads archaeologists to correct the mistaken conclusions of their predecessors. Before the re-excavations at Gezer, our position was somewhat uncomfortable because our discoveries at Hazor clashed with published findings about both of its sister cities in the Solomonic period. I proposed a theory about Gezer that would prove previous findings wrong, and the calculated hunch proved correct. Now, in following the description of checking excavations at Megiddo, the reader will see how persistence pays off; for not only did we find evidence to confirm the results of our dig at Hazor described up to now, we also acquired tools to help us understand the significance of discoveries yet to come.

Aerial view of Megiddo
(looking north-west), showing
the excavated area

14 Megiddo – Post Mortem Excavations

Megiddo (Armageddon of the New Testament), like Gezer and Hazor, is located in a highly strategic area. Situated in the middle of the country, it guarded the famous 'Megiddo Pass', which enabled the Via Maris to fork off through the southern Carmel ridge into the Plain of Jezreel and then continue on to the north-east to Beth-shan, Hazor, Damascus and Mesopotamia. Megiddo was one of the most heavily fortified cities in Palestine and always played an important role in key battles. In fact, one of the earliest battles recorded in history, that of Thutmose III in the early half of the fifteenth century BC, took place at Megiddo. The site was important even in the First World War, for it was through the Megiddo Pass that General Allenby managed to pursue the Turks and finally crush them. He was so proud of his victory that when he was later elevated to the nobility, he chose the title Viscount Allenby of Megiddo. Obviously, Megiddo was a vitally important city in the times of Solomon as well, and finding the city he rebuilt there became one of the objectives of the Megiddo excavators, just as we sought it at Hazor.

Megiddo had been excavated over a number of years by several archaeologists, beginning with the destructive dig carried out by the amateur archaeologist G. Schumacher in 1903–5 and terminating with the systematic excavations by a team from the Chicago Oriental Institute in 1925–9. This later dig, financed by the Rockefeller Foundation, was the most ambitious enterprise of its kind carried out in Palestine in that period. The entire mound was purchased and beautiful accommodations (including tennis-courts) were erected near the site to assure the expedition staff their comfort for many years, for the initial plan was to excavate the whole *tell* by peeling off layer after layer – an elaborate plan that was soon abandoned. Despite the methodical excavations of the Oriental Institute, quite a number of stratigraphic problems remained without satisfactory solutions, mainly because the constant change of expedition directors impaired the continuity, and efforts to bridge the discrepancies between the various expeditions were not always successful.

The main buildings attributed by the excavators to the Solomonic period were in their stratum IV from the top, where they discovered the by-now-famous two complexes of stables: one on the southern side of the western half of the *tell* (called the southern stables) and the second on the northern side of the eastern half of the *tell* (the

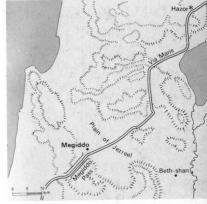

above The dominating position of Megiddo, guarding the 'Megiddo Pass', which connects the coast with the Plain of Jezreel

below Plan of stratum IV at Megiddo, showing the two groups of stables

northern stables). Stratigraphically, there was no doubt that the stables were contemporary with a solid offsets-insets wall (surrounding the whole mound), which the excavators ascribed to Solomon. Hence it followed that the stables, too, should be ascribed to Solomon. To this same 'Solomonic' wall, the excavators also attributed the six-chambered city gate, which we now know for sure was built by Solomon. Under the complex of stratum IV, the excavators of Megiddo discovered earlier strata still within the Iron Age, that is, from the twelfth century to the tenth century BC. Each of these strata consisted of at least two phases, and they were therefore labelled, from top to bottom, VA and VB, VIA and VIB, VIIA and VIIB (the last one turned out to be the final phase of the Bronze Age in the thirteenth century, contemporary with stratum XIII at Hazor. Thus we can say that the first Iron Age city in Megiddo is that of stratum VIIA). So far so good, and everything was relatively smooth from the chronological and stratigraphical viewpoints. Then came the first catch.

Stratigraphy set by Oriental Institute excavators

IV	Stables, offsets-insets wall (325) – Solomon
IVB	Palace 1723, building 1482 – Solomon? David?
VA	
VB	*Iron Age strata*
VIA	
VIB	
VIIA	First Iron Age city (12th century)
VIIB	13th century

Solomon the builder as wrecker?

The 'Solomonic' city wall (325) discovered above ruined building 1723, built in Solomonic style

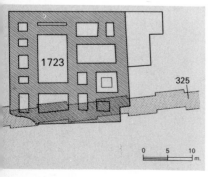

The first problem arose as a result of a surprising discovery on the south side of the *tell*, just east of the southern stables. Here a building measuring 20 × 22 metres was discovered (labelled 1723 by the excavator). It may have been a palace or a fort for it was built of beautifully dressed ashlar stones, similar – in fact identical – in style to those found in the Solomonic gate. The astonished excavators realized that the thick, so-called Solomonic city wall (325) had been erected *on the ruins* of that palace. Moreover, west of the palace, but stratigraphically contemporary with it, a huge, well-conceived structure (1482) was discovered partially under the foundations of the southern stables complex; so it, too, preceded the stables and the adjacent city wall! Once it became clear that one could not ascribe these two buildings to stratum IV, and since the number V had already been used up to mark other ruins, the Megiddo excavators ascribed the palace and structure 1482 to stratum IVB. But here they encountered a problem that defied explanation.

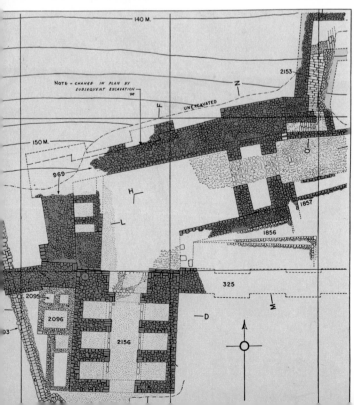

above The southern half of Solomon's city gate (looking south-west)

left Plan of Solomon's gate and the solid wall (325), as published by the Megiddo excavators (colours added by the author)

As the excavators were quite certain that the stables and the solid offsets-insets wall (325) had been built by Solomon, and that the palace and structure 1482 were also Israelite (for the style of their stone is identical to that of the Solomonic gate), they were left with one of two explanations, neither of which was logically or historically tenable. One possibility was that the palace was built at the beginning of Solomon's rule, before the city had been fortified, when it had been an isolated structure; the adjacent building 1482 may then have served as the governor's residence, with an excellent vantage point on the entire region. Later on – so they claimed – when Solomon's engineers were about to fortify the city, this palace stood in their way; and so they demolished it and built the offsets-insets wall on top of its ruins. This explanation was coupled with the assumption that the palace may even have been demolished before its construction was completed. Alternatively, the excavators postulated that the palace had been built by David, only to be destroyed by Solomon when he rebuilt Megiddo. Both these explanations assumed that Solomon himself destroyed the two grandest Israelite structures existing in Megiddo in order to build the solid wall and stables.

The first assumption is illogical because Solomon's architects and engineers were certainly competent enough to avoid making such a crude mistake. The second alternative is impossible for historical reasons: the Bible explicitly states that Solomon rebuilt Megiddo, Hazor and Gezer; David, busy enough with other affairs, did not engage in building enterprises and could not even build the Temple in Jerusalem. He certainly did not build a city in Gezer; and at Hazor, as we shall see, there were no Israelite fortifications prior to Solomon. Had David built a city in Megiddo, surely the Bible would stress the fact for its very uniqueness. And even were we to assume that it was David who built stratum IVB, we would have to conclude that the palace had been destroyed not by Solomon but by some enemy during David's reign or at the beginning of Solomon's reign, a conclusion that has no support in the written sources of any country in the region.

These problems were indeed baffling even before our excavations at Hazor and the subsequent identification of Solomon's fortifications at Gezer. Two foremost American archaeologists, W.F. Albright and G. Ernest Wright, made some ingenious and valiant efforts to clarify the stratigraphy of the discoveries. They proved conclusively that not only the palace and structure 1482 should be ascribed to stratum IVB, but also a number of other structures wrongly attributed by their excavators to what seemed to be another stratum, VA. Thus Albright and Wright introduced yet another 'new stratum' (which they called IVB–VA). But even they did not succeed in overcoming the main difficulty, for they accepted the assumption of the excavators that the Solomonic stratum was stratum IV proper, the one with

opposite Our last season of excavations, December 1971– January 1972, was carried out under a plastic shed for protection against the rain

the stables and the solid wall. In fact they, too, had to assume that the palace and other buildings were built in David's time, which, as we have seen, was historically impossible. These experiences made us realize that the stumbling block in ascribing the solid wall to Solomon lay not only in its architectural difference from the Solomonic casemate wall at Hazor and Gezer, but also in its very stratigraphy.

In order to clarify these problems of Megiddo's walls in Solomon's times, I began a brief excavation there in 1960. It lasted only a few days, but it resulted in startling discoveries. However, my subsequent archaeological activities in 1960–1 in the Bar-Kokhba caves and the enormous excavations at Masada in 1963–5 delayed the detailed report of our short Megiddo dig. When we were finally ready to tackle the problem for publication in 1965, I realized that it was imperative to re-examine the stratigraphic problems related to our 1960 discoveries, especially the dates of another important discovery made in Megiddo: the well-known water system. I therefore carried out other short digs in Megiddo, the first for about twelve days in 1967 and again for ten days as recently as the end of 1971 and beginning of 1972. All these explorations were regarded, in a way, as *post*

A series of brief digs

On the first day of excavations in an earlier season, students removed stones from city wall 325. The Plain of Jezreel can be seen in the background

The area of '*post mortem*' excavations can be seen in the centre left of this aerial view of Megiddo. The 'water shaft' is at the bottom right

mortems, operations on the 'prostrate corpse' of the partially excavated *tell*. Let us now see what was found during these digs.

The first surprise – another palace

I suspected that during Solomon's reign, Megiddo, like Hazor, had casemate-wall fortifications which were later (in Ahab's times) covered by a solid wall, and that this possibility escaped the earlier excavators. The area we selected for our trial dig in 1960 was located on the northern side of the eastern half of the *tell*, east of the Schumacher trench. In that area the offsets-insets wall had not been removed by the earlier excavators and was thus well preserved. Furthermore, an aerial photograph published by them showed some houses under the wall and near it that were neither marked on the plan nor discussed in the final report. We attached particular importance to the fact that the northern stable complex, which had been only partially dug, was also located here, and its remains were still strewn around the area.

The first day of excavation brought our first surprise. As we started

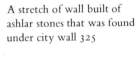

A photograph of solid wall 325 and earlier walls nearby taken by the excavators of Megiddo

A stretch of wall built of ashlar stones that was found under city wall 325

marking the exact spot for our trench, and while we were standing outside the offsets–insets wall on the slope north of it, we realized that what seemed to be the lower part of the wall foundations was actually built in a straight line, devoid of offsets and insets, measuring 28 metres. It also seemed that while the wall itself had been constructed of field stones (or small dressed stones) to strengthen the corners of the offsets and insets, this stretch of wall was built of ashlar stones, some of which had margins dressed in the same manner as Solomon's gate and the southern palace discovered by the earlier excavators. That part of the wall stopped abruptly in a straight and perpendicular line at its western end, with particularly large ashlars dressed and laid in header–stretcher fashion, similar to those of the six-chambered gate.

While contemplating this fact, it occurred to me that the offsets–insets wall here must have been built over the foundations of some external wall of a palace, or fort, built on the *tell*'s edge, like the southern

Detail of the ashlars, showing the typical Israelite style of stone dressing

The walls of the newly discovered palace 6000 found under the stables (see plan opposite)

Farewell to Solomon's stables

palace 1723. In order to verify that assumption, we decided carefully to peel off the foundations of the offsets-insets wall above the beautiful ashlars at what appeared to be the north-west corner of the building. Should our assumption prove correct, then the western wall of the building would be under the foundations of the offsets-insets wall, continuing south into the city. Sure enough, the wall was found as soon as the foundations were removed. It was about 1.5 metres thick and built of ashlars laid in header-stretcher fashion, both inside and outside – similar to the technique used in building the southern palace.

We followed that wall into the city and discovered that it extended not only under the offsets-insets wall but even under the foundations of the northern stable complex. This meant that if the Solomonic stratum was not the one associated with the offsets-insets wall, then the stables, too, were not Solomonic but belonged to a later monarch, perhaps Ahab. I remember that our conclusion shook the Israel Ministry of Tourism and the National Parks Authority, for Solomon's stables were one of the major tourist attractions in Megiddo. I suggested that they be labelled Ahab's stables – or perhaps Jezebel's stables, after Ahab's better-known half – but to no avail. To this day, visitors are being shown around Solomon's stables (though Solomon is now placed in quotation marks).

In due course, as we continued excavating this large structure, we succeeded in ascertaining its plan. We were particularly impressed by its southern front, where the thickness of the beautifully built wall reached over 2 metres. The building is rectangular in shape; its length from east to west is about 28 metres and from north to south about

21 metres, occupying a built-up area of 600 square metres, slightly more than the southern palace. The building's front faced south; in the north, on the very edge of the *tell*, were five rooms, while the east and west side had elongated halls. One of the structure's corners must have had a tower, and the other corner a square room. Although the excavations of this palace (marked 6000) have not yet been completed, the plan can be reconstructed, and a glance at it shows that it greatly resembles the type of palaces known from northern Syria and other sites on the Phoenician coast – all from the very early centuries of the first millennium, including the Solomonic era. This type of building served as a ceremonial palace. Those entering it from the wide front found themselves in a central court surrounded by rooms on three flanks. The similarity between this building and others in Phoenicia is particularly interesting, for it adds evidence to the biblical assertion of Phoenician influence on Solomon's building techniques. But it was the stratigraphic problem that concerned us most. Our dig clearly indicated that here, as on the southern edge of the *tell*, there existed monumental buildings identical in style to the

left Plan showing the position of Solomon's palace 6000, with its casemate wall, under the stables and above strata VB and VIA
right Store jars found in a palace casemate were evidence of sudden destruction

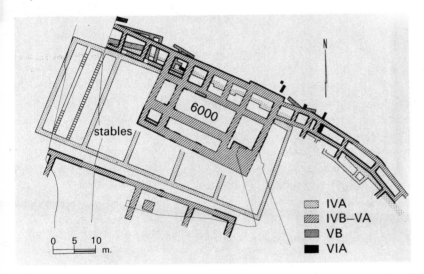

6000
stables

IVA
IVB–VA
VB
VIA

0 5 10
m.

Solomonic gate. In other words, what we found was not an isolated structure, but a large city with magnificent buildings. In some of the palace rooms we found much pottery *in situ* – store jars, juglets, dishes and cooking pots – all characteristic of the tenth century BC – in a state that indicated sudden destruction.

Who was responsible for the destruction of the Solomonic city? Fortunately we have a water-tight clue corroborated by no less than three witnesses: the Bible, Egyptian sources and the spade. When Solomon died, his son Rehoboam succeeded him. We are told in I Kings 14:25–6 that 'in the fifth year of King Rehoboam, Shishak king of Egypt came up against Jerusalem; he took away the treasures of the house of the Lord and the treasures of the king's house; he took

A peg for absolute chronology

away everything. He also took away all the shields of gold which Solomon had made . . .' These biblical verses state unequivocally that Shishak penetrated the heart of the kingdom to the capital. But they do not indicate what happened to the rest of the country, particularly the north. The Egyptian king's invasion is also recorded in II Chronicles 12, where the Bible elaborates somewhat:

> In the fifth year of King Rehoboam, because they had been unfaithful to the Lord, Shishak king of Egypt came up against Jerusalem with twelve hundred chariots and sixty thousand horsemen. And the people were without number who came with him from Egypt – Libyans, Sukki-im and Ethiopians. And he took the fortified cities of Judah and came as far as Jerusalem (2–5).

The chronicler here is mainly concerned with the Kingdom of Judah (one must remember that the kingdom of David and Solomon split after Solomon's death). But from Shishak's own records, which list the cities of Palestine occupied by him, we know that his troops penetrated far to the north; in fact, these records actually mention that he occupied Megiddo. But now comes the third and decisive piece of evidence. In previous excavations of Megiddo, a fragment of a monumental stele erected by Shishak was discovered. Small though it may be, the name of Shishak is clearly inscribed on it. Unfortunately the fragment was found in debris and not in a well-stratified *locus*, but it suffices to indicate that Shishak did indeed occupy Megiddo. All this data, and the fact that the crushed pottery on the floors of the Solomonic buildings are from the latter part of the tenth century, serve to prove that the destruction of Solomonic Megiddo was perpetrated by Shishak. Thus we also had an absolute date for the destruction of stratum 'IVB–VA', *circa* 923 BC.

Through careful examination of the ruins in the stratum under the stables – the Solomonic stratum – we came across an important technical phenomenon that helped us not only to locate another huge structure of the same period (south of palace 6000), but also to comprehend why the earlier Megiddo excavators had failed to locate the structures of Solomon's magnificent city. South of the palace, across a rather wide street, we discovered the remains of a large structure whose building style resembled that of other IVB – VA structures. But except for a few places where the lower stones were preserved, we noticed beautiful beaten-chalk floors extending up to what we assumed was the line of a wall and then stopping abruptly. It seemed that most of the beautiful ashlar stones of the Solomonic building had been uprooted. No doubt this was done mainly by the builders of the stables and the solid wall, who, we believe, were Ahab's builders – and why shouldn't they have exploited such excellent and available building material? This theory also explains why a number of stones bearing identical masons' marks were discovered in

Fragment of a victory stele erected by Shishak at Megiddo

Robbers' trenches

the IVB–VA Solomonic city and also in the stables. Once we realized this point, by closely following the floors and robbers' trenches we managed to uncover the remains of the huge structure, with a front at least 55 metres long and rooms and courtyards branching southwards (see plan on page 215). As stated, this structure was across the street from the palace, and unfortunately most of its southern section had vanished during the early excavations, which had gone to a great depth at that point.

Our primary objective in 1960 was to establish whether or not a casemate wall was hidden beneath the solid offsets-insets wall. The discovery of palace 6000 was a very important link in the clarification of the Solomonic stratum and its character, but our problem was the city's fortifications during that period. So we selected a section of the offsets-insets wall just east of palace 6000, only to find that the wall close to the corner of the palace was completely demolished, and both the offsets-insets wall and the upper coarses of the corner of the palace itself were missing. Surely this damage must have been the result of a relatively late destruction. We therefore started our trial trench about 10 metres east of the palace corner. After carefully peeling off the foundations of the offsets-insets wall, we hit a fill of earth and field stones, and immediately beneath it a casemate wall emerged! All told, we excavated about a 35-metre stretch of the casemate wall and found remains of three long and two short casemates.

above The first sign of the casemates: the outer wall and a room wall appear under the removed foundations of solid wall 325 (a worker stands on 325)
left The entire stretch of the eastern casemate wall (looking east)

The length of the long casemate is about 7 metres. Where the wall turns towards the fort at an obtuse angle, there are additional smaller casemates. The casemate wall here is weaker than the one at Hazor, a fact that is easily understandable since the much higher and steeper slope here makes attack from that side impossible. Even the later solid wall of the offsets and insets did not seem strong to the excavator Colonel P.L.O. Guy, who wrote about it as follows:

At Megiddo greater strength was hardly necessary for it crowned a steep and high slope of the tell itself; the distance which attackers would have had to climb from the plain to the base of that part of the wall . . . is well over 30 metres, and a wall of this thickness would have constituted a formidable obstacle to the reduced number who could survive such a climb under fire from the summit.

We were fortunate to discover between the palace and the city gate

above P.L.O. Guy's field box, re-used by us, is seen near a stone manger adjacent to a stable wall

Western casemates, as left by the Megiddo excavators (looking south-east)

The same western casemates during the course of excavations (looking north)

an even finer portion of the casemate wall – sturdier in structure and more beautiful in design. From the outset of our excavations, we discerned a walltop made of ashlar stones and constructed mainly of headers at a spot west of the palace and in a level below that of the solid wall and the stables. This wall had already been uncovered by the Megiddo excavators, but it was neither marked on their plans nor mentioned in their reports. The upper photograph on page 218 shows the area prior to our excavations. As soon as we began digging, it appeared that openings were interspersed in this wall at fixed intervals. Further examination proved that these openings led to casemates whose external (northern) wall was built of large, partially dressed field stones and extended in a westerly direction towards the city gate as a direct continuation of the northern wall of the palace. Its construction is similar to that of the casemates on the east side of the *tell*. In later years we also excavated these casemates, and altogether

The casemates between the palace and the gate

The eastern casemates (bottom, left) and corner of palace 6000 towards the end of the dig. Note the flimsy walls of stratum VB under the casemate's floor

opposite Close view of an eastern casemate (looking north). Note the 'headers and stretchers'

uncovered two complete casemates and one-half of a third.

We did not manage to uncover the western extension of these casemates, for here the Schumacher trench had destroyed all previous remains. As a result we cannot know what he discovered from actual evidence, nor can anything be learned from his publications. But there seems to be no doubt that these casemates continued westwards, towards the gate. Theoretically, as we stated at the time, it could be argued that the casemates belonged to the northern part of a court that might have surrounded the palace. But it became clear in the course of excavations that this hypothesis did not make sense, since no remains of such a court were found. Could it be that both Schumacher and the American excavators had come upon the casemates between our trench and the gate without discerning them? It is possible, since, as we already observed, some sections were marked in their plan while others, also uncovered by them, were not. On the other hand, it is feasible that the wall in this particular section was deliberately demolished by the builders of the offsets-insets wall in order to re-use its stones. It is from this section of the mound that a very sharp slope begins towards the gate, and it is conceivable that when the offsets-insets wall was built, the earlier wall could not support it, and as a result the entire area had to be rearranged.

Checking Solomon's stratum from below

Although the evidence demonstrated quite clearly that the newly excavated stratum and buildings under the stables and the solid wall actually belonged to Solomon, it was imperative to double check whether that particular stratum would fit Solomon's period when counting upwards from the strata below. Theoretically, it could be argued that the palace and fortifications we found – albeit older than the stables and solid wall – were in fact very much older. Here, of course, we were aided by the previous excavations, which demon-strated that under stratum IVB there were several strata belonging to the early Iron Age. Two of these are of direct interest to us. Stratum V had a lower (earlier) phase that the excavators marked VB. Below it were the two phases of what they marked stratum VI, the upper of which (VIA) was more important not only as a city, but also as a guideline for us archaeologists. Stratum VIA is a burned layer that is easily recognizable all over the site. Wherever we reached it, we struck a thick layer of ashes covering the remains of well-built brick buildings that contained great quantities of pottery typical of the eleventh century BC. It is generally believed that this city was sacked and captured by David, and the poor VB city – or rather village – was actually a small Israelite settlement of David's time that was later replaced by Solomon's royal city. From the very begin-ning, we occasionally probed under the floor of our newly dis-covered palace 6000 and the casemate wall. Two of these digs are worthy of special attention not only because they proved that, strati-graphically, stratum IVB–VA was indeed Solomonic, but also because

opposite Solomon's and Ahab's Megiddo. In red are Solomon's two palaces (1723, 6000) and other public buildings (including 1482), water gallery 629, the casemate wall and the city gate. In blue are Ahab's chariot city with its stable complexes (1576, 403), the palatial building (338), the solid wall (325), city gate and underground water system (shaft, 925; tunnel, 1000; and spring cave, 1007)

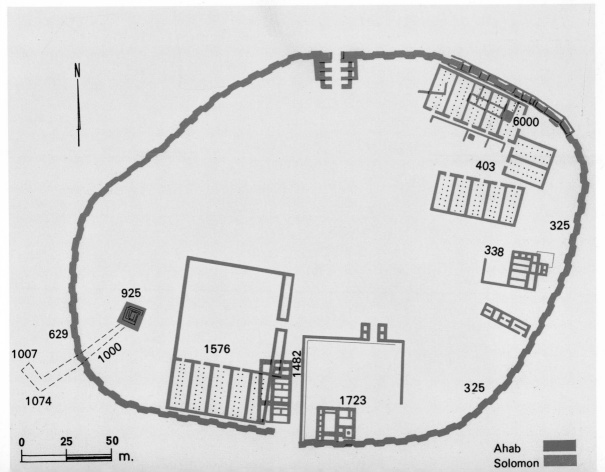

N

925

629

1007

1000

1074

1576

1482

1723

6000

403

325

338

325

0   25   50
            m.

Ahab
Solomon

A poor wall of stratum VB under the floor of Solomon's palace 6000

A huge quantity of pottery found among ashes, testimony to the violent destruction of stratum VIA (see next page)

of the important – though unexpected – finds of the previous periods.

We decided to dig under the floor of the north-west room of the palace in the hope of finding the remains of the huge conflagration of stratum VIA. Our hopes were not in vain. Beneath the palace floor we first came across the relatively poor walls of stratum VB (in itself a decisive point, because it proved that palace 6000 was of the IVB–VA stratum) and immediately under them we uncovered typical stratum VIA structures. These were completely covered by a thick layer of ashes in which we found a wealth of pottery, much of it lying in complete disarray on the floor. The pottery included the famous 'beer mugs' in the decadent Philistine style, ascribed to the second half of the eleventh century BC, and quite a number of flasks, all typical of the period. Thus we confirmed absolutely that the palace

belonged to stratum IVB–VA, whether one counted from the top downwards or from the bottom upwards.

This dig was aimed at double checking stratigraphic facts: walls, levels and *in situ* pottery. But even on this kind of expedition, the excitement among the excavators soared when we hit a veritable treasure that shed light on one of the interesting cultures of Megiddo – that of stratum VI, just preceding King David. When we removed the level of ashes and its pottery from the room under the threshold, we encountered a strange object, partially hidden and protected by a few surrounding sherds. It soon became clear that what we found were miraculously preserved remains of a woman's cloth bag. All of us are sometimes amazed and intrigued by the huge amount of objects that women manage to squeeze into their handbags. But we were absolutely flabbergasted when we 'emptied' *this* bag, which had been deliberately hidden under the threshold. Its anonymous owner managed to compress into it a huge amount of objects that must have been precious to her, such as nine ivory spindle whorls, two pomegranate-shaped pendants taken from a tripod (typical of the times), iron bracelets (among the earliest pieces of iron found in the country), a ring and hundreds of tiny beads and semi-precious stones.

A few of the vessels shown on page 222 (bottom), typical of the 11th century BC. Note the decadent Philistine 'beer mug' (bottom right) and the Philistine bowl decorated with a spiral (second row, second from left)

left A woman's bag, as found, covered with sherds
right The same with sherds removed, revealing the contents

The bag's contents after cleaning

opposite, above The small and elegant goat at rest held between two fingers, to serve as a scale of its size

opposite, below The two profiles of the apple-eating monkey

left The ivory spindle whorls
right A few of the semi-precious stones

left Two pomegranate-shaped bronze pendants
right A tripod base from Ugarit showing the position of pendants

The prize articles in this treasure, however, were two small bronze weights shaped like animals, one probably a goat at rest and the other a squatting monkey. The photographs on page 225 show them after cleaning. The horned animal is fashioned with outstanding delicacy. Before the haul was cleaned, we thought the monkey was of the 'see no evil, hear no evil, speak no evil' type; but after cleaning it appeared to be eating an apple-like object. We joked at the time about what seemed to be an artist's effort to depict Adam holding the apple in one hand and using the other to block his ears against Eve's importunate tirade!

A prototype of Adam

The 1966 dig left us with one problem that required thorough verification. We realized from the uncovered sections of the casemate wall that its foundations lay on the burned layer of stratum VIA. This meant that although we could attribute the wall (like palace 6000) to stratum IVB–VA when counting downwards, it could be argued that since it was built on stratum VIA, it was actually part of stratum VB. In that case, the casemate wall had been built before Solomon and had later been integrated into the Solomonic fortifications. Such a conclusion seemed illogical as city VB had no fortifications whatsoever. But it was nonetheless imperative to clarify the point. Towards that end I formed a special task-force in the 1967 dig headed by the expedition's chief architect, the late I. Dunayevsky, who was aided by two of the ablest graduates of our institute. Their mission was to come up with an independent verdict on the stratigraphy of that section. Work was deliberately slow and was carried out with the utmost care and delicate instruments. Those who have never participated in an archaeological excavation may think that the greatest joy of the excavator is to find hidden treasure or objects of artistic merit. Quite the contrary is true. For us the crowning discovery at Megiddo in 1967 was a few wretched walls of seeming insignificance; but in our case their importance was immense. These were the walls of stratum VB, sandwiched between the casemate wall above and the burned layer of stratum VIA below. Thus the circle closed. Here too, as in the palace, we had proof that the casemates belonged to stratum IVB–VA, counting both upwards and downwards. In short, our excavations proved that the Solomonic city of Megiddo – like Hazor and Gezer – was also fortified with a casemate wall, originally attached to the six-chambered Solomonic gate. Later, for a while, that gate was re-used together with the solid wall, until it was abandoned altogether and a new series of gates was erected in subsequent periods.

A 'dry' archaeological treasure

While digging at Megiddo to verify the stratigraphy of the fortifications, we also became involved with the problem of dating the city's magnificent underground water system. This point is important not only because of the new conclusion we arrived at concerning its date, but also because of the bearing this conclusion had on our future

A hidden water-supply system – Israelite or Canaanite?

'Gallery 629' (looking west)

excavations and discoveries at Hazor. To illuminate the problem in the context of our excavations, let me briefly describe the system and the dates attributed to it by previous excavators. The problem and its solution may seem a trifle complicated, but it is necessary to deal with them, and I hope that the plans will help the reader follow the 'whodunit' without much difficulty.

One of the most interesting and spectacular structures discovered by the Megiddo excavators on the south-east edge of the *tell*, near the southern stable complex, was labelled 'gallery 629'. This 'gallery' is none other than a narrow passage (slightly over 1 metre wide) that leads outwards from the city to the south-western slope of the *tell*, where a spring exists in a cave. The walls of the passage (revetment walls, since only the internal faces were well built) stood up to 2 metres high and were constructed of well-dressed ashlars laid in header-and-stretcher fashion. One may assume, as the excavators did, that the passage leading towards the spring was covered and camouflaged.

The fine ashlars of the gallery laid out in header-and-stretcher fashion and dressed in typical Solomonic style

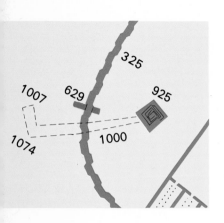

Stratigraphically speaking, the passage was found under the offsets-insets wall (which was, as said above, considered Solomonic by its excavators), and for that reason it was assumed that the 'gallery' had been built prior to Solomon. However, since it was impossible to ascribe this magnificent structure to the relatively poor strata of the eleventh century BC, it was attributed by the excavators to the reign of Ramses III (beginning of the twelfth century, *i.e.*, to their stratum VIIA), when Megiddo still retained some of its erstwhile splendour. Fixing the date of the 'gallery' was a cardinal point of departure for R. Lamon (one of the Chicago Oriental Institute archaeologists who published the report on the Megiddo water system) in dating the Megiddo water tunnel (which later gained fame as the subject of James Michener's best-seller *The Source*).

The water system consists of two parts: a vertical shaft and a horizontal tunnel that conducts the water from the spring to the shaft. The

above Water shaft 925, tunnel 1000, cave 1007, spring 1074 and city wall 325 – all of Ahab's period. Note the position of Solomon's gallery 629 under solid wall 325
right Plan and section of the water system as depicted for visitors on a National Parks Authority sign

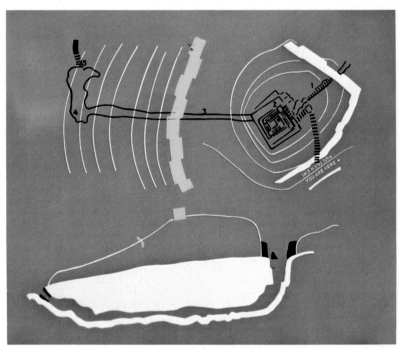

upper part of the shaft was cut by the original builders through layers of earlier strata, and its walls were lined with stone. Its lower part, on the other hand, was hewn out of rock. In order for the system to achieve its main aim – namely water supply in times of siege – the builders would have had to block the cave opening from the outside to prevent the enemy from poisoning the water or cutting off its source. And sure enough, when discovered by the Megiddo excavators, the entrance to the cave was blocked by a wall of huge stones. At first they sought to determine when the tunnel was cut by identifying the highest stratum through which the shaft was dug. It became apparent that higher strata bearing clear evidence of destruction by the shaft contained sherds from the Late Bronze period (the fourteenth or thirteenth century). The excavators could not check conditions above the highest stratum of the shaft as the strata above the shaft itself had collapsed in antiquity, together with part of the stone lining its walls. They concluded, therefore, that the latest possible date for the cutting of the shaft was the end of the thirteenth century.

Then, by the cave entrance, inside the blocking wall, the burned skeleton of a man was found. Lamon assumed that the man must have been the cave's guard, killed in enemy attack; and since there was no point in guarding the cave after it had been blocked, the guard must have died while the citizens of Megiddo still had access to the spring via a path down the slope, that is, before the shaft and tunnel were cut. Furthermore, the fact that the latest pottery found near the skeleton was of the twelfth century led to the assumption that the blocking of the cave – and therefore also the quarrying of the shaft and tunnel – took place in the middle of (rather than before) the twelfth century.

Having reviewed the conclusions held by archaeologists before we arrived at Megiddo, let us return to the point of departure: the 'gallery'. Lamon assumed correctly that the gallery's function was to provide access to the spring before the advent of the shaft-tunnel water system. In his opinion, therefore, it must have belonged to the first half of the twelfth century. Our approach to the dating problem was from another angle, however. Having spent so much time delving into stratigraphy, we decided to apply our finds to the question of the water system as well. Earlier I stated that the gallery was found under the offsets-insets wall. The previous excavators had attributed this wall to Solomon, but as early as 1960 we had already proved that this wall was post-Solomonic. Therefore, there was no further reason to suppose that the gallery pre-dated Solomon. On the contrary, the gallery's stratigraphic circumstances were identical to those of the southern palace and all the other structures in Solomonic stratum IVB–VA. Moreover, the method of construction and stone dressing used in the gallery matched to a startling degree the construction method employed in that stratum.

In 1960 I scraped the vicinity of the gallery just enough to verify that its foundations were built into the fallen, burned bricks of stratum VIA. We therefore assumed, once again, that the gallery had been built after the destruction of VIA but before the offsets-insets wall, and so wrote in our preliminary report. But as the dating of the water system is of paramount importance, in 1966 we decided to check our assumptions by actual excavations. The method was simple enough: since it was obvious that the gallery had been dug into previous strata, we selected an adjacent square to the south of it and began to excavate

The 'gallery'

When in doubt, excavate!

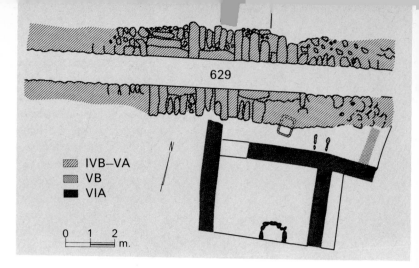

629

▨ IVB–VA
▩ VB
■ VIA

N

0   1   2
└──┴──┴──┘ m.

right Schematic plan showing how gallery 629 cut through earlier strata VB and VIA
below A stone from the gallery bearing a mason's mark identical to those found on other Solomonic buildings

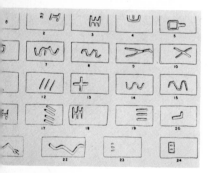

Masons' marks from Solomonic buildings at Megiddo

thoroughly. Our purpose was to date the uppermost stratum that had been damaged when the gallery had been dug. We were fortunate indeed! Descending down to stratum VIIA, we noted the whole array of strata familiar from our digs in other areas and even enriched the pottery repertoire of some. But more important, it became decisively clear that the creation of the gallery had damaged – in fact, cut through like scissors – the buildings of stratum VB. Thus the gallery was squeezed in between IVA and VB, stratigraphically speaking, both when counting from top to bottom and from bottom to top. It was built in the period of stratum IVB–VA, just like the palaces and Solomon's gate.

Had we needed further proof for the attribution of the gallery to IVB–VA, we now came across it accidentally. Since the excavation of the gallery by the previous Megiddo team, some of its stones had come loose and fallen to the ground. Upon overturning one such stone, we noticed that it bore a mason's mark identical to marks discovered in stratum IVB–VA structures and in secondary use in stratum IV. Thus it follows that the gallery must be dated to the Solomonic period. Taking this conclusion one step further, the magnificent shaft-tunnel water system must therefore have been post-Solomonic, that is, cut at the beginning of the ninth century during the reign of Omri's house or, more specifically, during Ahab's rule, when the stables were built.

We can say today that the city of stratum IVB–VA was undoubtedly the one built by Solomon. This conclusion is derived not only from the biblical statement that Solomon rebuilt Megiddo, but also from all the pottery, architectural (the style of stone dressing and the building plans) and stratigraphic evidence. No more are we confronted with merely a single fort, but with a metropolis of stately buildings clearly built to accommodate ceremonial functions. This city is surrounded by a casemate wall with a gigantic gate composed of six chambers and two towers, and it has a secret passage (the 'gallery') leading to the water spring. The passage is built in the same style as the other

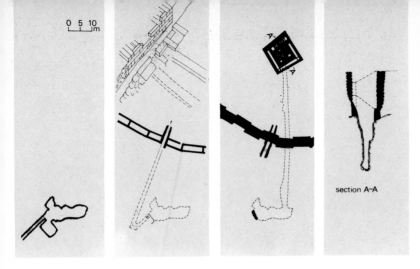

section A-A

structures and offers added proof for the existence of a wall around the city. The discovery of two palaces may lead us even to assume that the southern palace was the residence of Solomon's governor Baana, son of Ahilud (1 Kings 4:12), while the newly discovered northern palace (6000) served ceremonial purposes and perhaps even to house the king himself whenever he visited Megiddo.

The city that was built on top of the ruined Solomonic stratum differed considerably in character and plan. It was not just an administrative city, but a well-fortified chariot city (accommodating up to 450 horses) with a hidden water system for times of siege and, of course, a governor's residence. In this stratum (IVA) some repairs are visible, and there seems no doubt that it was used over a long period, reaching its height most probably in Ahab's days, as hinted in an important inscription of Shalmaneser III, king of Assyria. According to this document, it seems that among the coalition forces fighting against Shalmaneser in the battle of Qarqar (835 BC), Ahab's chariot force (2,000 chariots) was the largest of all. Indeed, it is interesting to note that the Megiddo excavators tended to ascribe this city to Solomon because of the biblical reference to chariot cities built by him. On the other hand, nowhere is it mentioned that Megiddo, Hazor and Gezer were chariot cities. Another interesting fact is that neither in Hazor nor in Gezer were stables discovered in the Solomonic stratum (or, for that matter, in any other stratum). Be that as it may, Megiddo's greatness as a fortified city in Ahab's times must have continued – as with Hazor – until its destruction by Tiglath-pileser III in 732 BC. If our excavations have deprived Solomon of his famous stables, we may console ourselves with the fact that we have returned to its glory his true city – which was no less magnificent than the cities of the northern kings of Israel who ruled after him – and that we were also able to date the two water systems found in Megiddo within the Israelite period. This latter point is a crucial one and, as promised, has direct bearing on the description of our next major discovery at Hazor. So we can now return to the original site of our inquiry.

left History of the Megiddo source (from left to right): the cave and source in the Bronze Age; in Solomon's period; in Ahab's period; and section of the water shaft (925)
right The Megiddo water tunnel

A stone manger in Ahab's stables

15 The Source

The problem of water supply to Israelite Hazor in times of siege intrigued me from the outset, but for years I postponed probing into it because there were no clear-cut clues as to where such an installation could be found, and the cost of digging at random in order to check a theory would have been prohibitive. After my digs at Megiddo – which established that the famous water system for times of siege had been constructed in the ninth century (approximately the period of stratum VIII on the *tell* of Hazor) and proved the similarity between the two cities from an historical and archaeological point of view – it became almost self-evident that a similar water system should have existed in Hazor. I remember the long discussions I had with James Michener about the problems of Hazor and Megiddo when he was researching his famous novel *The Source*. Later on Hazor served, in a way, as the model for his imaginary site of *Makor*. But for the water system – the source itself – Michener had to resort to Megiddo. Furthermore, the existence in other Israelite cities of some sort of underground installation to supply water in times of siege – like Hezekiah's famous tunnel in Jerusalem or a similar installation in Gibeon, just north of Jerusalem – was a clear indication that in the times of Ahab, a well-fortified city such as Hazor, and one of such highly strategic importance, must also have had a sophisticated system of water supply for siege conditions. Our deduction from comparative evidence was unequivocal: a water system existed. But where were we to look for it?

In addition to the logical assumption, we had two clues to help us locate such an installation, which should have had a vertical shaft inside the city ending in a tunnel that led to the external water source. South of the mound, near the present highway to the north, there is a deep ravine covered with green shrubs all year round. In it were – and still are – several natural springs, where the shepherds of Rosh Pinah water their flocks in the hot summer months. Nowadays, most of the springs are tapped by the Israel Water-Supply Company,

A deduction from comparative evidence

Two clues

opposite The scaffolding and wagon rail used to empty the silt and debris from the 'source' (looking east)

The springs of Hazor (looking south)

The depression on the morning of the first day of excavations

Workers surveying the area of the depression, where one of the field latrines had been built

Mekorot, but some still exist in various places. I believed that if Hazor had a water system similar to Megiddo's, it would have been on the southern edge of the mound, as close as possible to the springs. Indeed, in the southern area of the upper mound, we could discern from the outset – on aerial photographs as well as with the naked eye – a very shallow depression that could not be explained by any visible structural remains. In fact, it was here that we had built one of our field latrines in 1955, believing that somehow the spot was discreetly hidden from the rest of the mound.

When I returned to Hazor in 1968 after ten years of absence, I was determined to put to the test my theory about the possible location of a hidden water system in that shallow depression. I knew that if I were right, we would have to dig at least 40 metres below the surface to reach the water level indicated by the springs at the foot of the mound. Half the labour force at my disposal was put to this task at the newly chosen area, designated L. This is how it looked on the first day of excavations: nothing was visible on the surface. I might

add that quite a number of the members of my staff were very sceptical about the chances of our finding the water system there. The one member who stuck by me all along was Y. Shiloh, who was in charge of the work team in area L. And, to be fair, I should add that more than the fate of a theory was at stake here: quite a few bottles of whiskey were riding on the outcome of our probe both among and *beyond* the expedition staff.

The experience of the excavators in Megiddo, Gibeon and other sites in which water systems were discovered taught us that the most difficult problem in excavating a water system of this sort is to determine the date of its construction; dating its last use is, naturally, easy, because this can be decided according to the latest objects found within. The best, in fact almost the only dating method is to try and ascertain the date of the topmost strata cut by the builders of the vertical shaft (as we did at Megiddo). This would at least give us the *post-quem* date, meaning the date prior to which the shaft could not have been cut. Our first step was to obtain a definitive and objective picture of the stratification of the area by examining the layers and plans of the structures adjacent to the depression. Having established that data, we hoped to ascertain the dates of the strata cut through by the shaft by comparing them with the adjacent strata and structures for evidence of contemporaneity. The proximity of the shaft to the edge of the mound suggested that a good starting point for fixing the stratigraphy might be the Solomonic casemate wall that must have existed there, since we had found parts of it east and west of that spot. We began our excavations by cutting a long trench, 5 metres wide from north to south, just off the centre of the depression and tallying with the excavations' grid. Sure enough, after a few days of digging, the first casemate – filled with scores of storage jars of the Solomonic period – emerged

How to dig?

The trial trench dug across the depression (looking south)

left The Solomonic casemate
wall (looking east) – a
stratigraphic peg
right Store jars found in a
casemate (looking south)

A stumbling block

right on the edge. Another encouraging sign at the very start of work
in the depression was the lack of any proper structures belonging to
periods *prior* to the abandonment of the mound; in fact, the whole
area was filled with silt containing considerable quantities of late
artefacts, including Persian, Hellenistic, Byzantine and even Arab
pottery. Once the nature of this accumulation had been determined,
we employed even heavier equipment to help remove the debris.
It was indeed a good beginning.

Then for a while our spirits fell, because in the centre of the depression
we came upon a large area paved with field stones. The odds were
going against finding the water system here, for this looked like
remains of a pool built to collect rainwater. Furthermore, the sloping
terraces of the depression's side walls were lined with stones. The
wags among us began referring to the depression as 'the depressing
area'. But then I remembered that a similar phenomenon had been

The heavy equipment used for
removing silt

encountered at Megiddo. There the abandoned water shaft, which
had been clogged with debris, was later used as a water pool; so perhaps
the same applied here. The very possibility encouraged us enough
to continue digging and cut through this paved area. Below it unusual
crude structures began to emerge again. A number of terrace-like sub-
structures, almost circular in shape and made of small field stones,
surrounded the deepest point of the depression. But we again convinced
ourselves that this did not yet preclude the existence of a water shaft.
It may have been that soon after the shaft went out of use these structures
were built to facilitate the drawing of water collected here. Jars could
well have been placed on the terraces, which were found on two
consecutive levels. And considering that in a rainy year these terraces
could be covered with silt, it was not even necessary to conclude that
the two levels indicated two distinct strata, although such a conclusion
was, of course, possible. At this stage of the excavation, one fact

left A circular, paved area at
the centre of the depression
right The terrace of the
depression composed of field
stones (looking north)

The circular, terrace-like
sub-structures for resting water
jars

A corner of the revetment
wall – an encouraging sign

Some of the workers from
the neighbouring village of
Hazor

encouraged me and strengthened my feeling that we might still
find the vertical water shaft. In a corner of the depression we uncovered
part of a huge revetment wall whose foundations went much deeper
than the level of our excavations. If my theory proved right, this was
part of a revetment wall built above the upper part of the rock-hewn
shaft to line and protect that part of the shaft which had been cut
through the strata of debris. But at that moment we were still some
35 metres above the assumed water level. Before proceeding further,
however, we cut a section under the circular terraces to verify the
absence of structures and debris composed of fallen earth and stones.

A considerable part of the excavation season had passed when I
came to the conclusion that were we to proceed at the present pace,
digging mainly by hand, it might take us years to descend to our

A young worker admiring the energies of another

target – if it indeed existed. This thought was particularly depressing as most of our labourers, though good natured, were rather old. Not that I thought that at the current rate of progress the Angel of Death would beat us to goal. But although these workers excelled in the delicate technique of surface digging, they were hardly fit for the arduous task of excavating down another 40 metres; and the few younger workers preferred to sit back and admire the work of the young girl volunteers wearing bikinis. I therefore decided to employ a huge crane with two iron claws, and it was no mean operation just to haul it up onto the mound. I detailed a few archaeologists to work in close collaboration with the crane operator and carefully examine the contents of the earth and debris brought up by the crane. Finally the work progressed quickly, and soon came the first 'sign of the dove'.

The crane at work

The turning point: the rock scarp is uncovered (looking south-east)

In the south-east corner, not far away from the revetment wall and the remains of buildings nearby, we hit a vertical scarp of the rock. This could be none other than the uppermost part of the long-sought vertical shaft. Our excitement mounted. After many weeks of work, the shaft began to show through at various sides of the dig, and, even more important, broad steps had been cut out of its side for descent. The entire area was clogged with debris of the supporting walls,

The shaft emerges from the debris (looking south-east)

and the accumulation of silt swept down from the slopes probably began right after the destruction of the last defended Israelite city (stratum V) in 732 BC.

When we reached a depth of about 30 metres from the top, we suddenly had a hunch that something was 'wrong' in this water system. As we descended, the original width of the shaft's opening became progressively narrower due to the winding stairs hugging its walls, and we were still about 10 to 15 metres above the water level! When work began we all thought that the vertical shaft would descend as low as the water level itself and then turn into a tunnel leading to the springs outside the city – as it had at Megiddo. Yet at this point the shaft became so narrow that, according to our calculations, there was no possibility of it going straight down another 10 metres. There was simply no room left for a shaft plus stairs. Once again the odds turned against the water-system theory, and some of the staff thought we had found a pool or even a grain silo. Nonetheless, my hopes remained obstinate, and having come so far I was intent on pursuing this course to the end, bitter though it might be. Then, suddenly, the secret of the water system began to reveal itself, and though vindicated, even I could not resist a wry smile at our twist of fate. Although my faith that the system would be found here paid off, the reasoning behind it proved to be slightly off course. In fact, we all learned a

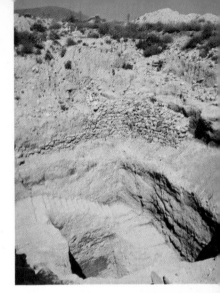

above The revetment wall and the shaft (looking north-west)

below Broad hewn steps for the dual carriage-way

The great surprise: the
discovery of the tunnel in the
west wall

lesson in humility that day, for it turned out that the original planners
and engineers of the system were far more clever than the archaeologists
who pursued their trail.

In the south-west corner of the shaft, we saw the pointed top of a
tunnel that seemed to lead not southwards, where the springs were,
but westwards. At first we could not grasp the meaning of what we
saw, but as soon as some of the debris near the tunnel's opening had
been cleared, we managed to descend into it and found ourselves on
top of a huge accumulation of fallen stones (from the revetment wall)
and other debris. Advancing about 25 metres first to the west and then
in a south-westerly direction, and at the same time descending another
10 metres due to the tunnel's downward slope, we arrived at the tunnel's
end. And there it was: pure water shone up at us! It is difficult to
describe how we felt at that moment. We breathed air that had been

The long-searched-for prize:
water

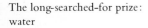

compressed in this tunnel for 3,000 years and touched the source of life of Israelite Hazor. It appeared that the original engineers knew – or at least suspected – that the water-table which fed the springs outside the city also existed within the confines of the settlement. Thus the water system here was even better protected than the one at Megiddo, as the entire installation was within the city wall and went down to bedrock.

Although the upper part of the tunnel was clear of debris, the rest of it was covered with fallen stones, particularly near the entrance. It took us nearly a year to finish clearing the tunnel of debris and it was an extremely difficult job! We had to build scaffolding and a miniature rail from top to bottom for a little wagon, operated by a generator, to haul up the cleared silt and debris. But eventually the whole installa-

The great tunnel, as found, looking from the entrance towards the west

tion was cleared and was a magnificent sight to behold, especially from the vantage of the inside looking out. The remains of buildings close to the top of the stone-lined shaft also gave us an exact date. Those of the Solomonic stratum (X) were sliced through by the builders of the shaft, while adjacent to the shaft we found structures related to the system that clearly belonged to stratum VIII, Ahab's period. So the water system must have been built during the times of Ahab, just as in Megiddo.

By the time our operation ended, we had a clear idea of the plan of the water system, which comprised three elements: an entrance structure, a vertical shaft and a sloping tunnel.

left Viewing the shaft from inside the tunnel
above An aerial view (looking west) of the shaft (compare plan), with Ahab's four-room structure on the left and Solomon's casemate wall on the extreme left

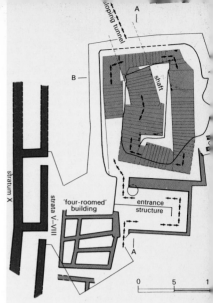

Plan of the water shaft and
vicinity (compare with aerial
photograph at left)

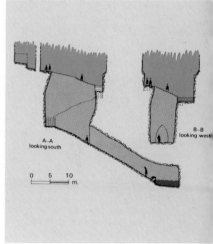

Two sections of the water
shaft and the tunnel

By the south-east corner of the top of the shaft, near the edge of
the mound, we found the entrance structure, which was carefully
planned to minimize the angle of the slope from the level of the city
to the top of the shaft. It comprised two ramps: one going from south
to north and ending on a landing, the second continuing from north
to south and on to the shaft.

The shaft itself consisted of two parts: the upper part had been cut
through the early strata of the *tell*; the lower one had been quarried
through rock. The upper part measures about 19 × 15 metres and its
depth from the top of the mound is about 10 metres. This section was
shored up by huge revetment walls mainly on the southern and western

sides (where the virgin rock was relatively lower due to the natural south-westerly slope of the area), and these supporting walls were well preserved up to a height of 4 metres, mostly in the corners. The depth of the rock-hewn part of the shaft is about 20 metres, so the total depth of the shaft is some 30 metres. (The horizontal dimensions diminish, of course, as one descends.) The descent is effected by means of beautiful rock-cut steps that reach up to 3 metres in width. The entire staircase extends down five flights, each flight running along one of the shaft's four walls, beginning and ending with the southern wall. But the fifth flight only begins on the southern wall and then widens out to take up the entire width of the shaft until it merges

The shaft, steps and tunnel
(looking west)

with the staircase of the tunnel (described below). The generous width of the stairs suggests the possibility that the water may have been carried by pack animals, and sufficient space had to be provided for simultaneous ascent and descent. At any rate, it is clear that the staircase was a dual carriage-way, and even if it were meant solely for the water drawers – most probably the women – it allowed ample space for them to go up and down without clashing with one another.

The tunnel is pointed in shape and 4.5 metres high. The entrance to it is about 4 metres wide, but the tunnel narrows slightly about 9 metres in before widening again; and at the end, which is a sort of pool, it is 5 metres wide. The tunnel is 25 metres long and covers a descent of 10 metres until the average water level is reached. The total depth from the entrance to the water level is therefore 40 metres! The rock-cut steps in the tunnel, some eighty in number, were thickly plastered to protect the soft stone, while the last eight steps – which were submerged in water when the level rose – were built of basalt slabs and broken orthostats (in secondary use). When preparing the area for visitors, we were advised to support the innermost part of the tunnel with wooden poles for safety's sake, and this is how it looks today.

below The basalt steps near the 'source'
bottom The end of the tunnel shored up by wooden poles

The discovery of this enormous water system and our ability to date it to the first half of the ninth century evoked a picture similar to that derived from the re-dating of the Megiddo water system. One may assume that from the beginning of the ninth century, when the Aramaean and Assyrian menace to Israel and the neighbouring countries became acute, defensive measures generally increased and fortifications, in particular, were strengthened to withstand a long siege. For the kings of Israel and Judah, the ability to hold out in face of a prolonged siege was the only hope for survival. And although the cliché had not yet been coined, they proved that necessity is the mother of invention. It was imperative to develop engineering skills that could create fortifications and underground water systems unsurpassed by any other nation. As a matter of fact, the Moabite king Mesha, whose inscribed stele was found many years ago in Dibon, Transjordan, recorded that he cut all sorts of underground water systems with the help of 'prisoners from Israel'. So these skills, once developed, were obviously envied and in demand.

So here we had reached 'the source' of Hazor, but having done so we find ourselves somewhat out of chronological order, at least as far as the framework of this book is concerned. When we left the site at the end of chapter 11 to pursue the search for Solomon, we had got down as far as the period of the United Kingdom of the Israelites in the tenth century BC. Working down from there – and further back in time – we come full circle to the major problem that enticed us to Hazor in the first place: who killed King Jabin and destroyed the last Canaanite city at Hazor, Joshua or Deborah?

16 The Enigma of Joshua and Deborah

The problem

In the opening chapter, while enumerating all the textual evidence concerning the history of Hazor known before the excavations, I quoted, nearly in full, two biblical verses: one from the Book of Joshua and the other from the Book of Judges. At that time I refrained from going into detail about the solutions proposed to overcome the apparent discrepancy inherent in these two traditions. According to the former, Joshua – at the head of the Israelite hosts and in the process of conquering Canaan – fought a decisive battle in the north against Jabin, king of Hazor. The Israelites prevailed, and the biblical text notes the fact that Jabin was killed and the city burned. But, as mentioned, it adds a gloss to emphasize that of all the cities of northern Canaan, Hazor alone was burned, for Hazor 'formerly was the head of all those kingdoms'.

Had we had only this single passage, there really would be no problem, for the history could be reconstructed with relative ease: after Jabin, king of Hazor, had consolidated his rule over the lesser or petty kingdoms of Galilee, the area was subjugated by the conquering Israelite tribes under Joshua's leadership. (The placement of this battle in the conquest cycle in Joshua also tells us that Hazor fell during one of the later stages of the conquest.) However, in the Book of Judges, we are given two versions of a crucial battle that took place later (namely in the era of the Judges), when some of the tribes had already begun to settle the lands they had conquered but were still fighting for their existence or for a hold on the remaining Canaanite cities. The battle – between Deborah and Barak, on the one hand, and Sisera, on the other – was immortalized in one of the most ancient literary pieces in the Bible, the famous Song of Deborah (Judges 5). According to this victory poem, as it may be called, the battle took place on the Plain of Jezreel, not far from Megiddo (more specifically, Mount Tabor and Megiddo), by the banks of the Kishon River. Neither Hazor nor its king are mentioned here. Sisera is defined as the main enemy, and we are not even told where he resided; but it is implied that he commanded the Canaanite hosts fighting the Israelite warriors, whom Deborah rallied to the battle from all over the country.

So far, so good – or at least no problem. However, in the preceding chapter of Judges there is a prose version of this same battle that provides more details. The headline of the chapter sets the historical scene: 'And the people of Israel again did what was evil in the sight of the

opposite The foundation deposit as found in the 11th-century BC high place (see pages 256–7) *below* The battlefield of Deborah and Sisera

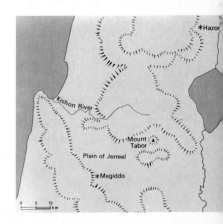

Lord, after Ehud died. And the Lord sold them into the hand of Jabin king of Canaan, who reigned in Hazor; the commander of his army was Sisera, who dwelt in Harosheth-ha-goiim' (4:1–2). Later on, although the prose narrative tallies with the poem in placing the battlefield on the Plain of Jezreel, near the Kishon River, we are again told, more than once, that Sisera was the commander in chief of Jabin's hosts; and then, after the Israelite victory, verse 24 states: 'And the hand of the people of Israel bore harder and harder on Jabin the king of Canaan, until they destroyed Jabin king of Canaan.' Now the obvious contradiction between the two sets of traditions reveals itself. If Joshua, who lived before Deborah, had already destroyed Hazor and killed Jabin, how is it possible that several decades (at least) later, Jabin was still alive and his commander in chief engaged in battle as far away from Hazor as the valley of Megiddo? This is indeed one of the most irksome questions of biblical research.

Solutions proposed before our excavations

Many explanations were offered by biblical commentators, but ultimately there is no escape from the conclusion that the contradiction cannot be resolved. The different types of explanations fall into three main categories. The first – and oldest – represents the views of ancient Jewish commentators and the more fundamentalist approach to biblical texts. This view stresses the fact that in Judges 4, Jabin is referred to in the past tense ('who reigned in Hazor'). It takes the whole Deborah story to mean that by the time the battle raged, Jabin was no longer alive; but since Sisera had *previously* been his commander in chief, the reason for mentioning Jabin is to help identify Sisera. This explanation implies, of course, that at the time of Deborah's battle, the city of Hazor may not have played an important role and Sisera was at Harosheth-ha-goiim (wherever that may have been).

Another, much more radical, theory is taken by some modern scholars (mainly German), who represent the critical approach to biblical texts. They deny the historicity of the narratives in the Book of Joshua and, in fact, regard the whole process of the conquest as a rather peaceful infiltration that culminated in local conflicts, some of which are reflected in the narratives of the Book of Judges. This school of thought therefore maintains that the clash between Jabin and the Israelites took place at a later stage, when Hazor must have been a city of some importance. In other words, they accept Judges as the basic source.

A third opinion, whose most prominent proponent was the late Professor W.F. Albright, attempts to explain the situation in nearly the opposite manner. For the followers of this school, the Book of Joshua represents a true historical nucleus. They stress the fact that in the Song of Deborah (which pre-dates the prose version in Judges) neither Hazor nor Jabin are mentioned at all, and the battle took place near Megiddo at a much later period. They explain the references to Jabin and Hazor in Judges 4 as a later editorial interpolation, influenced by the Book of Joshua. The editor of chapter 4 had no notion of Sisera's historical background, and he therefore connected this military commander with the great battles of the north recorded in the Book of Joshua. For this school of thought, Hazor had to be a very important city at the time of the Israelite conquest, while the question of Hazor's role in Deborah's times is left open as irrelevant. The city could have existed or not; either way, it had nothing to do with the biblical story in question.

A fourth view, which may be called a compromise, proved to be the important and influential one for us if only because one of its proponents actually joined our dig. This approach originated with Professor B. Mazar of the Hebrew University, Jerusalem. He considered the nucleus in both Joshua and Judges as reflecting actual historical events whose order was somehow reversed. He therefore places the destruction of Hazor as described in Joshua *after* the event narrated in Judges 4. Mazar's understanding developed from a careful reading of the text itself. Judges 4 states that 'the hand of the people of Israel bore harder and harder on Jabin the king of Canaan, until they destroyed [him]'. It does not say that they destroyed him at that time, nor does it suggest when they did so. Since the Joshua narrative is so definitive and detailed about the death of Jabin and the destruction of his city, he concluded that the Joshua version must be the answer to the question of when.

This view was further developed by Y. Aharoni, a student of Mazar's, in his Ph.D. thesis. Aharoni made a survey of Upper Galilee and found remains of many small hamlets and settlements with typical Iron Age (twelfth century) pottery. Accepting the German school's assumption of the peaceful infiltration of Israelites preceding the actual conquest, he explained these settlements as evidence of the first Israelite penetration into Galilee. Then, developing Mazar's view, he came to the conclusion – based on the date of the settlements – that the final and decisive battle with Jabin must have taken place towards the *end* of the twelfth century. In other words, he believed Jabin's Hazor was a flourishing city that reached its peak in the second half of the twelfth century. This theory prompted Aharoni to join the Hazor expedition in 1955, and in fact, at that stage, he was the only member on our staff who had some pre-conceived opinion about the solution to the problem. The rest of us lacked any vested interest in the results and wanted to excavate the site precisely in order to find out which of the approaches was correct, if any. Although, as we shall see, Aharoni's theory proved incorrect, his insistence and natural sensitivity to the excavations here led us to probe more profoundly into the question and even forced us to enlarge the areas of excavation until we were completely satisfied with results.

When we discussed the results of the excavations in the lower city, we stressed the fact that the city was totally destroyed by fire in the thirteenth century BC. The evidence of fire there tallied with the description in Joshua. Likewise, the date of the stratum could be ascribed to Joshua, rather than to the later era of the Judges. But since no later remains were found in the lower city, it could be argued that after the destruction of Hazor by Joshua – as the biblical narrative records – occupation was confined to the upper city alone, and it is to this city that the story in Judges refers. It was imperative, therefore, that we excavate on the *tell* below the Solomonic stratum. This phase of our excavations was probably the most exciting of the whole dig, and tension among staff members rose considerably. We were aware that as far as this biblical problem was concerned, we had reached the Day of Judgement.

We deepened our excavations under the Solomonic stratum and eventually found the Late Bronze city of the thirteenth century completely destroyed, as in the lower city. We called that layer stratum XIII (counting from the top), and for the first time could correlate the strata of the upper city with those of the lower one. Stratum XIII was parallel to stratum IA of the lower city, that is, to the last city of the Bronze Age. From now on, the equation was as follows:

	Upper City	Lower City
	XIII	1A
	XIV	1B
Strata	XV	2
	XVI	3
	XVII	4

The remains of city XIII were easily dated with the help of the Mycenaean pottery, as in the lower city. But the state of preservation of artefacts and structures on the *tell* was not as good as in the lower city, for after the upper city had been demolished – particularly from the time of Solomon onwards – the Israelite builders dug the foundations of their walls and buildings deep into the strata of the Late Bronze period and robbed most of its building material for re-use in their own structures. The fact that the last Bronze Age stratum of the upper city was numbered XIII implied that between it and stratum X (Solomon's city) we found two additional strata, which we marked XI and XII, respectively. If the Mazar-Aharoni theory were true and the battle recorded in Joshua occurred *after* the one narrated in Judges, and Hazor reached its climax under Jabin in the latter part of the twelfth century, then we should have found the Hazor of the Jabin-Sisera era in one of these two strata. But it was precisely the nature of both these strata that not only disproved this theory but enabled us to reconstruct what we believe to be the true course of events at Hazor after the destruction recorded in the Book of Joshua.

The semi-nomadic Israelites   Let us begin with stratum XII, the first occupation after Jabin's

An oven made out of an overturned storage jar from the 12th-century BC primitive settlement of semi-nomadic Israelites (stratum XII)

Hazor. Instead of a full-fledged city – or even a fortified settlement – stratum XII represented a settlement of semi-nomadic people with hardly any permanent buildings to be found. All over the mound we found remains of hut or enclosure foundations, generally composed of one course of field stones laid either in circles or in any other curved contours. In several areas, particularly A and B, ovens made of the upper parts of overturned storage jars, surrounded by a circle of stones, were found near these structures. Perhaps the most characteristic element of this settlement was the many pits dug all over the place. In area B, for example, twenty-two such pits were found within an area of 25 × 15 metres. At the beginning it was very difficult to comprehend their function, as in many cases they were detected only as a result of the different type of earth they contained or of the typical

Pits filled with stones found under the floor of stratum XI in area B (looking south)

An Israelite high place of stratum XI (11th century BC) found in area B (looking west)

The archaeological answer

pottery found intact in earlier levels. But soon it became clear that the pits served as silos or storage places for either vessels or grain. The typical feature of these pits when discovered was that they were filled with field stones. This strange phenomenon was understood only during the excavations of 1968, when one pit was found with its wall lining, made of field stones exactly like those of the filling, intact. It may therefore be assumed that the 'fillings' were only the stones of the collapsed lining.

Now it was quite clear that the destruction of the Late Bronze city was not followed immediately by the establishment of another city proper but by tentative efforts at settlement by semi-nomadic people. Who were they? Here the decisive clue was the pottery associated with the dwellings and pits. It is fundamentally different from that of the preceding Late Bronze stratum and is very reminiscent of the earliest phase of the Iron Age. One of the most prominent elements of this pottery is large storage jars, or *pithoi*, with a tall neck and a ridge at the base. More important is the fact that the pottery found in stratum XII is practically the same as that found in the small Iron Age hamlets in Galilee explored by Aharoni. There can be no doubt that these hamlets, as well as the occupation on the mound of Hazor, represent the earliest efforts of the nomadic Israelite tribes to settle in a more permanent fashion, and here in Hazor we had the clue to when this process occurred. Clearly it was after the destruction of the Canaanite city – that is, after the victories recorded in the Book of Joshua – and not a peaceful infiltration that preceded this fateful battle. The stratigraphic evidence at Hazor was definitive: stratum XII was above the wrecked city of Jabin.

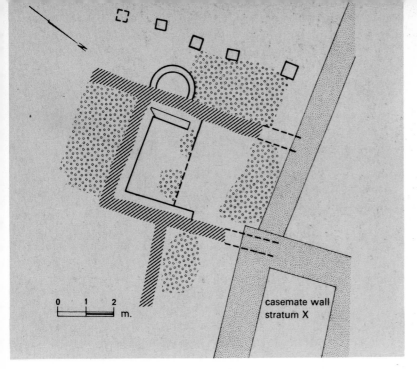

casemate wall
stratum X

0   1   2
                m.

An 'incense stand' (restored) found in the high place

Here, I believe, at long last, the excavations provided testimony to the true course of events; and it turns out to be exactly as described in the Bible – if one reads critically! First in sequence were the battles under Joshua, in which the great Canaanite centres were destroyed by the storming Israelite tribes. Then, in a very long process, some of these sites began to be resettled by the still semi-nomadic Israelites who slowly but surely turned the settlements into proper cities, particularly from the times of the kings onwards. The narrative in the Book of Joshua is therefore the true historical nucleus, while the mention of Jabin in Judges 4 must have been a later editorial interpolation.

The next stratum (XI), above the remains of stratum XII but still below the Solomonic layer (X), was also of great interest. It, too, represents an unfortified settlement, most probably of the eleventh century. Furthermore, its remains were not found all over, but were mainly concentrated in area B. This small settlement was most probably a later Israelite effort to settle above the ruined pits of the first semi-nomadic wave. The date of the pottery suggests that it belonged to the times of the late Judges, King Saul or even the early reign of King David. The most conspicuous structure found in area B was definitely cultic in nature. Stratigraphically, it was extremely well situated, for its walls were above stratum XII yet still under the Solomonic casemate wall. The building was rectangular, about 5 × 4 metres, and had a bench-like structure in its southern half. West of the building was a paved area with four stone pillars. Other paved areas were also found in the south and east, and in the southern one we found two broken incense stands, similar to those found at Megiddo in the

stratum just preceding David (VIA). This was the first indication that the strange structure may have been a 'high place', or cult place, but

opposite, above The votive objects being removed from the jar (see page 248)
opposite, below The votive objects: the deity, an axe and javelin heads and butts

The deity figurine and axe being photographed immediately after their removal from the jar

the decisive evidence came in a most unexpected place and in the form of a most unusual find.

In the south-west corner of the area, just under the floor, we found a jug full of bronze objects. It was evidently a foundation deposit or votive, but how strange were the objects inside! They looked like votives of thanks to a warrior god. The most prominent of them was a bronze figurine of a seated male deity with a cone-like helmet. The hole in his left hand indicated that at one time it must have held a weapon. Judging by the other votives found in the jar – a sword, two javelin heads and javelin butts, an arrow head and a lugged axe blade – this must have been a war deity. We were very excited when we emptied the jar, and I recorded every phase of the operation. The obvious pagan nature of the 'high place' does not rule out the possibility that it was Israelite. It looks like a chapel or 'high place' of the kind often mentioned in the Bible, particularly in the period of the Judges (*e.g.,* Judges 18). But whether these objects were Canaanite or Israelite, it is clear that the remains of stratum XI represented a small unwalled village soon to be replaced by the well-fortified Solomonic city of stratum X. Besides solving the enigma of Joshua and Deborah, this phase of the dig reconfirmed that the biblical verse stating that Solomon rebuilt Hazor is correct. His was the first proper city erected on the site after (about 300 years after) the last fortified Canaanite city had been destroyed.

Two views of the bronze figurine of the deity, which was originally fixed on a wooden base

17 Prologue – The Beginning

Standing among the ruins of stratum XIII, we found ourselves in the paradoxical position of simultaneously being at the end and at the beginning. Insofar as the questions about biblical Hazor were concerned, we had come to the end of our road, and the answers seemed to be clear: it was Joshua, not Deborah, who destroyed the Canaanite city of Jabin; Solomon did indeed rebuild Hazor; and the subsequent history of the city during the rule of the kings of Israel was faithfully reflected by the biblical account. At the same time, however, stratum XIII brought us back to the first days of our expedition in the lower city; and in an ironic way, after painstakingly making our way down through twelve layers of destruction, we were now back to where we had first started! Just because the biblical questions were out of the way, we were hardly about to pack up our equipment and go home. Under our feet were layers of earth that could corroborate evidence uncovered in the lower city and, hopefully, reinforce our earlier conclusions. But there was an even more important motivation for going on.

The nature of the high *tell* and the sherds of much earlier periods found scattered over the area indicated that Hazor was originally settled on the mound, near the spring, long before the establishment of the lower city. To unravel the early history of settlements in Hazor was no less a challenge to our spades. Now, with no written records to guide us, archaeology's singular role is manifested. The relics alone must recount history. All this meant that if we went down far enough we might well come upon the very first Hazor. We decided to aim for no less. One could say that we turned a popular phrase on its head and adopted the motto 'Bedrock's the limit!'

As mentioned in the previous chapter, we found the heavily destroyed and robbed remains of the last Canaanite city all over on the mound immediately below the layer of the semi-nomadic Israelite settlement. At first it was not easy to develop a clear picture of the stratigraphy of these periods because of Solomon's levelling operations and other incidents of re-use by later kings. One of the first encounters with the Late Bronze period was under the foundations of Solomon's gate. We deepened our trenches there for a couple of metres and our first find was beautifully dressed orthostats, identical to those found in the orthostat temple in area H. They looked like part of a door jamb or the entrance to a building. On top of them we

The foundations of Solomon's gate, under which the entrance shown opposite was found

Relative and absolute chronology

The orthostats entrance to the royal temple of the Late Bronze I period (16th century BC) found in area A (looking west)

A curved wall of the semi-nomadic Israelite settlement built on top of the ruined orthostats entrance to the Late Bronze I temple (see plan below)

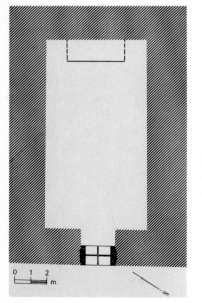

found the remains of a poorly built curved wall similar to structures typical of stratum XII, so we were convinced that the orthostats belonged to stratum XIII and tallied with the period of the stratum IA in the lower-city temple. Only about ten years later, in 1968, when we enlarged the area of excavations in this section, were we able to comprehend the full significance of our discovery.

The first discovery made then was that the orthostats formed an entrance to a temple of unusual plan, at least as far as Hazor was concerned. It was long and rectangular and measured 16.2 metres internally, from east to west, and 11.6 metres from north to south. Its thick walls were 2.35 metres on the average and were built of bricks on stone foundations. Opposite the entrance was a platform made of brick and plaster that measured nearly 5 metres from north to south and approximately 1.5 metres from east to west. A quantity of votive offerings and pottery, as well as remains of animals, were found on the platform around it. Clearly this temple was originally built in the Middle Bronze II period (eighteenth–sixteenth centuries BC), but the orthostats themselves, or rather the orthostat entrance, constituted a later addition to the temple. The most interesting fact, however, was the date of the temple's destruction. The entire area was covered with nearly 2 metres of debris composed of bricks that had fallen off the walls. The latest pottery found among this debris was of the Late Bronze I period (sixteenth–fifteenth centuries BC, *i.e.*, stratum XV). No remains of the fourteenth–thirteenth centuries (*i.e.*, of strata XIV–

The stratum XIII cult installation (13th century BC) near the derelict temple, with stelae and a votive bowl (looking west)

XIII, respectively) were found. This was a startling discovery, for it proved that the orthostats, both here and in the lower-city temple, were older than we had originally thought. Jumping back to chapter 6 for a moment, you will recall that we found the beautiful lion orthostat and the plain orthostats in the IB temple and therefore tentatively concluded that they were made for that fourteenth-century temple. Even then, however, we were uneasy about this dating because of the strange position of the orthostats in the IB stratum. Now we had proof that the Hazor orthostats originated at least in the Late Bronze I period (100–200 years before the IB temple), and (as explained in chapter 6) this discovery enabled us to understand the strange position of the orthostats in the fourteenth–thirteenth-century temples in area H (see pages 104–12).

A stigma

The thick layer of brick debris covering the remains of the Late Bronze I temple also indicated that after its final destruction, this temple was never again reconstructed. Nevertheless we observed that the sanctity of the area and its immediate surroundings was maintained through the fourteenth and thirteenth centuries (strata XIV and XIII). Several cultic installations were found all around the ruined temple's perimeter in a much higher level, dated by the typical fourteenth–thirteenth-century pottery. Of particular importance was a cult area discovered on a higher level – just in front of the (by-now) covered entrance of the temple – identified as such by the presence of one large and several small stelae. Two phases can be detected in this installation: one, in

The main stele, with head downwards, originally belonged to an earlier stratum

which a tall basalt stele with rounded top had been installed head downwards, most probably belonged to stratum XIV; the other, in which several small stelae (identical to those found in area C) and an offering bowl (found intact) had been added, probably belonged to stratum XIII. In addition, around the temple we discovered many heaps and pits containing sacrificial remains, bones and votive vessels, all associated with the late phases of the Bronze Age. Was it true that the temple itself was never re-built? If so – which seems likely – will we ever know the cause of the stigma attached to it? Apparently this phenomenon is not without parallel. I was rather struck by Sir Leonard Woolley's description of a more-or-less contemporary temple he found in Alalakh: 'It would seem that to Yarim-Lim's shrine there attached a stigma that prevented its re-use. The site of that shrine was left desolated and its ruins were riddled with the rubbish pits of levels VI and V.' That description – minus specific references to the ruler and the levels, of course – could easily apply to the temple we discovered.

The temple, which was built in the heart of the upper city (area A), was not an isolated find. It was, in fact, part of the royal palace found nearby, also heavily destroyed and robbed. Of that palace – which may also have originated in the Middle Bronze period – we found columns and bases, some of them very large indeed, strewn all over the area. We also discovered the staircase that led to the court. Then, among the ruins of the top Bronze Age strata (belonging to the four-

The thick and heavily destroyed walls of the palace of the Middle Bronze period (strata XVII–XVI, 18th–17th centuries BC) in area A. Note the pillared building of stratum VIII built on debris of seven strata (looking south-east)

A mould for jewellery (and cast thereof) found within the ruins of the palace

The ceremonial staircase leading to the palace in area A

teenth and thirteenth centuries), we came across the forepart of the lioness orthostat described in chapter 6. All these discoveries enabled us to correlate the strata of the Late Bronze period in the upper and lower cities and, even more important, to prove that the palaces of the kings of Hazor were up on the *tell*.

A self-maintained palace

One of the most impressive installations discovered between the remains of the palace and those of the temple was a huge underground water reservoir. It was about 30 metres long and consisted of two parts: a large, descending, rock-hewn tunnel, ending in a trefoil-shaped pool or cave; and, leading into it, a vaulted corridor with steps, some built and others rock cut. All told, it was a magnificent work of engineering! Its capacity was about 150 cubic metres, and in order to fill it (with an average rainfall of 600–500 millimetres per annum), the cobble-stone-floor area of the court would have had to have been at least 300 square metres, which is roughly the size of the area discovered. This was definitely a reservoir, and the tunnel was not meant to reach down to the natural water-level, as in the later, Israelite system in area L. Its walls were plastered almost up to the entrance; a channel led to it under the cobble-stone floor; and a basalt inlet was built into its inner walls. This reservoir may have been the water system for the palace in times of siege only. But as most parts of the palace are still hidden beneath the pillared building of stratum VIII, I am sure that once it is excavated in its entirety the answer to this question and a wealth of discoveries will be revealed.

Hazor in the times of Hammurabi

Our excavations had already indicated clearly that the lower city was established in the Middle Bronze IIB period, that is, the eighteenth century BC. Obviously, the *tell* proper must also have been occupied during that period, for otherwise the lower city would have been at the mercy of any armed group that seized the desolate mound. However, if we assume that the *tell* was occupied, then it must have been both the seat of the ruler and the site of the citadel precisely because of its superior topographical position. Moving from conjecture to evidence, remains of a great city of Hazor from the time of Hammurabi and the Mari letters were discovered all over the *tell*. It was certainly a strongly fortified city with palaces and a citadel. Basically, we found two strata belonging to this period, which we marked XVI and XVII (corresponding to strata 3 and 4 of the lower city). Earlier I said that the palace of the Late Bronze period in area A may have originated back in the Middle Bronze II period, as did the temple. While the huge foundations of the Middle Bronze II palace were found destroyed, and most of its stones had been removed by the Solomonic builders, two floors associated with it were nonetheless found intact and correspond to strata XVI and XVII. An object that turned up in the lowest stratum (XVII) was a fine Hyksos scarab typical of the period.

The disturbed state of the area is responsible for the fact that two

A fine Hyksos scarab found in the Middle Bronze II palace

The rock-cut and built roof of
the tunnel leading to the palace
water reservoir (looking west).
Compare with plan below

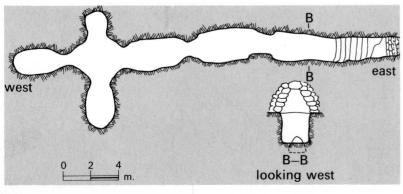

west

B
B

east

B—B
looking west

0 2 4
m.

A fragment of an old Babylonian Sumerian-Accadian dictionary found at Hazor in the hand of Professor H. Tadmor, who is to publish it

of the most important inscribed objects discovered there were actually not found *in situ* but were picked up later on, by visitors, in the dumps of the excavations. They are two small, broken, clay tablets: one has already been mentioned in chapter 1 as bearing an inscription concerning real estate in Hazor; the other is a tiny fragment of an old Babylonian tablet from the Mari period bearing parts of a Sumerian-Accadian dictionary, which indicates that the kings of Hazor at that time had scribes to handle their correspondence with the surrounding empires. We are left to hope that if and when that palace is excavated in its entirety, the archives of the kings of Hazor will be found.

Impressive fortifications

Impressive evidence of Hazor's grandeur during that period was found in connection with its fortifications, which we discovered in two areas. Under the Israelite fortification in area G, on the extreme

Plan of the *tell* (looking north) showing area G on the upper right, where the impressive *glacis* (opposite, above) was found

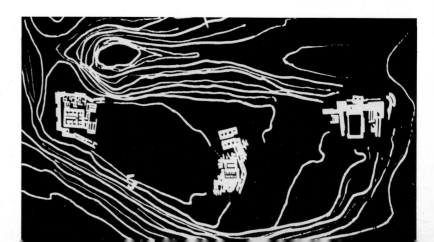

eastern end of the *tell*, we found a well-built stone *glacis*, or battered wall, fronted by a narrow and deep moat. This *glacis* is actually a huge revetment wall for the platform on which the defensive brick wall was most probably built. Most impressive are the rounded corners, protecting the eastern and northern parts of the city. The *glacis* is built of medium-size stones, quite similar in appearance and function to the famous battered-stone *glacis* in Jericho. This element of the fortifications may have been erected in stratum XVI. The defensive wall that protected the citadel was found in area A, in what we call the 'big trench', east of the middle terrace. It was 7.5 metres thick, built of bricks and set on a broader stone foundation. As it was on the terrace slope, its outer (eastern) face was 2 metres higher than its inner face, which was built on the natural rock. The brick construction was very

above The impressive stone *glacis* and moat of the Middle Bronze II period found in area G (looking south-east)

left The 'big trench' east of the pillared building (looking west) The brick city wall, shown right, was found here
right A section of the thick, brick city wall of the Middle Bronze II period found in the 'big trench'

interesting indeed, for the wall comprised three sections: outer, middle and inner. The outer and inner sections were built of dark bricks, and their exposed faces were covered with a sheath of lighter bricks made of some limy material. The middle section, or core, was built with less care of dark and light bricks. The outer face of the wall was further protected by a layer of plaster.

Near the wall and parallel to it, we found a section of fine drainage made of fitted clay pipes with inlet holes on top. These pipes drained the water accumulated in the square facing the gate and are further evidence of the high skill and town-planning ability of the Middle Bronze period, already attested in the drains and channels discovered in area F, and near the present-day museum, as described earlier.

Between the ruins of the Middle Bronze city (destroyed by the Pharaohs of the New Kingdom in the sixteenth century) and the Late Bronze I (stratum XV) remains, we discovered several graves with late Middle Bronze II pottery that were unrelated to any structure or floor above them. It may therefore be assumed either that they represented the occupation of squatters who returned to the site or that in the intermediate period the *tell* served as a burial place for people living in the vicinity. We became aware of this phase only in 1968, after the various strata had already been given numbers, so we called that spasm of a settlement 'Post XVI' – a name which, I believe, also fits the nature of the settlement, which was not really a proper occupation of the site in city form.

The main strata of the Middle Bronze cities coincided with those of the occupation in the lower city. Yet at the beginning we discovered in several places quantities of sherds that seemed to be slightly earlier than the Middle Bronze IIB period proper. Some of them may have belonged to the end of the preceding phase (Middle Bronze IIA) and some to a transitional period. In either case, they indicated that some sort of settlement existed here prior to the construction of fortifications on the mound. In 1955–8, however, we failed to detect any intact *locus* associated with these sherds. The exact nature of that settlement was of importance to our chronicle of the history of Hazor, which is why we probed deeper into those layers in 1968. The excavations un-

top A fine drainage system found near the city wall of the Middle Bronze II period in area A

above The clay pipes

right 'Post XVI' stratum represented by an infant burial on the derelict *tell* (16th century BC)

covered no substantial Middle Bronze II buildings under stratum XVII. Instead, some meagre structures, associated with graves and containing Middle Bronze IIA (or early Middle Bronze IIB) pottery, were found here and there. Unless we were unfortunate in our choice of areas to be excavated, it seems now that prior to the foundation of the large Middle Bronze IIB city, there was only a poor occupation, which was confined to the *tell* alone. Again, in order not to upset the strata numeration already in use, we called this phase 'Pre-XVII', a designation which conveys its transitory nature. It actually represents the very first Middle Bronze II settlers who occupied the site, which slowly but surely turned into a well-fortified city.

The best evidence for this phase of occupation came in a most unexpected manner. In January 1971, a burial cave was accidentally discovered by a team employed by the National Parks Authority to reinforce the southern flight of the rock-cut steps in the Israelite water system of area L after a crack had been observed along the shaft face. The safety engineers decided to drill a horizontal hole into the rock and fill it with concrete in order prevent the crack from expanding. As they were drilling, they came upon a cavity inside the rock, about 1 metre from the shaft face. It seemed that the drilling party had hit the back of a cave that had obviously just been missed by the hewers of the original shaft. This was a burial cave of that 'Pre-XVII', Middle Bronze IIA–B phase. As we entered the back of the cave through the hole made by the drill, we came into a cavern that was completely free of any silt or debris and contained about 150 vessels, mostly intact! We also found remains of between seven and nine skeletons, most of them pushed to the sides, with the one buried last in crawling position. The cave's original entrance – still blocked by its slab – was situated on the slope, probably underneath the city wall.

The variety of vessels confirms our belief that this phase should be dated to the end of the Middle Bronze IIA – or the beginning of the Middle Bronze IIB period – and it represents the pre-fortified settlement of Hazor. The position of the cave also supports that view. The cave is rectangular, with rounded corners, and measures some 4.5 metres from north to south and 3 metres from east to west. The blocked entrance is located in the middle of the southern end, on the southern slope of the mound. If our assumptions are correct, then the original entrance to the cave must have been under the foundations of the Middle Bronze IIB city wall, described above. It appears that the rocky slopes of the mound were used by these people for burials. This particular cave miraculously escaped the Israelite builders cutting the shaft, who may well have come across similar caves and demolished them. The 150 vessels are among the most beautiful pottery of the Middle Bronze period discovered in Hazor.

Under these phases of occupation we discovered great quantities of pottery of the Middle Bronze I period (2100–1900 BC), but as in

Repairing the crack (top); the drilled hole (centre); and the cave's original entrance (bottom)

other ancient sites in the country, we hardly found any structures associated with the pottery. Here we had further evidence that the people of the Middle Bronze I period were actually nomadic or semi-nomadic and occupied the site temporarily in huts or shacks. We called this phase of occupation stratum XVIII.

In various places the digging reached bedrock, and in the process we discovered the first three cities erected on the *tell* in the third millennium BC (the Early Bronze period). Remains of these cities – deep under the debris of later ones – were found in trenches or in narrow sections, which obviously told us rather little about their

above Typical Khirbet Kerak Ware of the Early Bronze III period. Similar fragments were found in stratum XX at Hazor
right This is a display of some of the vessels found in the burial cave described on the previous page, the finest assembly of Middle Bronze II pottery found at Hazor

layout. The latest of these, our stratum XIX, manifests a period of decline and may be dated to the last few centuries of the third millennium. As I said earlier, there was an intermediate period of semi-nomadic occupation in the Middle Bronze I period, and these people may have destroyed this last Early Bronze city. The city below it, our stratum XX, represents a period of growth. The few buildings discovered there were associated with the beautiful black-and-red, lustrous pottery called Khirbet Kerak Ware, after the site in which it was first discovered. Khirbet Kerak (Beth-yerah in Hebrew) lies south of Hazor on the western shore of the Sea of Galilee, and the pottery is

dated to the Early Bronze III period (*i.e.*, between 2600 and 2300 BC). Finally, on the bedrock (stratum XXI), was the very first city of Hazor, established in the first half of the third millennium BC (as were many other sites in the Holy Land), at the beginning of the urban period. Rock-bottom: the operation was over.

Epilogue

In the preceding pages, I have tried, with the help of the photographs, to present the main discoveries and historical results obtained from our five years of digging at the extraordinary site of Hazor, the largest site of its kind in the Holy Land and among the largest in the entire Fertile Crescent. Clearly, as early as the third millennium BC, people had been attracted to this spot by the springs in the vicinity, the fertile fields, and the strategic position of the nearby mound. At that time, the city was built on the mound only and did not differ from many other contemporary cities in the country; in fact, it was not among the largest. However, following the establishment of the extensive city – in both the upper and lower areas – in the eighteenth century, Hazor became the seat of the Canaanite kings who dominated the area of Upper Galilee and perhaps even further north, south and east of it. It was with the rulers of this Hazor that the kings of Babylon and Assyria exchanged emissaries and maintained active commercial and political relations. This was also roughly the period of the Patriarchs, who migrated to this part of the world from Babylon. Despite repeated destructions and reconstructions, Hazor continued to be the so-called capital of the area during the fourteenth century, as evidenced from the el-Amarna letters and supported by our excavations. Finally, in the thirteenth century, Jabin, king of Hazor, was defeated by Joshua and the conquering tribes of Israel.

Now we approach the period of the Israelite monarchy. Again, after an intermediate phase of decline, Solomon reconstructed Hazor (albeit only on part of the mound) as part of the strategic chain of cities established along the lines of communication between Egypt and the north, in order to expand his economic activities in these countries. When the great northern empire of Assyria became a real menace to the countries between Mesopotamia and Egypt, the later kings of northern Israel, from Ahab onwards, refortified the city to serve as a main bastion against the invading forces. Huge solid walls and underground water installations were built for times of siege, but to no avail. Eventually Hazor, like many other cities in many other countries, could not withstand the might of the Assyrian battering rams. From then on, the city was nearly forgotten – except for sporadic mention of a citadel, a castle or check-posts erected there from time to time – until it was excavated by us a few years ago.

Despite the fact that our expedition was among the largest of its kind in this part of the world, after five years of hard work we managed to excavate only a small fraction of the area. It would require another 500 years of digging – assuming financial means were available to

The heap of discarded sherds at the entrance to the expedition camp

us – to uncover Hazor's secrets completely. Perhaps future archaeologists will revise some of our conclusions and gain further important data for reconstructing the history of Hazor. I wish these future excavators one thing: that they be able to recapture the sheer excitement and drama that pervaded the work of the earlier excavators of Hazor, this amazing *tell* of twenty-two cities.

Farewell to Hazor

Table of Strata and Chronology

Stratum	Archaeological period and/or date/*historical source or period*	
I	**Hellenistic, 3rd–2nd century** BC *I Maccabees 11:67*	
II	**Persian, 4th century** BC	
III	**Early 7th century** BC *Assyrian*	
IV	**Iron II, end of 8th century** BC	
VA VB	**Destroyed 732** BC *II Kings 15:29* **Iron II, second half of 8th century** BC *Menachem*	
VI	**Iron II, first half of 8th century** BC *Jeroboam II; Zechariah 14:5, Amos 1:4*	
VII VIII	**Iron II, 9th century** BC **Iron II, 9th century** BC *Ahab*	
IXA–B XA XB	**Iron II, early 9th century** BC **Iron I, end of 10th century** BC **Iron I, c. 950** BC *Solomonic city, I Kings 9:15*	
XI	**Iron I, 11th century** BC *Pre-Solomonic*	

Stratum	Archaeological period and/or date/*historical source or period*	
XII	**Iron I, 12th century** BC *First Israelite settlement; apparent contradiction with Judges 4*	
XIII	**Late Bronze III, 13th century** BC *Joshua 11*	
XIV	**Late Bronze II, 14th century** BC *El-Amarna documents*	
XV	**Late Bronze I, 16th–15th century** BC *Thutmose III*	
'Post-XVI'	**Middle Bronze IIC, transitional**	
XVI	**Middle Bronze IIC, 17th–16th century** BC	
XVII	**Middle Bronze IIB, 18th–17th century** BC *Mari documents*	
'Pre-XVII'	**Middle Bronze IIA (?)–IIB** *Execration Texts?*	
XVIII	**Middle Bronze I**	
XIX–XX	**Early Bronze III**	

List of Staff Members

1955–8
Director, Y. Yadin.

Permanent area supervisors: Y. Aharoni (area A), Ruth Amiran (area B), Trude Dothan (area C, 1956; area G, 1957; area H, 1958), J. Perrot (areas C and E, 1955; area F).

Other area supervisors: A. Ben-Tor (area BA, 1958), M. Dothan (area M, 1958), A. Kempinsky (section in ramparts, 1965), Claire Epstein (area D, 1955; area H, 1957), E. Stern (area 210, 1957).

Architects: chief architect, I. Dunayevsky; field architects and surveyors, Hannah Brook, O. Ellenbogen, Y. Kolodny, E. Mentzel, Y. Mintzker, U. Pikarsky, A. Sever, E. Tronek.

Photographers: J. Schweig (1955), A. Volk (1956–8).

Pottery restorers: chief formatore, J. Shenhav; M. Kadishman, Tamar Licht, Naomi Nir, Lea Ofer, E. Shani, Ruth Shenhav, Zivia Sirottah.

Draftsmen: D. Aleph, Y. Bechar, D. Ben-Shaul, E. Engel, M. Laufer, Y. Leibovitz, M. Nissim, P. Levinger, N. Sever, Z. Yeivin.

Administrators: Lt. Col. Y. Pelz, Lt. Col. N. Raz (1955); Maj. A. Efrath (1956); Lt. Col. S. Rechavi, Capt. N. Offner (1957); Lt. Col. N. Raz, Lt. Col. S. Rechavi, Capt. N. Offner (1958); secretary, Aviva Rosen.

Foremen: chief foreman, Y. Alouf; assistant foreman, D. Uchovsky.

Field assistants and students (including single-season participants): Z. Adin, M. Aharoni, D. Allon, S. Avidor, G. Backi, D. Barag, S. Barkai, P. Beck, G. Ben-Ami, T. Benyamini, A. Ben-Ezer, Y. Ben-Yosef, A. Berman, R. Bieger, D. Blumental, M. Broshi, H. Chernobroda, R. Cohen, Y. Dayan, M. Enkin, U. Eylam, A. Eytan, N. Feigin-Foerster, G. Goerster, A. Fraenkel, E. Gelber, E. Hagolani, Z. Hasharoni, S. Havlin, J. Hawkins, M. Hershkovitz, A. Horowitz, Z. Horvitz, M. Kochavi, Y. Kronenberg, T. Kruglak, Y. Levy, E. Linder, D. Littman, M. Livne, I. Machover, M. Megiddon, R. Menashe, Z. Meshel, Y. Morgenstern, R. Nadel, J. Naveh, N. Naveh, A. Negev, H. Niessen, N. Popper, S. Ragger, A. Ronen, M. Saltman, Y. Shifman, S. Simon, E. Singerman, R. Sofer, Y. Solomon, G. Stauber, S. Tamari, Y. Tversky, D. Ussishkin, Y. Vinestein, S. Yadin, M. Yarhi, Y. Yedidyah, T. Yizraeli, Prof. and Mrs D. Young, I. Warshall, A. Ziegelman, A. Zussman.

1968–9
Director, Y. Yadin.

Area supervisors: A. Ben-Tor (area A), Malka Batyevsky (area M), A. Eytan (area BA), B. Hofri (area N), A. Mazar (area P), Y. Shiloh (area L).

Architects: chief architect, I. Dunayevsky; field architects, G. Kertes, G. Klir.

Photographer: Z. Radovan.

Pottery restoration and drawing done in Jerusalem.

Administration: Col. A. Braker; secretary, Aviva Rosen; general assistant, Petty Officer M. Cohen.

Field assistants: senior field assistants, N. Ne'eman, Y. Portugali; students of the Hebrew University, Jerusalem.

Index

The author and publishers wish to thank the following institutions and individuals for their kind permission to reproduce the photographs cited below: the Trustees of the British Museum, London, 13, 18, 176 (top right); Institute of Archaeology, Hebrew University, Jerusalem, 14, 15, 56; R. L. W. Cleave, 142, 206, 212 (bottom); W. G. Dever, 203. The photographs which appear on pages 196 (top) and 224 (bottom right) are from the author's private collection.